Stephen Dando-Collins is the author of the acclaimed *Captain Bligh's Other Mutiny*. *Pasteur's Gambit* was shortlisted for the science prize in the Victorian Premier's Literary Awards and won the Queensland Premier's Science Award. The World War I family memoir *Crack Hardy*, his most personal history, received wide acclaim. *Mistaken Identity* tells another episode of previously undiscovered Australian history, and his biographies include *Sir Henry Parkes: The Australian Colossus* and *The Hero Maker: A Biography of Paul Brickhill*. He also writes about American and ancient Greek history, and his series about the legions of ancient Rome has found considerable success in the US, UK and Australia and been translated into numerous foreign languages. Stephen has also written several successful books for children and young adults. *Heroes of Hamel* is his forty-first book. Stephen and his wife, Louise, live and write in a former nunnery in Tasmania's Tamar Valley.

HEROES
OF
HAMEL

STEPHEN
DANDO-COLLINS

VINTAGE BOOKS
Australia

A Vintage Australia book
Published by Penguin Random House Australia Pty Ltd
Level 3, 100 Pacific Highway, North Sydney NSW 2060
penguin.com.au

Penguin
Random House
Australia

First published by Vintage Australia in 2018

Addresses for the Penguin Random House group of companies can be found at
global.penguinrandomhouse.com/offices.

A catalogue record for this
book is available from the
National Library of Australia

ISBN 978 0 14378 760 0

Typeset in 13/17 pt Adobe Garamond Regular by Post Pre-press Group, Brisbane
Map by Ice Cold Publishing
Printed in Australia by Griffin Press, an accredited ISO AS/NZS 14001:2004 Environmental
Management System printer

Penguin Random House Australia uses papers that are natural, renewable and recyclable
products and made from wood grown in sustainable forests. The logging and manufacturing
processes are expected to conform to the environmental regulations of the country of origin.

'There are no finer troops on earth, nor have there ever been, than the Australian Corps.'
Colonel William K. Naylor, Chief of Staff, American 33rd Division, July 1918

'We Marines would happily storm Hell itself with your troops on our right flank.'
General James 'Mad Dog' Mattis, formerly US Marines, latterly US Secretary of Defense, to the Australian Special Air Service Regiment, 2006

TABLE OF CONTENTS

Acknowledgements

I wish to particularly acknowledge the assistance of Paul Grasmehr of the Pritzker Military Museum & Library, Chicago, for his prompt and detailed assistance with the provision of background on Corporal Thomas Pope, Colonel Joseph Sanborn, and the 131st and 132nd Infantry Regiments prior to, during and following the First World War.

I also owe my cousin Craig Searle a debt of gratitude for preserving and sharing the letters, diaries and photographs of Viv, Ray and Ned Searle, my great-uncles. These records thoroughly fleshed out the background of the Searle brothers that my own family provided over the years. Craig also passed on several wartime stories that his grandfather Ned had shared with him. Thanks, too, to Les V. Holloway of Ballarat, for sharing his Western Front remembrances of his father, Vic Holloway, that I refer to in this work.

The staff of the Australian War Memorial, Canberra

were, as always, extremely helpful in the research process. I also want to thank my publisher at Penguin Random House, Meredith Curnow, for her continued enthusiastic support, my editor at Penguin Random House, Patrick Mangan, for his always diligent assistance, and my New York literary agent, Richard Curtis. And for soldiering on beside me as always, I am eternally grateful to my CIC, my wife, Louise.

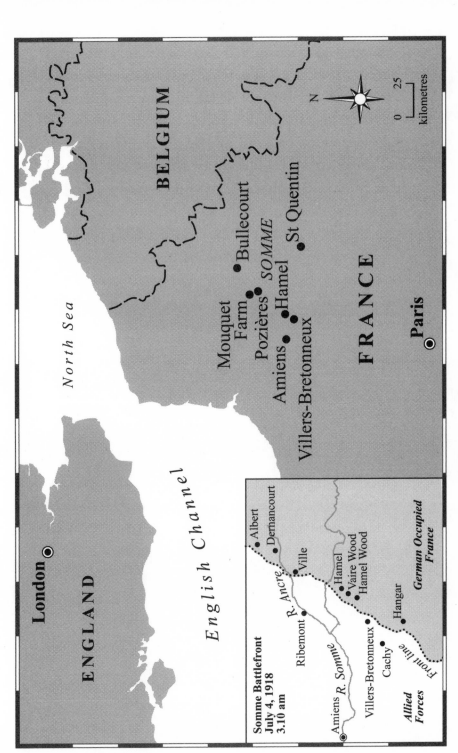

The Somme, The Western Front, 1918.

1.

The English War Correspondent's Mission

'In the hearts of these [American] men, the adventure of
battle is greater than its chance of pain or death.'
Philip Gibbs, English War Correspondent

THE LORRY BUMPED and swayed along the uneven, shell-
battered road from Amiens. Hanging on in the bouncing
cab beside the grinning Australian driver, forty-one-year-old
English war correspondent Philip Gibbs, a bony, hawkfaced
man, noted with surprise that, in all the French villages he
now passed through, French and American flags were flying
in equal number. It was 4 July 1918. Gibbs was aware that it
was American Independence Day, but he'd never imagined
the French villagers would also know it, and celebrate it.

The French civilian population clearly knew that
American troops were in this sector. That was why Gibbs was
here. Since 1915, the experienced journalist had been covering
this meat-grinder of a war for London's *Daily Telegraph* and

1

Daily Chronicle. He'd initially pulled back when the British Government imposed tight censorship on reporting from the battlefield, requiring correspondents to submit their articles for approval and frequently requiring cuts. But, determined to make the most of a bad situation, Gibbs had agreed to become one of five British war correspondents officially recognised by Whitehall and permitted to go into the war zones. Since then he'd been reporting the conflict with a mixture of pride in the men he saw fight and die and disgust for the inept and sometimes callous leadership he witnessed at the highest levels of the British Army.

The arrival of the Americans was the Allies' great hope to turn the bloody stalemate on the Western Front into victory. Since the United States had declared war on the Central Powers on 4 April 1917, it had taken more than a year for its first troops to reach the war zone. Now, they were here at last, on the Somme, and just days before this Gibbs had received a tip-off from British General Headquarters, or GHQ, that, tonight, Americans were going to participate in 'a little show' with the hardy Australians.

Gibbs had no doubts that the Aussies would give 'Fritz' a fright, as usual. 'The Australians have never lost the initiative since the day of March 26,' he would write, 'when at the end of the first phase of the German offensive they arrived on the [Somme] battlefield with one battalion, increased to four that afternoon when they thrust back the German outposts and helped to bar the way to Amiens. Since then they have made several successful attacks, driving the enemy's lines back from Villers-Bretonneux and the valley of the Somme in front of Moriancourt.'[1]

As far as Gibbs was concerned, the Australians were a known, and fearsome, quantity. He wasn't as convinced that the Yanks yet had what it took to make the Germans quake with fear. This would be the American Expeditionary Forces' first offensive action of the war, and Gibbs was keen to see and report on how they fared. Millions of fresh troops from across the Atlantic were expected to turn the tide against the 'Hun'. But what if, instead, the Americans turned out to be a flop as a fighting force? The USA had possessed only a small standing army at the time it declared war. The millions of men it was sending to Europe comprised a smattering of reservists and a host of conscripts.

Gibbs had been present at Pierregot several days before his visit to the Australian part of the front, and had heard the commander of the American 33rd Division, Major-General George Bell Jr, tell his assembled troops, 'America expects you boys to make good. You are going in with the Australians, and those lads always deliver the goods. We expect you to do the same.'[2]

The English war correspondent had seen the eyes of American 'Doughboys' light up at the sound of these words. 'They were ready to take all risks to prove their mettle,' Gibbs would write in a despatch. 'They were sure of themselves and tuned up to a high pitch of nervous intensity at the thought of going into battle for the first time.' They were clearly keen to accept General Bell's challenge. 'In the hearts of these men, new to war and fresh out in France, the adventure of battle is greater than its chance of pain or death, and calls to the hunter's instinct in them.'[3]

But what of their prey? The German Army facing the

untried Americans had close to four years' experience of war. The French called their Germanic foe *le Boche*, a contemptuous slang term of vague origin whose meaning ranged from 'cabbage-eater' to 'blockhead'. The Americans were soon also calling Germans by the derisory 'Boche' term; men of African-American regiments of the AEF, which were assigned to French commands, came to call the Germans the 'Bush-Boche'. But German soldiers, when well led, had shown they were tough and disciplined. What was more, the Boche had developed a constitution for trench warfare, living like rats in holes and then surging out to drive back their Allied opponents with bullet, bomb and bayonet. Could and would America's youth be up to this? That was what Gibbs was here to find out.

Jumping down from the truck when it halted by an Australian artillery battery nestled into the shelled-out ruins of a farmhouse on the outskirts of Corbie, Gibbs, wearing the uniform of a British officer without insignia of rank or unit, asked the way to the headquarters of the Australian 15th Battalion. Following direction from an Aussie traffic control NCO, Gibbs set off to find the battalion's HQ, and its commander, Lieutenant-Colonel Terence McSharry. Like all good war correspondents, Gibbs knew that a true and accurate picture of this conflict could only be told through the eyes of the individuals who fought it. The 15th Battalion would be 'going over the top' with men from the 33rd American Division in tow, and Gibbs wanted to see and talk to those Americans.

With heavy-smoking, hard-swearing Australian rear echelon troops paying him little heed as he passed, and the nearby bark of artillery reminding him he was perilously close to the front line, Gibbs, knapsack on his shoulder, began winding his way through the maze of communication trenches in search of the battalion HQ.

2.

The Australian General's Plan

*'A perfected modern battle plan is like a score for
an orchestral composition, where the various arms and
units are the instruments.'*
Lieutenant-General Sir John Monash

ON 18 JUNE 1918, the Australian Corps had its headquarters
at Chateau de Bertangles in Picardy, eight kilometres north
of the city of Amiens. That once pretty city, now in ruins,
occupied a vital Somme rail junction the German Army had
been striving to take as part of their spring offensive. From
Amiens, the Germans had planned to follow the Somme the
short distance it ran to the English Channel, thus splitting
Allied troops in northern France and Belgium from Paris and
the rest of France, and gaining the Channel ports.

Some time back, Amiens had been totally evacuated
of its population. It was now nothing but a ghost of a city.
Despite this, Amiens' ruin was exacerbated nightly by bombs
dropped by German Gotha bomber aircraft that droned in
from the east, whilst, during the day, massive 12-inch and

15-inch German naval guns mounted on rail trucks pounded the city from forty kilometres away.

Sprawling Chateau Bertangles on the other hand, sitting amid a park of chestnut and beech trees and rolling lawns, had avoided German attention and looked for all the world to be an oasis of charm and calm, far removed from the destruction of Amiens and the bloody, exhausting war being fought in the Somme trenches not so many kilometres to the east. Here at the chateau, the commander of the Australian Corps and his three hundred staff shared the mansion with its owner, the elderly Marquis de Clermont-Tonnerre, and ran this corner of the war as they plotted the downfall of their shared German enemy. And here, on this third Tuesday in June, a group of Australian generals sat down around a conference table to agree on a plan that would change the war.

Back on 30 May, two days before it was officially announced, a new commander had taken charge of the Australian Corps. Born and raised in West Melbourne, Lieutenant-General Sir John Monash was the first native Australian to hold the post. His predecessor, Lieutenant-General Sir William 'Birdie' Birdwood, who had been promoted to the command of the British Fifth Army, had been born in India to English parents.

In the present day, it would be unthinkable for anyone other than an Australian to have overall command of Australia's largest and principal fighting force, but back then it had taken several years of increasingly intense lobbying from Australia before the British Government had agreed to let an Australian lead the nation's fighting men. This was eight months after the Canadians had been permitted their own native-born corps commander, Lieutenant-General Sir Arthur Currie, who, like Monash, had been a part-time militia soldier before the war.

Whilst the Australian Corps was the largest to come under the aegis of the British Army – corps were ordinarily made up of four divisions – its five divisions comprised only a small part of the much larger overall British Army of fifty-three divisions of British and Empire troops on the Western Front, representing 9.5 per cent of British strength and five per cent of total Allied military strength in France.[4]

Just nineteen days into his new job, General Monash chaired this meeting of his divisional commanders and their chiefs of staff, the first time in history that commanders of the Australian divisions had come together under an Australian commander-in-chief. Just weeks away from his fifty-third birthday, Monash was the son of a German-speaking Polish Jew from West Prussia who had migrated to Victoria during the gold-rush years and become a shopkeeper. John, an only son, had attended Scotch College, excelling as a student. Going on to the University of Melbourne, he had taken three degrees, in art, law and engineering, at the same time helping found the university union and editing the university review.

By the time Monash began an engineering partnership in 1894, he had married local Jewish girl Victoria 'Vic' Moss and was a lieutenant in the part-time Victorian Garrison Artillery. Back then, his primary interest in the military was its ability to offer him an entree into business and social circles. With Australia in the depths of a severe economic depression, for the next seven years Monash had worked hard but struggled financially. He would be saved by reinforced concrete. In 1901, deeply in debt, Monash became a partner in the Monier Pipe company, which led, via hard work and influential friends, to his becoming a partner and supervising engineer with Reinforced Concrete & Monier Pipe four years later. This made him wealthy, enabling him to buy a mansion in the elite Melbourne suburb of Toorak. A decade later, he was one of Melbourne's most successful businessmen, controlling four companies and sitting on the boards of numerous organisations.

All the while, Monash had been progressing up the ranks of Australia's militia forces, which became the foundation of the Australian Imperial Force when war broke out in August 1914. When Monash sailed for Egypt that December, he was five feet ten inches tall, a portly fifteen stone (97.5 kilograms) colonel, a heavy smoker, and commander of the 4th Infantry Brigade. After the disasters of the Gallipoli campaign, during which Monash made his share of errors, but learned from them, he made his mark on the Western Front through 1916 and 1917 with promotion to major-general and command of Australia's 3rd Division. With that command had come the latitude to make many of his own decisions, and so to make his name.

Yet Monash was a reluctant general. 'I hate the business of war,' he had written to his wife Vic in 1917, 'the awful horror of it, the waste, the destruction, the inefficiency. Many a time I could have wished that wounds or sickness, or a breakdown of health, would have enabled me to retire honourably from the field of action.' Only his sense of duty to his Australian soldiers had kept him at the helm of his division, and now of his corps. Vic had suggested in one of her letters that he think about making the army his profession after the war, but he'd responded that he would only consider becoming a paid servant of the state as a last resort. 'I have fought all my life for personal independence, and shall not give up what I have won.'[5]

The past four years had changed him. He still retained his love of music, literature and art. He still had a keen sense of humour. But now, as commander of the Australian Corps, Monash was, in the words of one of his biographers, 'a slim, darkly handsome man, prematurely aged and greyed by the strain of war'.[6] In the fashion of the day, Monash wore a neat moustache, and his mature good looks made him attractive to women; at this very moment the married Monash had a mistress in London.

When Monash spoke, his words were chosen with care. Those words, sometimes used to stir and motivate, other times to console, showed his great compassion, his joy of life and a total command of his subject. His eyes took in everything. Behind those eyes worked as clever a mind as has ever led an army. 'No shrewder judge of men and things has ever lived,' Frederick Cutlack, his divisional intelligence officer in 1917, was to say of Monash.[7] Britain's World War Two Field-Marshal Viscount Montgomery later declared, 'I would name Sir John Monash as the best general on the Western Front.'[8]

Monash had an elevated ego; that he would never deny. Every general, like a brain surgeon, has to believe he has superior skills that equip him, or her, to perform their job better than anyone else as they make life and death decisions, and play God. Sometimes that belief is misplaced, and comes across as arrogance. But when self-belief is warranted, as it was in Monash's case, the result is an aura of confidence that is infectious, and inspiring. Besides, Australia's fighting men had gained such a reputation on the Western Front they gave Monash every reason to be confident, in them as much as in his own abilities.

Looking around his divisional commanders, Monash took in the faces of men he had come to know well over the past few years. Until recently, he had been their equal, a colleague in arms. His recent promotion had required a new mindset. 'I was now called upon to consider their personalities and temperaments as subordinates,' Monash himself would say. Monash was now the boss, but, as a superb man manager, 'the Old Man', as his staff called him, would let every general express his views before making a decision or issuing an order. Once that order was given Monash would expect every subordinate to make sure it was carried out, to the letter.[9]

Commanding the Australian 1st Division was Major-General Thomas Glasgow, a forty-two-year-old Queenslander. Serving in the Boer War as a lieutenant with the Queensland Mounted Infantry and winning the Distinguished Service Order, Glasgow had been a shopkeeper and cattleman prior to this war, which he'd entered as a major with the Australian Light Horse. Clean-shaven, well-built and forthright, Glasgow presaged the act of an American commander at Bastogne a quarter of a century later by telling Germans who'd surrounded his troops and called for their surrender to 'Go to Hell!' Monash didn't think Glasgow a great tactician, but credited his success as a commander to his strength of personality. 'He always got to where he wanted to get,' Monash said admiringly. Glasgow was, said Monash, 'consistently loyal to the Australian ideal, and intensely proud of the Australian soldier'.[10]

For the moment, Glasgow's 1st Division was engaged in the defence of Hazebrouck in Flanders, to the north, holding the front line there as part of the British Army. Monash was anxious to bring all the Australian divisions under his direct control and put Glasgow's driving determination to work for the success of the Australian Corps, but with British GHQ reluctant to release it from the Flanders front, the 1st would not join the rest of Monash's Australian fighting forces for some time yet.

Major-General Sir Charles Rosenthal commanded the 2nd Division. 'A massive man whose build belies his extraordinary physical energy,' according to Monash. Forty-three-year-old Rosenthal, from Berrima, New South Wales, had come to divisional command via the artillery. Another officer with a militia background, prior to the war Rosenthal had been an architect. Monash considered him a perpetual optimist. 'He always was,' said Monash, 'incapable of recognising failure.'[11]

Commanding the 3rd Division was forty-five-year-old Major-General John Gellibrand. Born and bred in Tasmania, Gellibrand had graduated from Sandhurst Military College in England and served in the British Army before returning to Tasmania to become an apple orchardist. An intelligent man, Gellibrand made a better philosopher than a warrior, but his determination to do his duty had seen him appointed to take Monash's place when Monash had recently been elevated from command of the 3rd to take over the entire Australian Corps.

The 4th Division had been commanded for some time by a Scotsman, Major-General Ewen Sinclair-Maclagan, a forty-nine-year-old professional infantry officer who had been loaned to Australia by the British Government prior to the war to help oversee the creation of the Royal Military College at Duntroon, Canberra, and train Australia's future fulltime military officers. Monash considered the Scot tactful, industrious, but a pessimist. Yet, despite his pessimism, Maclagan would always move mountains to achieve goals he frequently argued against.

Short, slight Major-General Sir Talbot Hobbs was commander of the 5th Division. Another militia officer, another architect, another artilleryman – he had commanded the artillery of the first Australian contingent that had sailed for Europe in October 1914 – and also another Briton, Hobbs was several months older than Monash. While 'he would be the last to lay claim to special brilliance, or outstanding military genius', Monash was to say that in his opinion Hobbs displayed 'sound common sense' and had a 'sane attitude to every problem that confronted him'.[12] Hobbs and Sinclair-Maclagan had both spent a number of years in Australia – Hobbs in Perth, WA, after migrating there in his twenties. In fact, Hobbs had become so Australianised he appeared to think of himself as an Aussie. Certainly, Monash credited him with being, 'first and foremost, a lover of the Australian soldier'.[13]

Monash was now in charge of more than 166,000 men. 'My command is more than two-and-a-half times the size of the British Army under the Duke of Wellington, or the French Army under Napoleon Bonaparte, at the Battle of

Waterloo,' he had proudly written to Vic in Melbourne in May. To put the size of Monash's new command in perspective, he controlled 10,000 more men than would be landed by the Allies at Normandy on D-Day, 1944.

In Monash's opinion, the Australian Corps was 'the backbone of the Allied armies' in 1918. It was by far the largest of any of the 'British' corps in France. Apart from the five Aussie infantry divisions it included the 13th Australian Light Horse, ten brigades of Australian artillery, two massive 12-inch railway guns, several battalions of British tanks, a battalion of cyclists, signal units, engineers, labour battalions, supply columns, ammunition dumps, mobile workshops, and the Australian Flying Corps' Number 3 Squadron.[14]

Close to a third of the men under Monash's direct command were not Australian. One thousand were non-combat troops of the American 108th Engineer Regiment, whilst 50,000 were British troops. Half of these Brits were regulars, with the balance conscripts, unlike the Australian troops, who were all volunteers. Many Australian officers and men had little time for British troops, considering them feckless at most times and useless if they lost their officers. This view would be reflected by Australian war correspondent Charles Bean who, in the postwar *Official History of Australia in the War of 1914–18*, would describe the British 'Tommy' as 'extraordinarily guileless' and 'humble-minded to a degree'.

General Monash had no problem with the British Army's rank and file, considering them no less courageous than any other soldier at the front. He did question the ability of many British field and staff officers. As a consequence, he relegated most of his British troops to support roles. Monash gave his

Australians the toughest assignments, because he knew they would not let him down.

At this stage of the war, the Allied armies in France were on the defensive, licking their wounds and catching their breath. The British north of the Somme and the French south of it were content to occupy the lines they had been driven back to by the German Army's spring offensive in March and April. That offensive, called the *Michael-Schlacht* or Operation Michael by the Germans, had been fuelled by the infusion of numerous German divisions transferred from fighting the Russians and Romanians on the Eastern Front after the Russians had sued for peace as their Bolshevik revolution took them out of the war.

Holding the line between the British and the French, the Australians on the Somme mounted regular surprise raids across No Man's Land to seize German prisoners and materiel and to generally keep Fritz uneasy, operating from the trenches they had been occupying since stopping the German advance short of Amiens in April. The Australians called these raids Peaceful Penetration. Perhaps there was an intended irony in this title, for the rationale behind these raids was to ensure the German troops facing the Australians never had any peace.

Monash's first order on taking over the Australian Corps at the end of May had been a defensive one, requiring the strengthening of the corp's support trenches behind the front line to enable his Australians to put up one hell of a fight if the Germans attempted a fresh push towards Amiens. Information from intelligence sources including the British Secret Service made available to Monash since he'd become a corps commander told him that Amiens had been and remained a key German objective. But Monash was itching to go on the offensive. 'It was high time,' he'd confided to his wife, 'that some commanders on our side of No Man's Land should begin to "think offensively", and cease to look over their shoulders in order to estimate how far it still was to the coast.'[15]

As British war correspondent Philip Gibbs had noted, in late March the Australians had made their mark on the Somme after an entire British corps had broken and fled at 4.00 pm on the 26th in the face of the German offensive. General Monash and troops of his 3rd Australian Division and others of the 4th Australian Division had stepped in and changed the course of the war. 'We have stood firm,' he wrote at the time, 'the road to Amiens is closed.' As a result, he said, 'we, and the 4th Australians, and the New Zealanders to the north steadied up the entire British line'.[16]

Then, on 4 April, the British 14th Division, holding the Allied line at and around the village of Le Hamel in the Somme Valley to the northeast of Villers-Bretonneux, had been routed by five German divisions and driven from the village and nearby woods. The German advance had swept on British heels to the outskirts of Villers-Bretonneux, where they were stopped by an unexpected charge from Australian troops.

The enemy's gains beyond Hamel had given the German Army a salient providing excellent artillery positions on high and well concealed wooded ground near Hamel, creating a 'bubble' in the Allied line that protruded well behind the broader front on the Somme. Back then, Monash had proposed a counterattack by his 3rd Division to eliminate this bubble, but to his frustration then corps commander General Birdwood had turned him down; in Monash's words, 'for reasons doubtless satisfactory at that time'.[17]

Ever since, said Monash, the enemy's Hamel salient had been 'a source of annoyance and anxiety to me'. Now that the proactive Monash was corps commander, he intended undertaking that operation to eliminate the salient, as a prelude to a much larger offensive. That was what this council of war at Chateau Bertangles was all about. By the end of the meeting, Monash and his generals had agreed a plan to retake Hamel and the nearby Hamel and Vaire Woods, popping the German bubble and smoothening the front line.[18]

'The main thing is always to have a plan,' said Monash when he took charge of the Australian Corps and at last had a certain freedom of command. 'If it is not the best plan, it is at least better than no plan at all.'[19] Monash, as events were to prove, would create a masterly plan or two before this war was over. He approached each problem with the mind of an engineer. Engineers work to plans, pulling together all the material and expertise necessary to build something solid that will serve its purpose well. This particular plan now being hatched by Monash would be unlike any drawn up by either side to date in this war. Incredible as it seems today, for the first time in the Great War this operational plan called for a surprise attack integrating infantry, artillery, tanks and air power, all with their assigned roles, objectives and timetables, working as one.

Monash had said in April, two days before the original British setback at Hamel, that to succeed in his task as a commander he had to inject optimism into all branches of his command and 'deal with every task and every situation on the basis of simple business propositions, differing in no way from the problems of civil life, except that they are governed by a simple [military] technique'. Just such a simple business plan was born at Chateau Bertangles.[20]

As Monash and his generals were meeting, General Sir Henry Rawlinson, commander of the British 4th Army, of which the Australian Corps formed part, arrived at the chateau. Scrawny, balding, a little taller than Monash, Rawlinson had the aura of a provincial bank manager. After Monash sent his commanders away bubbling with optimism and enthusiasm for the Hamel operation, he explained to Rawlinson, who was his immediate superior, his concept for an integrated attack on the Hamel salient spearheaded by tanks, adding that for the operation to succeed he would need more tanks, more artillery and more aircraft.

Rawlinson was a Briton, and an anti-Semite. Whether Monash was aware of, or was ever on the receiving end of, this anti-semitism, he never revealed, but, two years after this, Rawlinson would privately describe Monash as 'a clever, slippery, creepy crawly Jew'.[21] By comparison, in public at least, Monash was always complimentary about Rawlinson. 'His qualities of broad outlook, searching insight, great sagacity, and strong determination, tempered by wise restraint, never failed to impress me,' Monash would write just a year later.[22] 'Wise restraint' was Monash's code for 'overcautious'. Rawlinson, like all senior British commanders of the time, was ruled by a dread of failure. Years of British reverses and grievous losses on the Western Front had made him a cynic, and perhaps even a fatalist.

But then, Rawlinson also knew that Monash had the favour and the ear of British commander-in-chief Field-Marshal Sir Douglas Haig. Rawlinson, a 'ready talker, full of ambition and suspected to be not incapable of intrigue', according to Haig's biographer Duff Cooper, knew that his own present position and future prospects now largely depended on Monash's success.

Rawlinson warmed to Monash's idea for an integrated attack spearheaded by the Australians, especially as it involved straightening the front line in the sector he controlled. Experience had also taught him that any attack carried out by the Australians stood a very good chance of succeeding. And if it failed, the Australians could be blamed, not the English. Finding himself in a win-win situation, Rawlinson asked Monash for a concrete proposal in writing, one he could submit to Field-Marshal Haig for approval.

*

Within days of Monash taking charge of the Australian Corps, he had been invited to Vaux-en-Amiénois, a small village in a quiet valley to the northwest of Amiens. His host was Brigadier-General Hugh Elles, commander of the British Tank Corps. With British GHQ ambivalent about the potential role of tanks to defeat the Germans, General Elles had been determined to convince the most imaginative general on the Western Front of what they could do for his corps, and prove to Monash that his new Mark V was a very different animal from the unreliable old Mark IV.

Only arriving in France on 23 March, the first Mark Vs had re-equipped the 5th Tank Brigade at Vaux-en-Amiénois, replacing the unit's discredited Mark IVs. Now, the 5th Tank Brigade was on offer to the Australian Corps. General Monash and his chief of staff Brigadier-General Thomas Blamey had accepted Elles' invitation, and on a sunny mid-June day, as Monash, Blamey, Elles and Brigadier-General Anthony Courage, commander of the 5th Tank Brigade, watched on, the Mark Vs had gone through their paces.

'Sir John,' Elles had said as the massive twenty-three-ton monsters churned the grass in front of them, 'tanks are an arm which the enemy is not fully prepared to counter.'[23]

The Germans had yet to realise the potential of armoured vehicles. They had produced a handful of their own version of the tank, the massive and ungainly A7V, which required a crew of sixteen. The Australians would capture an A7V, *Mephisto*, on 22 July, and ship it back to Australia. There it remains today, on display, the sole remaining original A7V in the world. The German Army was also using a number of captured British tanks, but without any conception of the role the tank could and should play in infantry warfare. Instead, the Germans had invested heavily in anti-tank guns and armour-piercing machinegun bullets.

'The eventual counter to the tank can to my mind only be the tank,' Elles confidently told Monash, just as he'd told his GHQ. 'In the meantime, we have an opportunity. Once tank meets tank, the opportunity will vanish.'[24]

Monash the engineer nodded as he took in the smoke-belching metal beasts frolicking in the Vaux valley for his benefit. By the end of the day, he had come away convinced that Elles was right – the tank could be an infantry weapon *par excellence*, if deployed wisely. The Mark V tank had more powerful engines than its predecessor, meaning it travelled a little faster and had the capacity to get itself out of mud, snow and shell craters, which had invariably slowed or halted the Mark IV. The new tank also had thicker armour, and its internal efficiency was greater – instead of requiring four crewmen working together to steer it, as had been the case with the Mark IV, the Mark V needed just a single driver.

Like its predecessors, the Mark V did have one major fault. It was incredibly noisy and could be heard kilometres away, especially on quiet nights, the very time that Australian infantry moved into position to launch their surprise assaults. As things stood, that noise precluded the tank participating in such attacks – the enemy would be well and truly alerted to its presence long before it lumbered into view, and would be given precious time to take defensive measures.

Following the instructive Tank Corps demonstration, as Monash climbed into his Rolls-Royce staff car at Vaux to return to his HQ, he invited General Courage to send him a memorandum setting out how the Mark V could best cooperate with infantry in a surprise attack, as long as the problem of noise could be overcome.

On 21 June, Monash received Courage's memo, just as he was putting the finishing touches to his written Hamel proposal. The Tank Corps had developed a fixed mentality on how tanks should be used, and this dictated the first of

Courage's recommendations. He wrote that his new tanks could operate in an attack without the need for close artillery support. The tankers were worried that shells from supporting artillery could fall on their own advancing machines. Courage also said that tanks should advance in three waves, mixed with the infantry, with the infantry leading the assault.

As for the noise problem, Courage came up with a novel recommendation of his own. Only one other war machine was as noisy as a tank, the aircraft, and Courage suggested that aircraft be employed to fly low over the battlefield, drowning out the noise of advancing tanks and dropping bombs on the enemy's positions and keeping heads down, thus retaining the element of surprise as far as the tanks were concerned. Once Monash read Courage's report he dispensed with most of the tank man's recommendations, but was intrigued by Courage's original idea involving aircraft.

That same day, 21 June, Monash delivered the requested written proposal for the Hamel operation to General Rawlinson. Brief but precise, it read like a business plan. Covering seven points, it spelled out the pluses and minuses of the Hamel attack. As Monash and his divisional commanders had agreed in their council of war, this would be primarily an attack by 7500 infantry, but led by tanks. Contrary to Courage's recommendation, Monash's proposal called for extensive artillery support. But he did adopt Courage's idea for low-flying aircraft.

The main disadvantage of the operation, Monash wrote, was the potential depletion of his corps through casualties sustained in the attack. At this stage of the war, the supply of reinforcements from Australia had almost dried up, and heavy losses sustained from now on could not be replenished. A pitiful total of 5221 Australian reinforcements were then available at depots in England and Le Havre in France. However, the Australian divisions were already understrength by 8255 men as a result of casualties and illness. Major losses in this attack could make it necessary to abolish one of the five Aussie divisions and consolidate all remaining Australian infantry into four divisions.[25]

On the positive side, if the operation proceeded precisely as he proposed, with speed and precision, Monash said his losses would be minimal, and those casualties would be more than compensated for by the gain of the Hamel salient and the dent the success of the surprise assault would assuredly deliver to German morale. As for a date for the operation, Monash stated that his corps would be ready to mount it in the first week of July, when, his meteorological experts told him, he could expect clear weather and a waning moon; meaning, the surprise attack would not be illuminated by strong moonlight.

On 23 June, General Rawlinson submitted Monash's plan to Field-Marshal Haig at British GHQ at Montreuil-sur-Mer. This seaside town in the Pas-de-Calais region, where Jean Valjean served as mayor in Victor Hugo's *Les Misérables*, had been occupied by the British General Headquarters since 1916. Haig had his quarters in a chateau outside the town. Rawlinson added his recommendation to Monash's proposal that it be approved for implementation as set out by the Australian general, asking that a Royal Air Force squadron also be assigned to the operation to double Monash's air resources. Rawlinson expressed the opinion that the Hamel attack would be a great blow to German morale and a great launching platform for future larger attacks by the Australians.

Field-Marshal Haig liked and admired John Monash, and had been a prime mover in the Australian's recent promotion. An inarticulate man given to prolonged silences, Haig was also a man of little originality, and, indeed, according to some critics, of little compassion. Haig at least recognised talent in others, and in the articulate, urbane and sociable Monash in particular. Haig was delighted that, via the Monash plan, the British Army would be going on the attack after taking a battering in the Germans' spring offensive. Even if the Australians' attack was to be only on a relatively small scale at this point, it would still be, in Monash's words, 'the first offensive operation on any substantial scale' to be 'fought by the Allies since the previous autumn'.[26]

Haig was anxious to relieve pressure on Amiens, which he knew the Germans were keen to seize. The field-marshal also liked the fact that Monash was prepared to trust the much-maligned British tank. To Haig's credit, and to Monash's benefit, the commander-in-chief was a supporter of innovation. When, earlier in the war, others had scorned the introduction of tanks, considering them a desperate and last-ditch measure, Haig had encouraged their development and deployment. No one had been more disappointed than him by their failures to date. Monash's operation offered an opportunity to restore the tank's reputation. The field-marshal promptly approved the Hamel operation, and instructed Rawlinson and GHQ to give Monash all the tanks, artillery and aircraft he asked for.

Intensive, detailed preparations began at Chateau Bertangles, as General Monash, his department heads and staff began to quickly put together a detailed operational plan that would be both scrupulous and ingenious. In the end, it would involve 118 elements dictated by Monash, plus another eighteen added by subordinates, elements that had to be organised and integrated. These ranged, apart from the battlefield assault plan for 4 July, from supply to aerial reconnaissance, camouflage to diversions, in the days and hours leading up to the Hamel attack.

Monash considered an army a machine. According to his aide Frederick Cutlack, 'The work of the machine fascinated him, and its efficiency was a passion with him.'[27] Like the components of a machine, every one of the Hamel plan's 136 elements was vital to the operation's success. Should any component prove faulty, the whole thing might break down. Monash likened himself to the conductor of an orchestra, and his plan to a musical score. 'A perfected modern battle plan is like nothing so much as a score for an orchestral composition,' he said, 'where the various arms and units are the instruments, and the tasks they perform are their respective musical phases.'[28]

Some Australian officers who received General Monash's written 'score' for the Battle of Hamel complained there was too much paperwork. Others would later express the belief that the paperwork, and the detail, was the minimum required to ensure success. Either way, the 136 elements became the blueprint for the operation. With secrecy essential to ensuring the Germans had no idea about the build-up of men and equipment taking place opposite Hamel, or the reason for it, only very senior Australian and British officers were at this stage aware that an attack on the Hamel salient was being prepared. For the same reason, the movement of supplies and equipment towards the battle zone was restricted to the hours of darkness.

To undertake the Hamel assault, Monash selected General Sinclair-Maclagan's 4th Division, with Maclagan therefore the operational commander who would call the shots once the assault got underway. Monash bolstered Maclagan's force with the addition of the 6th Brigade from the 2nd Division and the 11th Brigade from the 3rd Division, with both brigades temporarily coming under Maclagan's command for the operation. When Monash informed Maclagan that he would be in charge of the assault, and that it would be led by tanks, the Scot flatly refused to have anything to do with tanks, having been badly let down by them in the past.

'Maclagan is not overjoyed by the prospect of tanks,' Monash told General Rawlinson.

'Don't worry,' Rawlinson responded, 'we will talk him round.' And they did.[29]

At this time, too, Monash had a brainwave. He knew that elements of the raw American 33rd 'Prairie' Division, which was part of the American Expeditionary Forces' II Corps, had been sent to the Amiens sector to train with the British Fourth Army for six weeks after landing in France from the USA on 30 May, the day Monash took over the Australian Corps. Monash was a great admirer of the United States. With his wife, he had visited the US in 1910 as part of a world tour, and it had excited him. 'Fascinating, stimulating and wonderful,' he had written to a friend.[30]

Over the years, too, Monash had studied America's military history in depth, the American Civil War in particular. So, Monash put in a request to General Rawlinson for 2000 American combat troops to be assigned to the Australian Corps to take part in the Hamel assault alongside the Aussies. Rawlinson would subsequently take credit for involving the Yanks. Certainly, he was the one to make the official request for them, but Monash would later make clear that the idea, and the original request, was his.

Ever since America had entered the war in April 1917, Monash had been looking forward to the arrival of American troops on the Western Front, envisioning their units being broken down to battalion size and distributed among British armies along the front. Nothing prepares a man for war better than war itself, Monash would have reminded Rawlinson. Since 13 June, a thousand noncombatants of the American 33rd Division's 108th Engineer Regiment had been attached to the Australian Corps, and all reports had them mixing well with the Australians. Knowing that no US combat troops had yet to be involved in an offensive action in France, it pleased Monash to think that he might be the one to give the United States its baptism of fire.

General Rawlinson thought Monash's suggestion a splendid idea, and contacted Major-General George W. Read, commander of the American II Corps. Rather than tell Read he wanted to throw 2000 Yanks into an attack against the Germans, Rawlinson suggested American participation with the Australian Corps in the most casual terms. 'Certain smaller units of your division might be permitted to take part in a raid of some kind which we contemplate making against the enemy some time in the near future,' he said. He added that Read should consider it 'valuable training' for his men. To meet Monash's request for 2000 American combat troops that could be spread through the Australian brigades, Rawlinson specifically asked Read for the American contribution to be in the form of platoons or companies.[31]

In General Monash's estimation, 'Read was a man of sound common sense and clear judgement.'[32] The white-haired, moustachioed, fifty-eight-year-old Read, an Iowa native, was a West Point graduate and professional soldier. For four years he had been assistant professor of military science at the University of Iowa, and during the Spanish-American War had served in Cuba as a captain in the ordnance department. General Read knew of the stellar fighting reputation of the Australians, and also knew that, while the British were content to sit pat in their trenches, the Aussies were making frequent raids across No Man's Land into the German front line and keeping the Kaiser's men on their toes.

Read, who had only been promoted from command of the American 30th Division to that of II Corps that month, saw this invitation to participate with the Aussies as an ideal opportunity to swiftly lift the level of battle preparedness of some of his men, without any risk of sending them into a situation where they might face defeat. To his mind, the Australians were guaranteed to succeed in any operation they undertook. According to Monash, who would develop an excellent working relationship with Read, 'His only desire was the success of his divisions.' So, without hesitation, Read agreed to the idea, and on 27 June his headquarters issued orders to the 33rd American Division to assign the 131st and

132nd Infantry Regiments to join the Australian Corps for the planned 'raid'.[33]

Read made just one stipulation when agreeing to his men joining the Australian Corps, that the Americans were not to be split up and scattered individually among Australian units. He required that they serve at the very least as complete platoons, and under their own platoon commanders. When Rawlinson passed this requirement on to Monash, the Australian general saw no problem, considering it a 'very proper condition'.[34] It was a condition he would adhere to, although some American medical personnel, runners and officers would be pragmatically salted solo or in small groups through Australian ranks as conditions dictated.

Three days later, at Chateau Bertangles, when General Monash held the final Hamel battle conference with his divisional commanders and departmental chiefs, including the commanders of Number 3 Squadron AFC and Number 9 Squadron Royal Air Force, after initially considering 2 July as the date for the assault he set 4 July as the day. 'This selection was prompted,' Monash would later say, 'partly by the desire to allow ample time for the completion of all arrangements.'[35]

Monash particularly wanted to involve his 11th Brigade, which had previously formed part of his 3rd Division command and which he considered the fittest of all the Australian brigades for the Hamel operation. The 11th was currently undergoing a scheduled spell behind the lines and was only due to return to the trenches the day before the Fourth of July. 'But there were also sentimental grounds, because this was the anniversary of the American national holiday.'[36]

American troops had already been involved in combat on the Western Front, in small defensive actions – two enlisted men of the 369th Regiment, an all-black National Guard unit from Harlem in New York City, had been awarded the Croix de Guerre by the French after fighting off a 14 May German raid on their guard post in the Argonne. But 4 July would be the first time American troops had gone on the offensive, and the Battle of Hamel, Monash's first operation in command of the Australian Corps, was quite deliberately and very confidently now set down by him to take place on American Independence Day, 1918, a day that Monash intended would give Americans every reason to remember and celebrate.[37]

3.

The American Colonel's Orders

'You're going into action with some mighty celebrated
troops guaranteed to win.'
Major-General George W. Read Jr, Commander
American II Corps

AS THE AMERICAN 131st Regiment marched to the front,
Colonel Joseph B. Sanborn smiled with satisfaction as his men
watched German shells lob in from long-range guns somewhere away to the east. The Americans observed this new
phenomenon more with fascination than fear. The enemy
guns seemed to be taking pot luck, firing without any precise
target in mind. Sanborn would later note that he saw only
a few of these shells cause casualties, while some destroyed
buildings, roads and bridges and occasionally obliterated a
British field gun or 'some luckless village', which, in Sanborn's
words, 'became a havoc of smoking ruin'.[38]

Like his Illinois boys, Joe Sanborn was in good spirits,
and ready to come to grips with the Germans. A stout sixty-
two-year-old with white hair and moustache, he was by any

standard rather old to be leading soldiers into battle. In fact, senior British officers who met him in June considered Sanborn a 'fussy' old man who should have been sent into retirement instead of being sent to the Western Front.[39] But Sanborn had made this regiment what it was. He was determined to fuss after the needs of his boys, and to do no less than he asked of them when the order came to go into the attack.

The Chicago-based 131st Regiment had started life in 1874 as the 1st Regiment of Infantry, Illinois State Guard. Retitled the 1st Illinois Volunteer Infantry, it had served in the 1898 Santiago campaign in Cuba during the Spanish-American War, with a younger, fitter Joe Sanborn one of its battalion commanders. As it happened, back then Sanborn had outranked his later corps commander, General Read, who would experience rapid promotion once the United States entered the Great War. Sanborn, a native of New Hampshire, had joined the 131st in Chicago as a twenty-four-year-old private in 1880, receiving a commission as a second lieutenant two years later. After a series of promotions, Sanborn had been made a colonel and commander of the regiment in December 1898. By that stage, he had also found success in business in Chicago as head of his own mercantile agency, J. B. Sanborn Co.

Sanborn had continued to command the regiment over the next seventeen years, and led it south in 1916 when the US Government mobilised 300,000 National Guard troops and sent them to the southern border to deal with the marauding Mexican general Pancho Villa, whose troops had raided Columbus, New Mexico and killed eighteen American citizens. Under Sanborn's efficient leadership, the 1st Illinois had been the first National Guard unit to reach the border, but, like all the other American troops sent to confront Villa, they had failed to see any action. Instead, the Illinois boys had spent four months kicking the Texas dust in camp at San Antonio. They had returned to Texas the following year to train for Great War service. This time reconstituted as the 131st Regiment and assigned to the 66th Brigade, which was in turn part of the 33rd Division, the unit had spent close to a year training at Houston's Camp Logan before finally being shipped to Europe.

After landing at Brest on 30 May, the regiment had been billeted there before being transferred east by rail to billets at the town of Eu. From Eu, Colonel Sanborn and his personal staff had proceeded to spend 12 to 16 June attached to the Australians, at the headquarters of Brigadier-General G. E. 'Pompey' Elliott's 15th Brigade. Simultaneously, Colonel Abel Davis, commander of the American 132nd Regiment, had spent these four days at the HQ of General Charles Brand's Australian 4th Brigade. Davis, an Illinois state senator and county recorder in civilian life, was Sanborn's protege and junior, having for some years commanded the 131st Regiment's 1st Battalion. Davis's appointment to lead the 132nd, the old 2nd Illinois, had been on Sanborn's recommendation.

At this stage, the Americans had no idea that General Monash would soon ask for them to join his corps. Sanborn was to say that over these four days at 15th Brigade HQ he had many talks with Pompey Elliott, a no-nonsense veteran of Australian campaigns on Gallipoli, in Flanders and on the Somme. Elliott and Brand, who had taken over command of General Monash's one-time brigade in 1916, were just the men to school Sanborn and Davis in the realities of trench warfare. Sanborn and Davis, for their part, were eager to listen and learn. Following this four-day attachment, Davis promptly wrote to Brand, thanking him for his invaluable time and advice and telling him how much he had enjoyed the experience. Davis had added, 'I hope that I shall have the opportunity to serve with you and your troops.'[40]

Australian officers had been equally impressed with their American counterparts. Said the 4th Brigade's Lieutenant Ted Rule, 'These Yanks view things much the same as we do, and their general trend of ideas was very sensible indeed.'[41]

On Friday 21 June, the day that General Monash submitted his written Hamel plan for approval, Colonels Sanborn and Davis obeyed orders from American II Corps HQ to move their regiments to Pierregot, northwest of Amiens, to join the British 4th Army's III Corps for training, with the front line and the Germans just fifteen kilometres to their east. At Pierregot, both the 131st and 132nd had received orders on 29 June to join the Australian Corps for 'a raid of some kind' against the Germans. This, said the written order that came out of the American II Corps headquarters, was 'considered valuable training'.[42]

Major-General George Bell Jr, commander of the American 33rd Division, had told Colonel Sanborn about instructions he'd received from General Read regarding the move. Read had urged Bell, when addressing his troops, 'Tell them, "You're going in with some mighty celebrated troops guaranteed to win, and you've got to get up to their level and stay with them."'[43]

Bell was a career soldier who'd graduated from West Point military academy the same year that Joe Sanborn enlisted in the part-time State Guard as a private. Field-Marshal Haig described Bell as 'a typical Yankee, with a little goatee beard and moustache'.[44] In fact, to modern eyes, the handsome Bell would look a great deal like Colonel Sanders of Kentucky Fried Chicken fame. With no time for delay or excuse, Bell had gained the nickname of 'Do It Now' from his troops. He had duly exhorted Sanborn to ensure his boys made ready to make good when they went over the top with the Australians. 'The bravery, efficiency and skill of Australian soldiers,' he was to say, 'are fully appreciated by this division as they are known to the entire world.'[45]

Neither Sanborn nor his troops had been impressed by the lethargic, unenthusiastic, war-weary British III Corps troops and their overcautious officers they encountered at Pierregot. 'The British were not contemplating any offensive, but were rather picking out the points on which to retire if pressed,' Sanborn would later say.[46]

The Americans were not alone in their critical assessment of the British Army. Privately, General Monash said, 'The best troops of the United Kingdom have been long ago used up and we now have a class of man who is without initiative or individuality. They are brave enough, but simply unskilful. They would be alright if properly led, but their officers, particularly the junior officers, are poor young men from the professions and from office stools in the English cities, who have had no experience whatever of independent responsibility or leadership.'[47]

The Germans also considered British troops the weakest

35

link in the Allied line, and were secretly planning a strike against the British Army in Flanders at this very time, a strike that would be cancelled once Monash went on the offensive. So, the Americans were thrilled to be joining the Australians. Just as the fighting prowess of the Australians was well known to the Americans, it was acknowledged by the Germans, whose press declared that the British were trying to climb to victory over the corpses of their Australian and Canadian troops.[48]

'There were great manifestations of joy,' Sanborn would say, when the order came in from brigade HQ at 2.35 pm on 29 June for the regiment's C and E companies, plus one platoon from K Company added to bring E Company up to full strength, to march to Allonville and report 'for training' with the Australian 4th Brigade.[49] The following day, a further six companies from the 131st were ordered to move south to take up reserve positions in the rear of the front line held by the Australian Corps and make ready to also participate in the Hamel attack. As Sanborn and his men marched into the Australian sector they were met by Australian officers and men who welcomed them warmly.

'Are you going to win the war for us?' one wisecracking Australian called to the Americans with a grin as they passed.

'Well,' a Yank came back, 'we hope we fight like the Australians.'[50]

Far from boasting that they were going to win the war, the Americans only wanted to learn from and emulate the Australians, which immediately enamoured them to the men from Down Under, who welcomed them like long-lost brothers. 'The Australians appeared to be more akin to our class [than the British and French],' Colonel Sanborn would say, 'in that they were an independent, alert, energetic lot of men and splendid fighters.'[51] As Sanborn noted, the Americans and Australians had a lot in common. Not only had both their nations been born out of British colonialism, Yanks and Aussies valued individualism. These men also looked much alike, being generally taller and stronger than the average short, pale British squaddie as a result of more protein in their diet while growing up, and more of an outdoor life.

The Aussies were in fact a sight for sore American eyes. 'From the first when our soldiers came in contact with them,' said Sanborn, 'they mixed well and took kindly to each other.'[52] As the two forces assimilated, word quickly also reached Australian commanders that their men considered the Americans 'good blokes', with similar outlooks. 'They swear a little less, they drink coffee rather than tea,' one Australian officer reported, 'but otherwise might as well be our own fellows.'[53]

An Australian war correspondent who saw the American troops arriving in the Amiens sector was immediately impressed by what he saw. 'Fine looking men,' he would write, 'just arrived by march today in their dusty boots, green-yellow canvas gaiters, coats shaped to the waist, and felt Puritan hats.' At a glance, once the Americans donned the same British-style steel helmets that the Australians wore, Yanks and Aussies were difficult to tell apart. Same impressive height and build, and a similar tunic design, of a similar khaki-colour, which the Yanks called 'drab'. On closer inspection, the American tunic had a stand-up collar that differed from the Australian tunic's flat collar.[54]

As Colonel Sanborn's headquarters and medical staff also

joined their Australian counterparts, the 131st Regiment's Company C dossed down with the Australian 42nd Battalion, and Company E, with the addition of the platoon from Company K, joined the 43rd Battalion. Simultaneously, the 132nd Regiment's Company A joined the Australian 13th Battalion and its Company G amalgamated with the 15th Battalion.

At 2.00 in the morning of 1 July, Indiana native Captain Carroll M. Gale, a police inspector in Chicago until a little more than a year before this, led his weary Company C men of Colonel Sanborn's 131st Regiment to the Australian 11th Brigade reserve trench line, where they were to join the Aussie 42nd Battalion. Thirty-eight-year-old Gale knew that something big was in the wind, but still didn't know exactly what. As he was departing Pierregot, a bright-eyed General Bell, who knew all about the planned Hamel attack but was sworn to secrecy by General Read, had told Gale as much as he dare. 'The Australians might let us take part in a show they are planning,' he'd said with a sparkle in his eye.[55]

At the reserve trenches, Gale was met by Major Edward Dibdin, who was commanding the 42nd Battalion, a Queensland unit. Prior to the war a company secretary in Rockhampton, Dibdin now warmly welcomed Gale and showed him where his men could bed down. Gale was surprised by how the Australian battalion had been reduced in numbers by its years of fighting the Germans, a fact he remarked on to the Australian major.

Dibdin shrugged philosophically. 'Yes, my companies are small,' he agreed. 'The entire battalion is little stronger than your company.'[56]

Gale nodded. His company was sixty men strong, while, in his estimation, the entire 42nd Battalion contained just one hundred men. That compared to a full-strength battalion of 900, although every one of the hundred Queenslanders Gale saw looked tough and battle ready. So, Gale made a suggestion. 'So that my men can mix more with your Australians and learn more from them, I suggest I detail one of my platoons with each of your companies.'[57]

Dibdin readily agreed, and the American platoons split up and divided themselves among the Australian companies, with much handshaking, backslapping and friendly banter exchanged. In daylight, more American platoons arrived. Some of the new arrivals were also distributed among the Australian companies, while fifty Americans and an equal number of Australians were sent to the rear to form a battalion reserve that could be quickly brought forward in an emergency to support the men of the first line.

Nearby, when Captain James W. Luke's Company E from the 131st Infantry joined the South Australians of the 43rd Battalion, a similar division of Americans was made among the Australian companies. The addition of American reinforcements permitted the equally understrength 43rd to re-establish its fourth company. The same sort of division and union took place when Colonel Davis's 132nd Regiment joined the 4th Brigade. Commented one 4th Brigade staff officer, 'These American soldiers seem an exceptionally smart lot and are most keen to learn. They are getting on exceptionally well with the officers and men of the brigade.'[58]

It was a marriage made in soldiers' heaven, and both the Australians and the Americans were eager to go into action together as soon as possible, but with different motives. The hard-bitten Aussies were determined to do whatever it took to bring victory and an end to the war closer. Meanwhile, the Yanks were keen to impress the Aussies with their enthusiasm and courage, and to win their share of glory.

4.

The Australian Sergeant's Reluctance

'It failed for a variety of reasons.'
Major-General John Fuller, British Tank Corps, on the
disastrous 1917 Bullecourt tank assault

AT THE VERY time the Americans were moving down into the Australians' sector, the Australian 15th Battalion's Sergeant Edward George Searle, or Ned to his friends and family, was standing looking at brown metal monsters arrayed before him on the grass of a French valley.

'Bloody tanks!' he cursed.

Blue-eyed, fair-haired Ned, of average height and build, was the eldest of four boys who had been raised in the northern Tasmanian farming village of Westbury. Commencing life as home to a British Army garrison when Tasmania was still known as Van Diemen's Land, Westbury had housed a detachment of British troops in the early nineteenth century, with retired veterans from the Duke of Wellington's army at the Battle of Waterloo being settled there. Three of the four Searle brothers had enlisted in the Australian Imperial Force in 1914, shortly after the outbreak of war in Europe. Ned, the eldest, had been the last to volunteer.

All the Searle boys had been accustomed to the outdoor life. Almost 1600 years earlier, Roman writer Vegetius, who penned a military handbook for the emperor Valentinian, had felt that country boys made the best soldiers: 'For they, from their infancy, have been exposed to all kinds of weather and have been brought up to the hardest labour.'[59] This well described the Searle brothers, who all worked as farm labourers, seasonal apple pickers and blacksmiths' assistants. Yet each differed from the next enormously.

Ray, the youngest, the most idealistic and the most naive of the brothers, had been in the militia when war broke out. Within days, rash Ray had been the first in the family to enlist in the new AIF. Middle brother Viv, a gifted, bowtie-wearing poet and teetotaller who had ambitions to become a clergyman after the war, had quickly followed suit, to look after his little brother. Twenty-six-year-old Ned was the black sheep of the family, a typical hard-drinking, hard-smoking, hard-gambling, hard-swearing Australian 'larrikin', or lovable rogue. He had resisted volunteering at first, only signing up a month after his younger brothers to impress his schoolteacher girlfriend Win Watson, being convinced that the war would be over by Christmas.

Three-and-a-half years later, come the eve of the Battle of Hamel, Ned was the only one of the three brothers still alive. Middle brother Viv had been with the 12th Battalion in the first wave of the Gallipoli landing in April 1915. Three months later, a temporary corporal, Viv had been shot in the head by a Turkish sniper while leading an Australian sniping detail. Ned was also on Gallipoli by that stage. Twice wounded there, he survived to be sent to the Western Front with the 15th Battalion.

There, Ned had reunited with baby brother Ray, who was serving with the 52nd Battalion. Ray was subsequently killed near Messines, in 1917, when a German shell collapsed his trench and entombed him. Ned had been wounded twice more, firstly by shrapnel when collecting water and then taking a German machinegun bullet in the hand while leading a patrol. Recovering in an English hospital, Ned had learned that back home Win Watson had dumped him for another man.

Having lost his two brothers and the love of his life to this war, Ned had spiralled into depression. The shattered metacarpal bone in his hand should have knitted in six to eight weeks, but every time it looked like healing Ned would surreptitiously smash it against the corner of a table, maiming himself anew. Ned had had enough of soldiering. 'I have no true friends in the army,' he'd written home to his mother. All his 15th Battalion friends from the Gallipoli days had been killed by this time. 'I hold all men in contempt,' he told his mother. 'Whether it is the army that has done this I do not know, but I am different from other chaps.'[60]

In hospital, Ned had kept to himself, shying away from other wounded Aussies who had only recently tasted battle for the first time and boasted of what they would do to the Germans once they got back to the front. 'I do not make friends and am really sick of hearing men talk,' Ned confessed to his mother. 'You can imagine how the army has had an effect on me.'[61]

When the Germans launched their spring offensive in March 1918, Ned was still in hospital in England, and wooing a Scottish nurse. Reading in April in the British press of the tough fighting the Australians had put in to halt the Germans on the Somme, he had been overcome with guilt, and let his hand heal. On Saturday 18 May, Ned had rejoined the 15th Battalion's D Company near Villers-Bretonneux. Being a rare Gallipoli veteran in his platoon, and surrounded by strangers, Ned, now promoted to sergeant, was put in charge of a six-man section.

Ned returned to the front with a determination to take out his bitterness on the Germans, avenging his brothers and making a name for himself. A medal would be nice. The Victoria Cross would be nicest of all. The highest gallantry award for British and Empire soldiers and the equivalent of the American Medal of Honor, the Victoria Cross had been inaugurated in 1856 during the Crimean War. The 999th VC had only recently been awarded. No one in the 15th Battalion had yet to receive a VC, and the idea of showing off the 1000th VC ever minted in the pub back in Westbury was an appealing one. And, perhaps, winning a VC would finally secure Ned the approval of his mother, Elizabeth Annie Searle.

Throughout the war, Elizabeth Annie had treated her sons with outward equality, writing to each of them every Sunday night and sending identical gift packages at special times such as Christmas, birthdays, and following family weddings. But Ned knew that Viv had been the apple of his mother's eye, and that young Ray had not come far behind in her affections, with Ned about as popular with her as the Westbury night-cart driver. Just as his heavy drinking had offended his Methodist mother, it had temporarily lost him his girl-friend Win just prior to the war. It was only by enlisting in September 1914 and promising to straighten himself out and marry her on his return from the conflict that Ned had won Win back after she had ended their relationship that autumn.

Yes, Ned had no doubts it would take a VC to elevate him to the top of the popularity table in the Searle house-hold. The fact that Ned still kept his former girlfriend's photo in a breast pocket of his tunic suggested that he thought he might even win her back a second time with a spectacular feat of bravery on the battlefield. He'd had his hopes of a medal raised following the Battle of Bullecourt. 'All of us that were left were recommended,' he'd written home, 'but our colonel [McSharry] is a Roman Catholic, and all the chaps that got anything were Micks and Pats, so we missed out, this time.'[62] As he rejoined his unit, the lustre of a Victoria Cross shone bright in Ned's ambitions. All ranks had to salute a Victoria Cross winner. Even General Monash would have to salute Ned if he won a VC!

Ned had been back with his battalion in the Somme trenches for forty days when he and all the other 15th Battalion platoon and section leaders had been ordered on 29 June to the rear, to the village of Vaux-en-Amiénois, for a training exercise. When they arrived in a field outside the town, Ned and his comrades saw that they were joining fellow platoon and section leaders from three Australian brigades for a day of training with British tanks. The sight of the lumbering armoured vehicles was enough to make Ned vomit.

In April the previous year, Ned and thousands of other

Australians of the 4th and 11th Brigades had launched an assault on the Germans' Hindenburg Line at Bullecourt, north of the Somme. The 'Inderbugs Line', Ned called it. The Aussies were supposed to be supported in the attack by newfangled tanks of the British Tank Corps; this had been the first experience Australian troops had of armoured vehicles.

After the Mark IV tanks assigned to the assault had been caught in a blizzard and failed to reach the starting point, the operation's start had been put off for twenty-four hours.[63] Uneasy Australian commanders, seeing how the tanks had succumbed to the wintry conditions and doubting their reliability, had asked for the Bullecourt operation to be suspended. Overall British commander Lieutenant-General Sir Hubert Gough had dismissed the Australian concerns and insisted the assault proceed. It was Gough who would ultimately be dismissed, relieved of his post by the high command, but that would be no consolation to the Aussies.

When the Australians finally charged across No Man's Land on the day of the assault, the tanks had failed them, badly. Some had broken down. Others had been quickly knocked out by German artillery and machineguns. The crews of the remaining tanks seemed to have no stomach for the fight and deserted the Aussies, who, in savage fighting and with heavy losses, nevertheless seized and occupied the heavily defended German trenches they had been ordered to take.

On top of the failure of the tanks, further troops had not been sent in after the first wave to consolidate the gains. British commanders also failed to provide the Australians with artillery cover, overconfidently believing that the tanks would sweep all before them. As the Germans mounted fierce counterattacks to retake their trenches from the Australians, Ned and his mates had fought them off until they ran out of ammunition. In a hopeless situation, the Australian survivors decided they had two options – surrender, or try to run back over open ground under heavy German fire to the trenches they had started out from. Ned was one of the few who made a run for it and miraculously made it back unharmed. Wounded Australians in the German trenches were going nowhere and had no choice but to surrender.[64]

Of the 3000 men of the 4th Brigade who had gone into the Bullecourt assault, 2339 had been killed, wounded or captured. Ned Searle had been one of just eighty-two from the 4th Brigade's 15th Battalion to make it back to Australian lines. Ned, a master of understatement, had said, after the battle, 'We had a rough time of it while it lasted.' No wonder Ned and fellow Australian survivors had lost faith in British generals, and in British tanks.[65]

Major-General John 'Boney' Fuller, then a colonel and a senior staff officer with the Tank Corps, blamed the failure of the Bullecourt operation on a variety of factors: haste of preparation, changes in the plan of attack the night before the assault, 'unavoidable' lack of artillery support, 'insufficiency of tanks for such an operation', and 'the lack of confidence on the part of the infantry in the tanks themselves'.[66]

If the Australians had lack of confidence in tanks prior to the battle, following it Ned Searle and his comrades absolutely detested the beasts and would have nothing to do with them for the next fifteen months. General Monash knew this well, yet he still made tanks the centrepiece of his Hamel battle plan, later declaring, 'That tanks, appropriately utilised, were destined to exert a paramount influence on the course of the war was apparent to those who could envisage the future.' Monash, for one, could envisage the mechanised future of land warfare.[67]

He had several reasons for his confidence in armoured vehicles. Since the Bullecourt disaster, the new Mark V tank had been developed. The Battle of Hamel would be the first time it was deployed in combat, and the Australians and accompanying Americans would be the first infantry to go into battle with it. At Monash's request, Field-Marshal Haig assigned the entire 5th Tank Brigade to the Australian Corps for the Hamel operation, and the brigade's commander Brigadier-General Anthony Courage gave General Monash all the more reason to be confident that the Tank Corps would not let down the Australians a second time. Courage, who possessed only half a jaw, the other half having been shot away by a Boche bullet during fighting at Ypres, was a capable organiser and an inspiring leader. According to Major-General Fuller, 'No detail escaped his eye, no trouble was too great.' Courage was just the man for detail-conscious Monash.[68]

With fifty-eight tanks at his disposal for the battle – roughly the same number as the Australian Army operates in total today – Monash had to convince his own troops to willingly work with them. This was a particularly difficult task because, as it happened, the very same Australian brigades that had been butchered at Bullecourt because of the failure of British tanks were to take part in the Hamel operation. In his initial written proposal of 21 June, Monash had said it was imperative that a day be set aside to demonstrate the new Mark V's capabilities to his men leading up to the battle, to rebuild his troops' trust in tanks.[69]

Under different circumstances, Monash would almost certainly have asked the British to hand over fifty or sixty of their new tanks for Australian crews to man. In March that year, British GHQ had in fact offered the Australians enough tanks to form their own armoured battalion, but Australian Corps commander General Birdwood had turned down the offer. One Mark IV tank did end up in Aussie hands; it was sent to Australia to support recruitment drives. That machine is today at the Australian War Memorial in Canberra.

There was no question that Australian infantry would storm the gates of Hell if they had Australian-crewed tanks supporting them. But it would have taken weeks, if not months, for Australians to train to operate tanks with proficiency. Monash didn't have the luxury of weeks or months. Eager to strike quickly at Hamel, he was prepared to use British tanks with British crews as long as they did what he told them to do, and as long as his Australian infantry willingly cooperated with them. That was what this training day at Vaux was all about.

Ned Searle saw a group of generals standing across the field to watch the fun as he and numerous other men from the Australian 4th, 6th and 11th Brigades stepped down from buses that had brought them to Vaux from their positions just behind the lines. To begin with, the Australian troops formed up by battalion and were conducted on manoeuvres with the tanks. Red flags had been placed to indicate the location of supposed enemy machinegun posts. Between the Australians and the flags stretched lengths of dreaded barbed-wire entanglements. Australian infantry platoons, each pairing up with a tank, advanced with fixed bayonets towards the flags.

At eight kilometres per hour, a little faster than the speed of the walking troops, the tank rolled ahead, mashing the wire into the earth and creating a path through the entanglement via which the troops poured through. With bloodthirsty yells the infantry charged past the tanks towards the flags, and, with grins, captured them and lifted them, fluttering, aloft.

Next, the tanks showed off their ability to climb over trenches dug for the demonstration, and to straddle said trenches and fire into and along them using the cannon and machineguns in the cupolas on their sides. Selected infantrymen were then equipped with rifle grenades and shown how, after they fired a grenade at a supposed enemy strongpoint, the grenade emitted white smoke, which summoned a tank. That tank then came lumbering up to the strongpoints indicated by the white smoke, and, in the words of General Monash, who was watching on with keen interest, 'Pirouetting around and around, [it] would blot them out, much as a man's heel would crush a scorpion.'[70]

The impressive display was followed by a picnic lunch on the grass. This affair was a long way from the normal wartime grind, although Ned would have liked a beer to wash down his sandwiches. The tanks then held 'open house', with the Australians encouraged to clamber all over and inside them. Following this the tankers took the Australian NCOs for joyrides all over the field, with some even given a chance to drive them. Meanwhile, Australian junior officers in charge of companies and platoons debated the merits of various combined tank and infantry tactics with British tank officers and agreed ways of improving their interaction.

Whilst wireless sets had been introduced to higher level HQs for the transmission of messages, tanks were not at this time fitted with radios for communication. To send messages to their headquarters they were equipped with carrier pigeons. For communication between individual tank commanders and troops around them on the battlefield, there was a bell attached to the rear of each machine. When this bell was rung, the commander, in theory, would open a 'port' and speak directly with an infantry officer who required tank support to attack a particular target. In addition, the tanks would fly small flags to indicate their status. A red, white and blue flag would indicate 'I am coming out of action', while a red and yellow one would signify 'I am broken down/ immobilised'.

None of these communication methods engendered a great deal of confidence among the already sceptical Australian infantrymen. What if the tank commander didn't hear or respond to the bell? What if a flag had been shot away, or wasn't raised in the first place? Then there was the question of the use of white smoke grenades to mark targets for tanks. Whilst fine in theory, the effectiveness of this method was doubted by the Australians, who pointed out that this grenade smoke could be obscured by smoke emitted by the hundreds of smoke shells lobbed onto the battlefield in the opening artillery barrage.

So, two important improvised battlefield signals were also agreed between the Australians and the tankers. Firstly, to indicate 'Tanks needed here', the infantry were instructed to jam a bayonet into the ground, place a helmet on top, and lie down and wait for a tank to come to their aid. There was also great concern in infantry ranks that tank drivers would not see wounded men lying on the ground and roll right over them, killing them, especially if the wounded were lying in wheatfields. To prevent this, the location of a wounded man would be marked by a rifle jammed into the ground and white tape tied around the top of a nearby stand of wheat.

By the time the Australians reboarded the buses to return to their bivouacs, all were in good spirits, and General Monash was convinced the day's outing had converted his rank and file into tank enthusiasts. Certainly, the Australians felt warmer towards tank crews, but for a number of men, like Ned Searle, it remained to be seen whether the tanks and their Tommy crews could and would meet their promise and back them up on the battlefield.[71]

5.

The Objections of General Courage

'I can never be sufficiently grateful to
Brigadier-General Courage.'
Lieutenant-General Sir John Monash

Two THOUSAND YEARS ago, the Romans turned the employment of artillery into an art form. Every Roman legion through the first several hundred years of the imperial era had its own artillery section firing a variety of missiles. Catapults called ballistas – from where we get the word 'ballistic' – fired specially rounded stones that were the equivalent of later cannonballs. These ballista stones, which were delivered to the catapult crews packed in crates like apples, ranged in weight from a few kilograms to a massive missile called a Wagon Stone, which was so large it required a wagon to carry it. Primarily used to batter down enemy emplacements, ballista stones were fired with such a velocity they could and did take the head off any human opponent unfortunate enough to be in their path. The scorpio was another Roman artillery piece, a light anti-personnel weapon on wooden legs that fired large arrows called 'bolts'. Numerous skeletons have been unearthed at Roman siege sites with the metal heads of scorpio bolts lodged in their spines as a consequence of falling victim to legion scorpios.

By the nineteenth century, artillery was an indispensable part of any field army. Napoleon commenced his military career as an artillery officer, and just as Napoleon always took great care in the effective provision, placement and use of artillery in his many campaigns, a century later General John Monash, who had also started out with the artillery, was well aware of the extraordinary power of artillery to influence the outcome of an infantry battle, and laid his plans accordingly.

For the Battle of Hamel, at Monash's request General Rawlinson attached his efficient personal artillery adviser Major-General Charles Budworth to Monash's headquarters, to act as overall artillery commander, and Monash took full advantage of Budworth's expertise. When Monash took over the Australian Corps it already possessed a powerful artillery arm: 'More than six times as numerous and more than a hundred times as powerful as that commanded by the Duke of Wellington,' in Monash's own words.[72]

From the eight he already had on the Somme, Monash also asked for his artillery brigades to be doubled for the Hamel operation. And, with Haig's full support, this was what Rawlinson gave him, sending elements of nine British artillery brigades with hundreds of additional big guns to supplement the Australian Corps' existing Aussie artillery. By the night of the Battle of Hamel, Monash would possess a total of 639 artillery pieces to pound German positions on a Hamel front just 5.6 kilometres wide and 1.5 kilometres deep – 326 of them would be field guns, 313 heavy guns including howitzers.

According to remarkably accurate intelligence reports in Monash's hands, the enemy had 477 artillery pieces in place to cover the Hamel salient and capable of countering his assault. Monash's multi-point plan required that his hundreds of additional artillery pieces all be secretly moved up and into place on the night of 2 July. In the meantime, in preparation for the guns' arrival, labour battalions and engineers were secretly building and camouflaging new gun emplacements by night. Ammunition would also be moved up to all guns in darkness.

At one point on the River Somme, every night for several days at the beginning of July engineers built a temporary bridge to speed the arrival of supplies, artillery and men for the Hamel assault, then took it down again before dawn so the Germans had no idea what was going on, only to rebuild it the following night. To fool Fritz, a dummy bridge was also prepared further along the river, but it wasn't used in the end because the local artillery commander protested that German artillery would shell it and probably hit his nearby camouflaged gun positions.

Monash had a hand in, and an eye on, all the details of the preparations in every unit and department. According to one of his aides, 'Without interfering with their work he insisted upon knowing every detail of the organisation under his command in all operations.'[73] As part of his 118-point plan, Monash gave his artillery commanders precise instructions, requiring a nightly barrage in the days leading up to the attack and a barrage that accompanied the assault itself.

July was the height of the northern summer, and in central France at this time the sun sets late in the evening and rises early in the morning. On 4 July 1918, the sun was expected to rise around 3.30 am. Australian commanders invariably launched their infantry attacks at dawn, as this allowed their men to move up to the start line in darkness undetected. Monash therefore specified that 'Z Hour', the time for the commencement of the Hamel operation, would be 3.10 am on 4 July. This meant that by the time the infantry reached enemy positions as they advanced behind a supporting artillery barrage, they would go into attack mode at first light.

From the moment that Field-Marshal Haig approved the Hamel operation, Monash ordered his existing artillery to fire an eight-minute barrage at German positions in the Hamel salient every morning from 3.00 am. This preliminary barrage, which had a sneaky tactical purpose that would only become apparent on the morning of the assault, was made up of a combination of heavy explosive, smoke and gas shells. In 1915 the Germans had been the first to use chlorine gas as a weapon; it became known as mustard gas because of its yellowy colour. The Allies had been quick to follow suit, and both sides now routinely lobbed poison gas of various kinds at each other. As a result, every British soldier always carried a gas mask, the Small Box Respirator, which he quickly pulled over his face after hearing an alarm gong sounding or the shouted warning: 'Gas! Gas! Gas!'

To support the tank and infantry advance on 4 July, after a two-minute pause following the end of the regular preliminary barrage, Monash's plan called for what he referred to as a 'jumping barrage'. Others called it a 'creeping barrage'.

Monash specified that from 3.10 all his guns would fire at the same target range just ahead of the waiting infantry and tanks for three minutes, then lift their range by precisely one hundred yards and fire for another three minutes, before another one hundred yard lift, and so on, until the barrage had jumped forward a total of half a mile, the halfway point in the planned advance.

Meanwhile, the tanks and infantry were to steadily advance immediately behind the barrage at walking pace, taking twenty minutes to reach this halfway point by 3.30. There would be a ten-minute pause to allow tanks and infantry to attack enemy front-line positions as the sun began to rise, before the creeping barrage resumed. This would bombard enemy reserve lines for four minutes at a time before again lifting range by a hundred yards, and so on. In all, Monash called for twenty-five lifts of range in the mile-deep advance, as far as an old British line of trenches on the ridge east of Hamel, which the Australians were to occupy and make the new Allied front line, linking up with Allied lines north and south of the Hamel salient.

However, Monash's plan for the massive use of artillery was directly at odds with the tactical principles that the Tank Corps had established for the deployment of its tanks. General Elles and his subordinates were of the belief that the new Mark V was such a superior weapon it could eliminate an entrenched enemy without the need for artillery support. So, they were dead against any form of creeping barrage, fearing that their precious beasts would be damaged or destroyed by shortfalls of friendly fire. Monash appears not to have told the 5th Tank Brigade's CO Brigadier-General Courage about his planned 'jumping barrage' in support of the assault, because when Courage and his deputy Lieutenant-Colonel J. D. Y. Bingham attended their first operational planning meeting at General Maclagan's 4th Division HQ at Bussy-lès-Daours, both made strenuous efforts to have the artillery barrage eliminated from the assault plan.

With Maclagan's bitter dislike and distrust of tanks, anything the tankers were likely to propose would not have gone down well with the pessimistic Scot. And Australian infantry officers would have been incensed that the British tank men were fearful of their metal boxes on tracks being hit by the barrage, when the Aussie infantry was fully prepared to advance out in the open, under the same barrage and facing the same lethal risk, without the protection of centimetres of armour plate. Maclagan and every other Australian Corps officer attending this meeting were unanimous in their agreement that the artillery barrage was essential, to protect the advance and ensure the assault's success. Courage and Bingham were shouted down.

Courage subsequently complained about this to Major-General Archibald Montgomery, General Rawlinson's chief of staff at British Fourth Army, and Montgomery, fully endorsing Courage's position, complained to his superior Rawlinson. But with Rawlinson a total enthusiast for Monash's plan, all such complaints fell on deaf ears. So, Monash's plan went forward unamended, with tanks, even though the operation's commander Maclagan despised them, and with massive artillery support, even though the Tank Corps was vehemently opposed to it.

In the end, General Courage applied his renowned powers

of organisation and leadership to meeting General Monash's requirements of the Tank Corps at Hamel, even if he did doubt the wisdom of the Australian commander's insistence on close support of tanks by artillery. Monash would later say, 'I can never be sufficiently grateful to Brigadier-General Courage of the 5th Tank Brigade for his diligent assistance, and for his loyal acceptance of the onerous conditions which the tactical methods that I finally decided upon imposed on the tanks.'[74]

6.

The American Corporal's Destiny

'[American] officers and men were most anxious to learn,
and eager for the fight.'
*Lieutenant-Colonel John Farrell, Commander Australian
43rd Battalion*

On Sunday 30 June, the day after Ned Searle and his 15th
Battalion mates played with the tanks at Vaux, officers
and NCOs of the American 131st and 132nd Infantry
Regiments also took part in the tank exercises. Unlike the
Australians, the Americans had no previous experience
with tanks, good or bad, and they participated with great
interest and enthusiasm. The 131st's commanding officer
Colonel Sanborn rated the day as 'most instructive, as it
gave the men some idea of tank tactics and promised confidence in action'.[75]

One of Sanborn's NCOs practising tank cooperation that
day was twenty-three-year-old Corporal Thomas Alexander
Pope from Chicago. Tom Pope had been born and raised in
Edison Park, a predominantly Irish area on the northern rim

of Chicago named for inventor Thomas Edison. On leaving school, Tom had gone to work for the busy Cook County Highway Department. To this day, Chicagoans will tell you: 'We only have two seasons in Chicago – Summer, and Repairing the Roads.'

Tom also joined his brother J. J. and a bunch of school friends in enlisting in the part-time National Guard's 1st Illinois Regiment. Tom, a solidly built, long-faced, thoughtful boy who was slow to smile, had gone to Texas with the regiment in 1916 during the Pancho Villa crisis, then returned there the following year as the Prairie Division trained for the war in Europe.

By the time the 131st and 132nd arrived in France in May 1918, the Chicago National Guard units had been brought up to full strength by the addition of draftees from throughout Illinois. Voluntary enlistment in the US military after the United States officially declared war on the Central Powers on 4 April 1917 had not met expectations, and the government of President Woodrow Wilson had instituted conscription. This had met with legal challenges, going all the way to the Supreme Court. In the meantime, the draft had been suspended. This was one of the reasons why the US was slow to send troops to Europe; it was intended that when the Americans arrived they did so in force, as an independent entity and not as piecemeal reinforcements the French and British could throw into their own battered units.

On 7 January 1918, the US Supreme Court had decided in favour of conscription, and the draft got underway in earnest across the US. In Los Angeles on 8 January, Carl

Laemmle, boss of Universal Studios, laid off 1500 of his 2100 employees. With the US Government talking about sending more than three million men to the European war by 1919, Laemmle foresaw a drastic dropoff in US movie-house attendances in 1918. Other Hollywood studios quickly followed his lead, and soon Los Angeles was so flooded with out-of-work actors who couldn't pay their bills that rooming houses and restaurants put up signs: 'No dogs. No actors.' More than one Hollywood actor was drafted into the US military as conscription built the nation's army in 1918.

As the political and legal games played out in Washington DC, to the frustration of the 131st Regiment's longtime volunteers like Tom Pope, who were chafing to get into the fight against Kaiser Wilhelm II's men, their training in Illinois and Texas had been stretched out for close to a year, without a hint of action. Meanwhile, hundreds of thousands of Allied soldiers died at the front.

Despite the lengthy training, during which Tom and his comrades practised defending and taking trenches time and time again, the brutal realities of trench warfare were as yet unknown to them. By the time they marched into Allonville in France, they were still novices, yet to see or be exposed to an artillery bombardment or experience the maiming and death of buddies around them. On the way to Allonville, the appearance of a German aircraft overhead had sent the men of the regiment diving for cover at the roadside, where they nervously remained for some time, delaying the march.

General Bell and Colonels Sanborn and Davis were acutely aware of the inexperience of their men, and keen to let them taste action without putting them too far into harm's way. Participating in a 'show' in company with the Australians offered just such an opportunity. But, for the moment, the Hamel secret remained confined to them; they could not tell their men that within days they would be coming face-to-face with the Boche.

In the National Guard units it was the experienced guardsmen who received promotion to officer and NCO ranks, and in this way Tom Pope had become a corporal in charge of one of the squads in the 131st Regiment's Company E. His company commander was Captain Jim Luke, who had only recently taken over this command, and Pope's platoon commander was First Lieutenant Alfred N. Clissold. As Company E was attached to the Australian 43rd Battalion on 30 June, the company's lively intelligence officer First Lieutenant Herman H. Weimer and his assistants eagerly partnered with the 43rd's experienced intelligence men. Lieutenant-Colonel John Farrell, commander of the 43rd Battalion, was impressed by Tom Pope and his Company E comrades, reporting: 'Officers and men were most anxious to learn and eager for the fight.'[76]

That night, from the reserve trenches at Allonville they were now sharing with Australians, Tom Pope and his comrades watched a display that had become common-place to the Aussies. 'The sky was lighted along the entire northern horizon by fireworks as numerous big guns shelled the trenches and roads to the front and rear.'[77] The same day the American units were absorbed into the Australian units, all junior officers were informed for the first time that they and their men would be attacking the Hamel salient on the fourth of July. It would be another two days before Tom Pope and all other NCOs and enlisted men were brought into the secret. Little did mild-mannered, duty-bound Pope know that, before long, he would make American history.

7.

The Blindsiding of General Pershing

'As the use of Americans at this time was directly
contrary to the arrangement, naturally it did not meet
with my approval.'
*General John J. Pershing, Commander-In-Chief, American
Expeditionary Forces*

THROUGHOUT THE DAY on 1 July, officers from the
American 131st and 132nd Regiments were taken in small
groups forward to the front line by Australian intelligence
officers, to see the lay of the land and to familiarise themselves with the Australian methods of issuing orders, so that
there was no confusion during the assault. From concealed
vantage points such as a ruined farmhouse in the village of
Vaire-sous-Corbie to the east of Corbie, the Americans were
shown the landscape that was destined to become a battlefield in three days' time.

'Rolling, hilly and wooded with flats,' Colonel Sanborn of
the 131st noted following his viewing. Sanborn had already
established that Hamel was located about 2000 metres south

of the River Somme, 5500 metres southwest of the town of Chipilly, and 5000 metres east of the town of Corbie, which was in Australian hands.

Checking what they saw via the naked eye against aerial photographs, the American officers were able to put into perspective the battle plan's main objective, that of seizing the old British trenches on the 100-metre-high ridge beyond Hamel. They were also able to size up the three individual primary objectives on the way to securing those blue line trenches. Objective one: to the left, three 11th Brigade battalions would take Notamel Wood and Hamel township. Objective two: in the centre, three 4th Brigade battalions would take Vaire and Hamel Woods and a large defensive redoubt forward and to the right of Hamel; for obvious reasons, the Australians had dubbed this redoubt Pear-Shaped Trench, and it became known simply as Pear Trench. On the right, two 6th Brigade battalions would clear enemy posts all the way to the blue line trenches.

As the Americans surveyed the ground through field-glasses, fields of wheat that would only be harvested by war stood high out in No Man's Land. These wheatfields, which would conveniently mask advancing troops, ran through Notamel Wood to the north and swung southwest along high ground towards Pear Trench. The remaining gently undulating terrain was mostly surfaced with clover. In the far distance, east of the town of Hamel, the hazy heights of Hamel Ridge could be seen rising up.

Those officers whose platoons were slated to go in on the left of the assault could see that the enemy were dug in about 700 metres away from them and were not particularly active.

In contrast, on the right, Americans noted with surprise that the enemy were just 200 metres away, and as they watched, they spied flickers of flame as German heavy machineguns there opened up and sent lead spewing towards the Australian front line, just to annoy opposing troops and keep heads down.

The 131st's Captain Luke, whose Company E men included Tom Pope, would be advancing towards Hamel township. Carefully studying the approaches via field-glasses, Luke spotted indications of a trench system, in front of the village. That line of trenches was accurately marked on the map he'd been given. 'What about the enemy's defences in Hamel itself?' Luke asked the 43rd Battalion's intelligence officer.

'We anticipate that he has fairly strong garrisons in Hamel,' the Australian replied, 'stationed in deep dugouts.' This would prove to be the case.

In the same way that the Americans were given a first-hand viewing and verbal briefing about the battleground, Australian battalion, company and platoon commanders were also taken to the observation posts and briefed. When field officers returned to their units, they were equipped to brief their senior NCOs once operational HQ gave permission for details to be released on the morning of 2 July. The NCOs would then pass on the details to their men.

At this point, while the officers knew that the operation was scheduled for 4 July, or Z Day as it was labelled by the operation's planners, no one apart from the most senior officers at divisional and corps HQs knew what time Zero Hour would be. To ensure that Fritz didn't know they were coming, and when, secrecy was paramount.

*

Australian Sergeant Ned Searle was no longer thinking about tanks. His thoughts were now on Yanks, and the prospect of having green Americans fighting beside him. His battalion commander, Lieutenant-Colonel McSharry, as short as a jockey but cheery, energetic and almost suicidally brave, went to great lengths to welcome the Americans who stumbled wearily into 15th Battalion positions on the night of 1–2 July.

Said Captain William J. Masoner, commander of the 132nd Regiment's Company G: 'Lieutenant-Colonel McSharry, in command of this battalion, guided us to a reserve trench a few hundred yards from his camp, and remained in our camp until all men found sleeping places and dugouts. The following morning, the four platoons were attached to the four companies of the battalion and were given instruction in the specialty weapons and were given a rehearsal for the attack.'[78]

McSharry was relying on his senior NCOs, men like Ned Searle, to take the Americans under their wing, and as the Doughboys joined with the Aussies for instruction in the use of the Mills Bomb Number 5 hand grenade and the Lewis Gun Light Machinegun – which the Americans called an automatic rifle – Ned had a chance to assess the Yanks firsthand. He had never met an American before in his life. He'd never left Tasmania prior to the war, and had never travelled aboard a ship before he sailed for Egypt with the AIF in 1914, so his horizons had been limited. Yet, he had revelled in the new faces and cultures he saw on the way to his first battle on the Gallipoli Peninsula in Turkey, and had befriended Maori and Ghurka soldiers on Gallipoli.

The English Tommy had not proven Ned's favourite fellow soldier, nor that of his late brother Ray, who had written home about the typical Tommy he'd encountered: 'If he does not have an officer or somebody to tell him what to do, he is lost, and then loses his head.'[79] On the Western Front, like Australian troops generally, Ned mixed well with New Zealanders and Canadians. Having visited the Edinburgh family of the Scottish nurse he'd taken a fancy to, again, like all Aussies, Ned got on well with Scottish soldiers, too.

But Ned's first words to the Americans were caustic. 'You're late!' he said to the Yanks of Company G, 132nd Infantry who joined his 15th Battalion company after sun-up that morning of 2 July.[80]

The Americans thought the caustic Australian sergeant was referring to the hour of their arrival at the Australian position.

'No, four years late!'[81] Ned added. Australia had been in this war for close to four years. Ned himself had been fighting for more than three. Still, after gently ribbing the Yanks on their government's tardiness in bringing the USA into the war, Ned took the Doughboys as he found them. And he found them a pretty likeable lot, ready to learn, and keen to give the Germans hell.

*

Late that morning of 2 July – X Day, as far as those involved with the Battle of Hamel were concerned – Field-Marshal Sir Douglas Haig arrived at General Monash's Chateau Bertangles HQ. Haig was excited by the prospect of the

Australian assault on Hamel, and asked Monash to personally go through the battle plan with him, which Monash was
pleased to do.

'As ever,' Monash wrote home in a letter to his wife
three days later, 'Sir Douglas was affability, courtesy and
consideration personified. He always expresses the greatest
confidence in me.' Haig spent more than an hour with
Monash before hurrying away to attend Inter-Allied War
Council meetings at Versailles. Haig's chief artillery officer
Major-General Noel Birch stayed behind and lunched with
Monash, discussing the Australian's intended use of artillery in the Hamel assault.[82]

In the early afternoon, as Monash and Birch wrapped up
their lunch at Bertangles, the Australian 11th Brigade was on
the march from its bivouac at Allonville, heading towards the
front line. They were accompanied by the Americans of C,
E and K companies from Colonel Sanborn's 131st Regiment.
Heading for the River Somme, and with a 200-metre break
between platoons, the column of thousands of soldiers passed
through Querrieu in good order, then tramped along beside
the dry bed of the River Hallue. At the same time, Ned Searle
and the men of the 4th Brigade, and those of the 6th Brigade,
had commenced to march in the same direction with their
accompanying American companies.

*

Late that afternoon, another VIP came to pay a visit to the
Amiens sector – John J. Pershing, the four-star American
general who was commander-in-chief of the American

Expeditionary Forces. The stern, unsmiling fifty-seven-year-old had the longstanding nickname among his troops of 'Black Jack'. This went back to the days when Pershing had commanded a black 'Buffalo Soldier' regiment. Pershing, a West Point graduate and professional soldier, had a lot of respect for blacks from the years he had spent soldiering with them, but his president Woodrow Wilson, who pandered to bigoted Southern Democrats, did not. So, to keep his president onside, Wilson had relegated some of the AEF's black units to labouring duties at French ports and loaned the remainder to the French Army. Pershing had even sanctioned a warning to the French people issued by his HQ to beware of black American troops because of their supposed propensity to rape and kill civilians.

Black Jack Pershing arrived at the American 33rd Division's headquarters in the chateau at Molliens-au-Bois at 4.15 pm on 2 July. The commander of the American II Corps, General Read, was there along with his subordinate, the 33rd Division's commander, General Bell. Read, a handsome man with a distinctive handlebar moustache that made him look a lot like the late British commander-in-chief Lord Kitchener, used maps to enthusiastically show his CIC the disposition of his American troops in the sector, Proudly, Read told Pershing that all the assigned units from the 33rd Division were in position for 'the Fourth of July show' with the Australians.

'What show is that?' asked a frowning General Pershing.

In response, Read told him about the Hamel assault that was due to take place in a little under thirty-six hours.

Pershing was far from happy, and he let Read know it,

reminding him that his agreement with Field-Marshal Haig was that 'our troops behind the British front were there for training and were not to be used except in an emergency'. There was no emergency that Pershing was aware of. 'As the use of Americans at this time was directly contrary to the arrangement, naturally it did not meet with my approval,' Pershing later said. 'Better they fought together than dispersed with the troops of other armies.'[83]

A disappointed Read glanced at a crestfallen Bell. Both had been looking forward to sending their men into action with the Australians.

In case he had not made himself clear, the inflexible Pershing spelled it out for his subordinates: 'Our troops should not participate.' He then ordered the withdrawal to the rear of the men of the 131st and 132nd then in position with the Australian Corps.[84]

General Read acknowledged the order, and said that it would be passed onto General Rawlinson at British 4th Army HQ to be acted upon. When General Pershing left Read and Bell at 5.45 pm, he was still seething at the thought that, without his permission and against his orders, his American boys had almost been thrown piecemeal into their first battle. 'The British made constant efforts to get them into their lines,' he later complained. Still, to his mind, he had corrected the situation in time.[85]

Following Pershing's departure, General Read rang General Rawlinson, reluctantly telling him that American involvement in the Hamel assault had been vetoed by General Pershing. 'He does not want partially trained troops to participate.'[86]

Rawlinson rang General Monash with the news, but softened it by telling him that, 'The matter having been reconsidered, only 1000 Americans are to be used.'[87] It is unclear whether Rawlinson had taken it upon himself to only require the withdrawal of half the American troops, or whether Read was behind this.

Even so, Monash was not a happy general at having to halve the American numbers in his now integrated assault force. He was to say, '[I was] strongly averse [to] embarrassing the infantry plans of General Maclagan, to whom I had entrusted the conduct of the actual assault.' To Rawlinson he put the case that this would reduce his Hamel attack force from 7500 infantry to 6500, and that he didn't have the time or the men to train 1000 Australian replacements in the tank cooperation tactics that the existing troops slated for the assault had undergone.[88]

When Rawlinson asked whether the Hamel operation could still be successfully accomplished with 6500 infantry, Monash conceded it could. But he added that if 1000 Americans were pulled out, Maclagan would have to totally reorganise the distribution of the remaining 1000 Americans to fill gaps the withdrawn platoons left in the assault line structure.

To which Rawlinson asked, 'Is it not now too late to rearrange the distribution?'

'No, it is not too late,' Monash unhappily confirmed.

So, Rawlinson asked that 1000 Americans be ordered to withdraw the following morning, with the remaining American troops redistributed among the Australian units accordingly.[89]

*

At 5.00 pm, when General Pershing was still at General Read's HQ, the 11th Brigade column had halted beside the Somme where an Australian Corps element waited with hot food. The troops were permitted to bathe, then, after much splashing and larking about, and in high spirits, the Australians and Americans ate a meal. American officers would several times comment on the fact that Australian headquarters made a point of providing hot food for their men at important junctures of their operations.

While the troops were halted beside the Somme, Australian intelligence officers and their American shadows handed out intel material to officers and men. General Monash had become a devotee of the new art of aerial reconnaissance, taking delight in poring over aerial photographs of enemy positions with a magnifying glass. So, as part of his Hamel operational plan, every Australian and American officer and senior NCO was provided with an aerial photo of their objectives. In addition, every single man in the attack force was given a map of the battlefield, with enemy positions clearly marked and with a blue line beyond Hamel showing the old trench line that had been occupied by British troops until they had been ejected by the Germans in April.

That blue line, 1.5 kilometres east of their starting point, was as far as Monash wanted his attacking troops to go. Once the assault force reached that line on 4 July and occupied the old British trenches, the Australians and Americans would have eliminated the bubble of the Hamel salient and would be able to link up with British troops holding the existing front line to their north and French troops entrenched to their south. This provision of intel materials, involving thousands of maps and photographs which were prepared in little more than a week after the operation received the 'Go' from Field-Marshal Haig, was another of Monash's pre-planned 118 elements, and was performed with precision.

In the early evening the column was reformed, and the march resumed. The roads they tramped along now were clogged with troops as the 4th Brigade and 6th Brigade columns also neared their destinations, together with motorised and horse-drawn vehicles, all moving in the same direction, towards the Germans. At one point, an Australian stretcher-bearing party passed the 11th Brigade column on foot, going the other way, carrying a badly wounded Australian soldier. For the Americans, it was a reminder that pain and death awaited them just a few hundred metres ahead.

And then they were descending into zig-zagging communications trenches. Shadowy figures passed the 11th Brigade men in the narrow confines of the trenches as they moved up. Exchanging whispered greetings with men of the 42nd and 43rd Battalions who were going forward, these were withdrawing men of two battalions of the Australian 12th and 13th Brigades who'd been holding the front line. The new arrivals, outnumbering the men coming out, filed into vacated trenches and made themselves as comfortable as they could in the front line. With only No Man's Land separating them from the Germans, they would sit here all through the following day, and into the next, 4 July, before going into action.

All along the 5.6 kilometre front of the Hamel salient, just like the men of the 11th Brigade and their American shadows, the assault troops of the Australian 4th and 6th Brigades and their American cohorts moved into position then tried to get some sleep. At the same time, hundreds of additional field guns and howitzers were readied to be brought up to their previously prepared secret gun-pits behind the front line.

'The men were sheltered in holes dug in the side of the [trench] ledges, covered with shelter tents,' said Lieutenant E. K. Emerson of Company F, 132nd Infantry. At 9.00 pm, not long after Emerson's men had settled in, and with night-fall still forty-five minutes away, six German shells dropped onto their position. Fired randomly, without any specific target in mind, these shells hit a section of trench occupied by Company F men. Four Americans were wounded, and calls of 'Stretcher-bearers!' soon had medical help on the scene. The wounded quartet was carried away to the nearest Casualty Clearing Station for attention by Australian doctors.[90]

At 3.00 am the following morning the now daily eight-minute barrage of enemy positions in the Hamel salient by existing Australian artillery commenced, sending high explosive, gas and smoke shells raining down on German soldiers who pulled on their gas masks and scurried for the protection of underground dugouts. And then the front went silent. A little later, when the sun began to rise at 3.30, a clear, bright summer's day dawned. It was Y Day, and the Battle of Hamel was just twenty-four hours away.

*

From mid-morning on Wednesday 3 July, telegrams containing the American withdrawal order and carried by runners began reaching the commanders of the Australian battalions to which the American platoons had been attached. They in turn passed the telegrams on to the American company and platoon commanders in the trenches. Some American officers would not get their copies until late in the afternoon – Captain J. R. Weaver of the 132nd Infantry, who had been assigned to take command of the Australian 13th Battalion's B Company for the battle, did not receive orders requiring him to personally not take part in the fight until 4.00 pm. 'I would have to remain out,' Weaver later unhappily lamented, although he stubbornly stayed put at the Australian battalion's HQ to observe the assault.[91]

Other American officers who were ordered to pull their men out were seen by the Australians to be dumbfounded by the command. Worse, a number of their men were inclined to disobey and went close to mutinying. At the 16th Battalion trenches, American troops of one 132nd Regiment platoon first argued violently with their officers about the order, then went and sat down among the Australians, refusing to budge.

Which platoon from which company went this far is unknown, but for platoon commander Lieutenant Emerson and his men of F Company, their withdrawal was particularly bitter, having seen four of their comrades carted away wounded, and now the opportunity to avenge their buddies had been denied them. The rebellious troops were eventually talked around by their officers and reluctantly rejoined American ranks for the withdrawal, although some were seen to be in tears as they marched away.

Said one American officer about men under his command who were forced to withdraw, 'They were cut to the heart.'[92]

According to Charles Bean, two Americans pulled on

borrowed Australian tunics and joined the 42nd Battalion to take part in the battle in Australian ranks, although there is no official record of this having taken place. Certainly, a number of Americans were seen to be 'visibly distressed' as they withdrew, Bean noted.[93]

The first withdrawn platoon of the 132nd parted from the 14th Battalion at 10.00 am, filing back through the communication trenches then marching despondently to Allonville. The last platoon of the regiment to be pulled out, the one that had almost mutinied, departed the 16th Battalion's trenches at 12.45 pm. The men of the 131st who had been ordered out withdrew to a similar timetable. The Aussies, for their part, thoroughly commiserated with the departing Yanks, telling them they'd soon get their chance for some action. 'Relations between Australians and Americans were the best throughout,' remarked Lieutenant Emerson.[94]

In contrast, Captain Carroll Gale, the former Chicago police inspector commanding the 131st's C Company, which was remaining for the battle, was livid at the withdrawal of two platoons of his regiment's Company D from around him. 'This caused an almost total rearrangement of the forces of the [42nd] Battalion for the attack,' he would fume after the battle, 'which rearrangement was made so late that many of the troops engaged could not be clearly shown the work they were to do.' Potentially, this disruption put the lives of the remaining Americans at risk.[95]

In addition to the 1000 American infantrymen who had been permitted to remain for the assault, a small number of American officers and men who had been attached to Australian battalion HQs as observers also stayed behind, as did a medical detachment. Meanwhile, everyone seemed to have forgotten the men of the 108th Engineers. This American unit, commanded by Colonel Henry A. Allen, remained where it was in the reserve area, even though, as part of General Monash's operational plan, the engineers had been tapped to carry out support work in the territory gained in, and immediately after, the infantry's advance. They were apparently overlooked because, technically, they were not involved in the assault itself.

*

That same morning, just as the disruptive orders for half the Americans to be withdrawn were being received in the front line, General Monash had to put up with an interruption that no commander would have appreciated so close to the launching of an operation that had the capacity to make or break his career. Two Australian politicians arrived at Australian Corps headquarters, accompanied by a pair of Australian war correspondents.

The war correspondents were Gordon Gilmour and Keith Murdoch, the latter the father of future media magnate Rupert Murdoch, and who, as Sir Keith, would be a leading Australian newspaper proprietor in years to come. The politicians were Billy Hughes, Nationalist Party of Australia leader and Prime Minister, and Navy Minister Sir Joseph Cook, a former prime minister. This pair had just travelled from Australia to France via the United States, and had sent a request to address as many AIF men at the front as possible in a day. Monash and Hughes were not huge fans of one another, but each respected the other's position, and Monash made arrangements to escort the pair around Australian units to address them. On Monash's orders two hundred men at a time would be assembled in woods near their posts to see and hear the politicians.

Back home, Prime Minister Hughes had divided the nation. The Australian Government had the power to conscript men into the army, but only for service within Australia. In 1916 and 1917, British-born PM Hughes had twice put a proposition to the Australian people via referenda that conscription be extended to allow him to send conscripts overseas for service at the front and so further assist the 'Mother Country' in her European war. Those referenda had violently split opinion, caused riots, and failed. The men already at the front also had a say in these referenda, and in each case they had voted overwhelmingly against extending conscription. The troops only wanted men serving beside them in the trenches who had chosen to be there, not those who were sent there by the government and didn't necessarily have a commitment to the fight.

Despite this background, the men assembled for the ministerial visit of 3 July gave Hughes and Cook a warm welcome when they drove to their positions. The novelty of seeing the short, idiosyncratic PM in the flesh, so close to the battlefront and so close to their next battle, made the men of the Australian Corps an interested audience. Hughes was a curiously hokey personality. There was a lot of the actor in him, as was evident when he made his political speeches. In fact, back in his youth, he had appeared on the Sydney stage as an extra in several plays, including one of Sarah

Bernhardt's French dramas during the international super-star's 1891 Sydney season.[96]

After lunch, a small convoy of motor vehicles sped away from the Bertangles HQ, as General Monash escorted Hughes and Cook on flying visits to the 11th, 4th and 6th Brigade units that were preparing to take part in the Hamel assault in the early hours of the following day. With the troops arrayed in front of them in full battle gear, both Hughes and Cook addressed the men, heaping praise on them for the blood they had shed and bravery they had shown, and were about to shed and show. While Cook spoke, Hughes stretched out on his back on the grass and looked at the sky and at the bemused men around him.

The visit was undoubtedly good for morale, but was a distraction General Monash and his commanders could have done without. Politicians on the battlefront were always an irritation, if not an annoyance, to military commanders, but, for Monash, on the day before a crucial operation it was an unnecessary extra burden. He was to tell his wife, 'It proved a most highly inconvenient day.'[97]

*

That afternoon, while on his way back from the Versailles conference, Field-Marshal Haig dropped in to see General Pershing in Paris. Pershing was irritable, telling Haig that he had only learned the previous evening, while meeting with General Read of his II Corps, that American troops of the 33rd Division had been slated to go into action with the Australians on 4 July. This, Pershing complained, was in direct contravention of his order that American troops only train with British armies and not be used in battle by British commanders at this stage of the American build-up in France, other than in an emergency.

The Hamel matter had troubled Pershing so much that he had, only shortly before Haig's arrival, put in a telephone call to General Read. In Pershing's own words, 'Further and positive instructions were given that our troops should not participate.'[98] Pershing seems to have instructed Read, as part of these 'further and positive instructions', to go over General Rawlinson's head and relay Pershing's order to General Sir Herbert Lawrence, Chief of the British General Staff and Haig's deputy, at British GHQ, for this is what Read did.

Haig played dumb when Pershing now raised the Hamel matter with him, pretending to know little about it. According to Pershing, Haig responded, 'I entirely agree with your point of view, Pershing.' Haig was to note in his diary that he added, 'Do you wish me to intervene?'[99]

'No, no,' Pershing came back. He said he'd called General Read on the matter only a short time before, to reiterate his instruction of the previous day and make it perfectly clear that no American troops take part in the Hamel operation. 'Read has it in hand with your man Lawrence,' he told Haig.[100]

Read had indeed rung General Lawrence at British GHQ following the terse call from Pershing, as a result of which Lawrence agreed that the Americans would be entirely 'left out' of the Hamel operation. Lawrence advised that he would pass on the instruction to Rawlinson.[101]

Following Haig's departure from the meeting with Pershing there seems to have been a further call from

Pershing's HQ to General Lawrence, to say that Pershing had just met with Marshal Haig, as Pershing referred to him, and that Haig had said he entirely agreed with Pershing's point of view in the Hamel matter. This information was relayed by Lawrence to Rawlinson at his Fourth Army HQ at Flixecourt. Accordingly, as far as all were concerned, the order to withdraw the last 1000 Americans from the Hamel operation had been endorsed by the British Commander-in-Chief. As far as Pershing was concerned, the matter was now at an end, and he forgot all about it.

*

As 4.00 pm approached, General Monash arrived at Australian 3rd Division HQ at Glisy as part of his usual daily round of visits to his brigade and divisional head-quarters, having detached himself from Prime Minister Hughes and Minister Cook. That pair had gone on to pay a visit to the airfield of the AFC's Number 3 Squadron – Hughes even sat in the cockpit of an RE8 fighter that would take part in next day's battle, as squadron commander Captain Lawrence Wackett from Townsville explained the controls to him.

Monash hadn't been at the Glisy HQ long when a telephone call came in for him from General Rawlinson.

'Monash, look, I'm sorry,' said Rawlinson, 'but it has now been decided that *no* American troops are to be used tomorrow.'[102]

Monash was thunderstruck. He would later say that he was never told why the decision had been taken 'in the upper realms of high control' to withdraw all the Americans. He said he could only guess it had been a matter of General Pershing's policy, or 'an underestimate of the fitness of these troops for offensive fighting'. If it was the latter, his own officers had assured him these Yanks looked fit and ready for the fight.[103]

Monash's immediate inclination was to resist this latest withdrawal instruction. It had been bad enough sending back half the Americans that morning. A further withdrawal, one that didn't attract German attention and bring a rain of German artillery shells on the Americans and on Australian troops assembled for the attack, could only be safely under-taken after dusk. Even then, the withdrawing Americans would clog roads over which reserve troops and supplies would be pouring up in preparation for occupying the front-line trenches once they were emptied by the advance of the assault force.

So, Monash asked Rawlinson for a face-to-face meeting. He knew from experience that he had a better chance of winning over his superior when they met in the flesh. Rawlinson possessed a 'charming and sympathetic person-ality', in Monash's estimation. Meaning, Monash might be able to change the Englishman's mind.[104]

'I'm far from my own station,' was Monash's excuse for an initial delay. 'Can I request that you be good enough to come at once to the forward area and meet me at the headquar-ters of Maclagan at Bussy-lès-Daours. Maclagan being the commander immediately affected by this proposed change of plan.'[105]

Those words *proposed* change of plan' must have fore-warned Rawlinson that he had a fight on his hands as far as Monash was concerned, but he nonetheless agreed to the meeting at Bussy. He and his Chief of Staff General Montgomery drove at once to Maclagan's 4th Division HQ, and the pair met there with Monash at 5.00 pm. From Monash's point of view, this meeting proved to be both tense and 'of grave import'. On the drive to Bussy, he had stiffened up his determination to retain the last thousand Americans. 'I resolved to take a firm stand and press my views as strongly as I dared,' he later said. Now, he let his superior have it.[106]

'At this very moment,' Monash began once he and Rawlinson came together, 'the whole of the infantry destined for the assault at dawn tomorrow morning, including those very Americans, is already on its way to its battle stations. The artillery is in the act of dissolving its defensive organisation with a view to moving forward into its battle emplacements as soon as dusk falls. I well know that even if orders could still with certainty reach the battalions concerned, the with-drawal of those Americans will result in untold confusion and in dangerous gaps in our line of battle.'

'I entirely agree with you, Monash,' Rawlinson responded, 'but I feel myself bound by the terms of a clear order from the Commander-in-Chief.'

'General, it is already too late to carry out the order,' Monash retorted. 'The battle will have to go on with the Americans participating, or not at all. Unless I am expressly ordered to abandon the battle, I intend going on as originally planned.' This was bold indeed, coming from a subordinate. More than that, it was a big and confident call.

Rawlinson countered that, if, after refusing to withdraw the last Americans, Monash went ahead with the operation and it proved a costly success, or a failure, it would cause 'an international incident'. For the outcry in America would be enormous.

Monash pictured a very different sort of international incident. 'If all the Americans are withdrawn, no Australian would fight beside an American again!' he declared. He was exaggerating, but this showed how emotional he had become, and how he had nailed his colours to the mast in this affair. In effect, he was challenging Rawlinson, and Haig, to back him in his first offensive operation in charge of the Australians, or to sack him.

Rawlinson didn't know what to do, feeling caught between the devil and the deep blue sea. Monash, on seeing this, gave him an out. 'General, I feel perfectly sure that the Commander-in-Chief, when giving such an order, could not have had present in his mind the probability that compliance with it meant the abandonment of the battle. And that, under the circumstances, it is competent for the senior commander on the spot to act in the light of the situation as known to him, even to the extent of disobeying an order.'

Rawlinson, that senior commander on the spot, was 'very much upset', in Monash's words, and retorted, 'Do you want me to run the risk of being sent back to England? Do you mean it is worth that?'

'Yes, I do,' Monash resolutely replied. 'Unless I receive a cancellation order before 6.30 pm,' he went on, 'it will in any case be too late to stop the battle, the preliminary phases of which are just on the point of beginning.'

Rawlinson thought long and hard, then said, 'I shall take it that your view is correct, provided the Commander-in-Chief is not accessible for reference.'[107]

On Rawlinson's instruction, a call was put through to British GHQ at Montreuil-sur-Mer, to make contact with Field-Marshal Haig and let him decide the matter. Haig wasn't yet at GHQ, and no one there seemed to know precisely where he was or when he would arrive back from his trip to Versailles. Increasingly desperate, Rawlinson put in a call to Montreuil every ten minutes, as Monash sweated on the future of his battle, and of his military career. Each call elicited precisely zero information about Haig's whereabouts.

As 6.00 pm approached, Rawlinson succeeded in making contact with the Chief of the General Staff, General Lawrence. Rawlinson told Lawrence that four American companies remained with the Australian Corps for the Hamel assault and could not be withdrawn in time before the operation commenced. If Field-Marshal Haig still wanted all the Americans out, said Rawlinson, the assault would have to be called off. But, to take effect, that order must be received by 6.30.

Lawrence advised that Haig had left Paris, 230 kilometres due south of Montreuil, by road some time before, and his two vehicles were expected to arrive at GHQ within half an hour. When Lawrence mentioned the time that Haig had departed Paris, Rawlinson estimated that the CIC could not possibly reach Montreuil until after 7.00 pm, so told Lawrence that if he did not hear from the Field-Marshal by 7.00, the Hamel operation would go ahead as things stood. Realising that Rawlinson was in a bind, Lawrence promised he would have Haig call him as soon as he arrived.

Monash would not have been pleased that his deadline

had been stretched by half an hour. With the atmosphere between Rawlinson and himself still tense, the pair parted, climbed into their Rolls-Royces, and set off for their respective headquarters.

At the same time, General Lawrence at British GHQ rang General Read at his II Corps HQ. 'Your four remaining companies have become fully committed to the operation,' Lawrence informed the American. 'General Rawlinson can make no change without instructions from the Commander-in-Chief, Field-Marshal Haig. And he cannot be reached.'[108]

Read accepted this advice without argument. He seems to have been as eager as his subordinates General Bell and Colonels Sanborn and Davis for their men to taste action with the Australians on the Fourth of July, to make a name for themselves and for American force of arms on America's national day. Read did not relay this latest piece of information to General Pershing. Instead, Read would go to his bed that night no doubt hoping and expecting that his boys did him proud in the early hours of next morning, but dreading Pershing's subsequent reaction.

*

Arriving back at Chateau Bertangles, Monash rejoined the waiting Australian Prime Minister and Navy Minister. In a private moment, Monash informed Hughes he was aware that a campaign had been waged behind the scenes to remove him from Australian Corps command, and said, quite bluntly, if push came to shove, he would not go quietly. Hughes proceeded to deliver a speech to the HQ staff in praise of

Monash, who kept checking his watch as the PM waffled.

By this stage, Monash was banking on Haig failing to arrive back at Montreuil in time, meaning the Hamel battle would go ahead with the Americans involved as he had demanded. But, as he later said, 'To me, it had taken the form of a very serious crisis.' His prime minister would be of no use to him in this, carrying no weight with the generals. This was a military stoush, but one that Monash was perfectly capable of fighting alone. He was determined to carry his point, for it wasn't just this Hamel operation that was at stake. As far as he was concerned, the success of this battle would have 'far-reaching consequences' that would affect the future tactics and outcome of this war.[109]

Hughes had let slip to journalists Murdoch and Gilmour that Monash was launching a surprise attack the following morning, and now Monash told the politicians and journalists about the 6.30 deadline he had set for calling the whole thing off, a deadline that General Rawlinson had extended to 7.00 pm. 'Monash told us with a smile,' one of the war correspondents would later reveal, 'that General Haig was in a motor car between Paris and GHQ and was unlikely to be back by 7.00, so that it would apparently be alright.'[110]

The clock kept ticking, and still no word came from Field-Marshal Haig. But just when Monash thought he was in the clear, the phone rang from Fourth Army HQ. 'Just before 7.00,' Haig's biographer Duff Cooper was to say, 'the decision came.'

As it happened, Haig had arrived back at Montreuil before 7.00. Lawrence was waiting for his weary CIC, and quickly brought him up to speed on the Hamel dilemma, and the deadline imposed by Monash and Rawlinson. 'Six American companies have been withdrawn,' Lawrence explained, 'but about four companies cannot be withdrawn in time. Should the operations be stopped in order to do so?'

Haig didn't hesitate to answer. 'No!' he said firmly. 'The first essential is to improve the situation east of Amiens as soon as possible. The attack must therefore be launched as prepared, even if a few American detachments cannot be got out before Zero Hour.'[111]

Lawrence immediately rang the waiting, sweating Rawlinson at Flixecourt with the decision, and Rawlinson promptly, and delightedly, rang Monash to convey it.

'The Chief directed the withdrawal of the Americans in deference to the wishes of General Pershing,' Rawlinson explained to Monash. 'But, as matters stand, he now wishes everything to go on as originally planned.'

Monash was more than a little relieved. 'The crisis passed as suddenly as it had appeared,' he would later say. 'Great issues had hung for an hour or so upon the chance of my being able to carry my point.'[112] Carry his point he had. Now Monash was free to get on with winning the war. With a confident smile, he farewelled Prime Minister Hughes and Minister Cook as they set off for Versailles to take part in the Inter-Allied War Council meetings. The politicians in turn wished the general every success with the 4 July operation, and asked to be updated with the battle's outcome the following day.

When the politicians took their leave, war correspondents Murdoch and Gilmour stayed behind to report on the Hamel assault. The pair dined with Monash and official Australian

Government photographer Captain George Hubert Wilkins – known as Hubert, and later as Sir George after he was knighted. Unusually for a photographer, Wilkins had just weeks before been awarded the Military Cross for gallantry. Within months he would be awarded a second MC, for leading to safety American troops who had lost their officer on the battlefield. South Australian-born Wilkins would settle in the United States after the war and become a noted polar explorer. Following Wilkins' death in Massachusetts in 1958, the crew of a US Navy nuclear submarine would spread his ashes at the North Pole.

Monash was extraordinarily gracious to include Keith Murdoch in his inner circle that evening. He knew that Murdoch and another influential Australian war correspondent, Charles Bean, had lobbied Hughes and the British government to have him removed from command of the Australian Corps. Officially, the journalists had pitched their argument against Monash around his military suitability, as a former militia officer, not a permanent soldier, putting their support behind professional soldier General Brudenell White for the role of corps commander, and pushing for Monash to be promoted upstairs to the purely administrative post of head of the AIF. The journalistic pair had even gone as far as approaching British Prime Minister David Lloyd George to argue against Monash's retention.

Although Monash never articulated it himself, there was, and remains, a strong suspicion that Bean and Murdoch were motivated by anti-semitism. Monash knew that the pair was lobbying against him. Writing to wife Vic on 25 June, he had told her, 'An intrigue going on is taking all sorts of subtle forms.' He didn't name Murdoch or Bean, but he knew very well they were the instigators of this intrigue. 'These proceedings are being undertaken in London,' he had told his wife, 'in order to put pressure on Mr Hughes.' Monash had felt he would win this political battle, not least because 'both Rawlinson and the Chief will see me through'.[113] As indeed they did. With Generals White and Birdwood also refusing to be a part of this intrigue, Field-Marshal Haig's recommendation that Monash be retained as corps commander had been endorsed by both the Australian and British governments.

Well aware of what Murdoch and Bean had been doing behind his back, Monash could have been churlish on the night of 3 July and excluded Murdoch from his company, giving journalistic competitor Gilmour the opportunity to secure a scoop on the eve of the important battle. But Monash was as wily as he was wise. He well knew the power of the press, and had appreciated for some time that his reputation as a general depended on the reports of the war correspondents. So, overlooking his personal opinion of them, he courted Murdoch, Bean and Gilmour.

Charles Bean, who would become Australia's greatest World War One historian, when he would, to his credit, lavish praise on Monash's generalship, was to say that it was Monash's practice to deliver 'wonderfully lucid explanations of his battle plans' to the war correspondents. These were explanations which they 'deeply appreciated', said Bean. Now, following dinner and as the clock ticked down toward Zero Hour the next morning, Monash gave Gilmour, Murdoch and Wilkins an insight into his plan for the Battle of Hamel.[114]

Monash explained his 'musical composition' for the battle, summing it up neatly: 'The whole program is controlled by an exact timetable, to which every infantryman, every heavy or light gun, every mortar and machinegun, every tank and aeroplane must respond with punctuality. Otherwise there will be discord which will impair the success of the operation, and increase the cost of it.'[115]

Monash also told the war correspondents, 'If the tanks fail to get to the strongpoints, the infantry cannot try. They are to let the tanks flatten out any serious opposition which they locate. They have been told, in such cases, to lie down and let the tanks go ahead.'[116] This was the infantry-tank cooperation technique that the Australians had been schooled in at Vaux. It of course depended on tanks actually turning up, and the past negative Australian experience of the metal monsters meant that many men such as Ned Searle would go into this battle fully intending to ignore this order and deal with German strongpoints themselves.

Meanwhile, just as General Read had failed to alert his commander-in-chief that Americans would still be going into offensive action with the Australians within hours, the British didn't bother to inform General Pershing that Field-Marshal Haig had gone back on their understanding that all Americans would be withdrawn from the battle. Clearly, Haig was prepared to weather the storm of Pershing's indignant protestations and accusations following the battle, rather than see it cancelled as Monash had threatened.

So it was that General Pershing was blindsided by both the British and his own corps commander. He would be in for a rude shock come the morning.

8.

The Gamble of Two-Gun Harry

'It [was imperative] not to arouse the suspicions
of the enemy.'
Captain Carroll Gale, Company C, US 131st Infantry

ANY SOLDIER WILL tell you that some of the longest hours
of their lives can be those leading up to a planned attack.
Sitting in the front-line trenches through the daylight hours
of 3 July, the Australians did what they usually did before
a battle: checked their weapons and ammunition, sharpened bayonets on whetstones, wrote cards and letters home,
updated their diaries, wrote a little poetry, played cards, and
tried to catch up on sleep – because sleep would be the last
thing they would be able to do on the forthcoming night.

As this was the Americans' first taste of an assault, pre-
battle nerves made them restless. Unlike the generally calm,
silent Aussies, the Yanks talked nervously and excitedly among
themselves, with men often popping their heads up over the
trench parapet to try to take in the fields of wheat and clover
that they would be advancing over within a few short hours.

Before long, this generated a command that swept along the front line, for the Americans to 'shut their gobs' and keep their heads down.

This was necessary, as Captain Gale of the 131st Infantry noted, 'in order not to arouse the suspicions of the enemy as to the increase in the strength of the trench garrison'.[117] It was imperative that the Germans on the other side of No Man's Land thought that it was business as usual in the trenches facing them, and that they had no inkling that twice as many men as usual were in the Australian front line and poised for an attack on them.

Gale's superior for this operation was the 42nd Battalion's Major Dibdin, who was taking no chances. During the daylight hours of 3 July, Dibdin summoned all his Australian and American company and platoon leaders to the battalion's observation post at Vaire-sous-Corbie, one at a time. Cross-referring his lieutenants to their maps and aerial photos, and the ground and landmarks in front of them, Dibdin carefully went through the operational plan and their specific objectives with them.

Captain Gale witnessed these briefings with satisfaction. Irked by the loss of his comrades of Company D as a result of General Pershing's withdrawal order, and unhappy that he hadn't had the chance to make a close reconnaissance of the ground his men would have to cross, he appreciated the personal briefings. 'This made up to a large extent for the lack of actual reconnaissance of the ground,' he would remark.[118]

Perhaps alerted that something was up, or perhaps purely by chance, in the afternoon German artillery began unexpectedly shelling areas just behind the 42nd Battalion's front line. One of these shells caught two officers standing talking outside the battalion's Corbie headquarters. Captain William MacDonnell, adjutant of the 42nd, was killed instantly by the blast. The other, Major Harry Cheney, commander of the 131st Regiment's 1st Battalion, was severely wounded in the shoulder and was evacuated to an Australian Casualty Clearing Station.

In the hours leading up to the assault, Australian and American infantrymen were equipped by Australian quarter-masters with the additional weapons and equipment they would carry into battle. Apart from standard issue 'tin hats' and rifles, the latter fitted with bayonets by the time the men went into the attack, in pouches each man carried 200 rounds of .303 ammunition, two grenades and rations for forty-eight hours (essentially tea and canned bully beef). Strapped to his belt, each man also carried two filled water bottles and either a small pick or a shovel. The same way Roman legionaries on the march had carried two stakes that would be contrib-uted to the top of the defensive wall they built around their legion's overnight camp, these twentieth-century footsoldiers each carried three empty sandbags, which, theoretically, they would fill with earth on reaching their objective, to strengthen their newly won piece of trench. Some men threaded these sandbags through their belts; others tied them around their lower legs like additional gaiters.

There were exceptions to these equipment-carrying rules. Officers were only armed with revolvers. They even went into battle wearing collar and tie. Signallers and Lewis gunners assigned to each platoon were exempt from carrying sandbags and picks and shovels, to free them up a little. The members of each of the two Lewis gun teams per platoon were given just 100 rounds of small arms ammunition, to allow them to also carry nine filled Lewis gun magazines each. Lewis gunners also carried a holstered revolver.

The 15th Battalion's Henry 'Harry' Dalziel was another exception to the rule. Twenty-five-year-old Harry, who'd been born at a mining camp near Irvinebank in Far North Queensland, had quit his job as an apprentice fireman on steam locomotives running on Queensland Government Railways' Cairns-to-Atherton line to enlist in the AIF in January 1915. Arriving in Egypt as a private with reinforcements that July, he'd joined Ned Searle and the rest of the 15th Battalion for the last stages of the ill-fated Gallipoli campaign. Harry had subsequently gone to France and Belgium with the 15th, and played his part in fighting the Germans to a standstill in the 1916 battles of Pozières, Mouquet Farm and Flers. Then it was the 1917 battles of Gueudecourt and Lagnicourt, before the disaster of Bullecourt with the Mark IV tanks, where, like Ned Searle, Harry had been one of the few 15th Battalion men to survive.

Harry had subsequently been wounded during the battle of Polygon Wood, after which he was evacuated to England, or 'Blighty' as the British called it, for treatment and to recover. He had enjoyed that break away from the war, sleeping between sheets and being pampered by pretty nurses. When Harry rejoined the 15th Battalion in January 1918, the Australians were experiencing a lull in the fighting that would be rudely terminated by the German spring offensive in March. Like a number of Gallipoli veterans who returned to their units on the Western Front after recovering from battle wounds, back in the 15th Battalion Harry was again given a noncombatant role. Attached to battalion HQ, he found himself a driver, behind the wheel of a truck and behind the lines.

When the Hamel operation was first mooted in late June, non-vital HQ staff were asked if they wanted to help fill the 15th's depleted infantry ranks by volunteering for active duty. For better or worse, Harry put up his hand. Volunteering to go into battle was a bit of a gamble. No one in Australian Corps ranks doubted that hundreds, and perhaps thousands, of Australians would be killed and wounded in this operation. Harry was a bit of a gambler at heart. He considered himself lucky in many ways; when he was a kid, he and his brother Vic had stumbled on tin samples that had resulted in the founding of the Boulder Tin Mine near Emuford.

But, Harry asked himself, what was the worst that could happen now? He could be killed. Or maybe he'd end up having another long stint in hospital in England, a prospect that quite appealed to him. Later, Harry would philosophically say he accepted that one way or the other this battle could result in him being despatched – back to Blighty, or to his final resting place.

So, just days before the Battle of Hamel, Driver Harry Dalziel joined the 15th Battalion's A Company, where he was assigned to a Lewis gun team as the gunner's offsider. This was when Harry bent the regulations as far as the equipment he would carry into battle were concerned. Onto his belt he affixed an ornate German knife in its original scabbard. Harry never said where it had come from, but he probably bought it from another Australian who'd souvenired it from a dead

German on the battlefield. Some entrepreneurial Aussies, against all regulations, made a tidy profit from collecting and selling German uniforms and equipment from and to comrades as souvenirs.

In addition to his regulation revolver, Harry armed himself with a second handgun, contrary to regulations, making him look like a gunslinger from the Wild West. 'Two-Gun Harry', his new comrades in A Company branded him with a nudge and a wink. But Harry would soon have the last laugh.

9.

The Countdown to Z Hour on the Fourth of July

'Once a commander's orders are issued, there is little left for him to do but watch and wait.'
Lieutenant-General Sir John Monash

AT 6.00 PM on the evening of 3 July, about the time that General Monash set off from Bussy to drive back to his corps HQ at Bertangles – still with his ultimatum to Field-Marshal Haig hanging unanswered, meaning that within an hour the entire operation might be called off – telegrams were sent by Monash's HQ, as prearranged, to all company commanders involved in the Hamel assault.

These telegrams advised that Z Hour was set for 3.10 am next day, Z Day, and also set out the staggered times for each platoon to move forward to the 'jumping off' point out in No Man's Land, in preparation for the assault's commencement. Word of Z-Hour's exact time was passed along the line. Men like Ned Searle, Tom Pope and Two-Gun Harry Dalziel knew their wait for action would soon be over.

Their jumping-off point, 100 metres in advance of the Australians' front-line trenches, would be marked by white tape to be laid at 11.00 pm by company intelligence officers with the help of engineers. Already, at midnight the previous night, those intelligence officers and engineers had crawled out and marked the point with pegs which they had hammered into the chalky ground. Tonight, it would simply be a matter of crawling out again and stringing the white tape from peg to peg, creating a starting line along a front of 5.6 kilometres. They would also lay tapes all the way back to the front line, which each platoon would follow to reach its designated position on the jumping-off tape, or JOT.

As the sun set at 9.45, the tension grew in the trenches, and in the battalion, brigade, division and corps HQs. Behind the lines, the fifty-eight tanks allocated to the operation rumbled into the villages of Fouilloy and Hamelet in the twilight, and commenced to wait in long lines at the roadside. Accompanying the fifty-four battle tanks were four fully loaded carrier tanks that had originally been built with small armoured cabins and large flat trays to mount a heavy gun – the forerunner of the self-propelled artillery piece that would emerge in World War Two. When the mounted gun proved unsatisfactory in practice, the Tank Corps had turned the machine over to the carrying of supplies. The carrier tanks allocated to the Hamel assault would follow the advance and each deposit 4.5 tonnes of small arms ammunition, grenades, rolls of barbed wire, water and ration containers just behind captured enemy positions, then withdraw.

That evening, too, at the airfields at Villers-Bocage and Argenvilliers that were now temporary homes to the AFC's

Number 3 Squadron and the RAF's Number 9 Squadron, aircrews and groundcrews made final preparations. As set down by General Monash's plan, there would be four types of aircraft mission involved in this operation: reconnaissance, bombing/strafing, supply drop and contact – which involved intercepting enemy fighters and preventing them from attacking the aircraft flying the other missions. The Australians, operating eighteen two-seat RE8 biplane fighters in three flights, would conduct the recon, bombing/strafing and contact missions. The British, also using RE8s, would fly the supply drop missions, entailing the delivery of heavy machinegun ammunition by parachute, the first time such a thing had been attempted in the Great War.

The problem of resupply of his advancing troops had occupied General Monash's mind for some time. The carrier tanks would solve the bulk of his problem, but not one crucial part. 'The "consolidation" of newly captured territory,' Monash was to say, 'implies its organisation for defence against recapture.'[119] For this reason, to defend against German counterattack, his operational plan called for Vickers heavy machineguns from the Australian 4th Machine Gun Battalion to be carried forward by their crews at the rear of the infantry advance and sited in newly taken ground, at preselected locations based on a chequerboard pattern.

In action, these machineguns went through 1000 rounds in five minutes. For resupply, each additional ammunition box containing 1000 rounds would normally have to be carried by two men more than two kilometres, over open ground and under enemy fire, with heavy casualties among these carrying parties and with much of the ammunition failing to reach its destination. 'It was therefore decided to attempt the distribution of this class of ammunition by aeroplane,' said Monash.[120] This had never been done before, and was made possible by a parachute release mechanism invented by the Australian Flying Corps' Major David Blake, a native of Parramatta, and implemented by the visionary commander of the AFC's Number 3 Squadron, Captain Wackett.

As Wackett had demonstrated to the general shortly after Monash took charge of the Australian Corps, most of Number 3 Squadron's aircraft were equipped with bomb racks beneath each lower wing. When a cockpit lever was pulled, bombs were released. On the same principle, said Wackett, a 1000-round ammunition box had been fitted under each wing and could be released by pulling the lever.

However, the box would not reach the ground undamaged unless suspended from a parachute that slowed its descent and softened its landing. Whilst the parachute had been invented by this stage in history, aircrew were not permitted to use it – senior British officers felt that a pilot would be more likely to bring a damaged aircraft back to base if he didn't have the option of bailing out. So, using Major Blake's mechanism, Wackett had experimented with parachute drops of full boxes of machinegun rounds, determining the right size of parachute and the ideal height from which to allow the box to float to earth intact and find its target – a thousand feet.

Once the RAF's Number 9 Squadron was allocated to the Hamel operation it was given the ammunition drop role, with Wackett personally training British aircrew in the supply drop technique and devising the targeting method to be used.

The Australian Vickers machinegun crews were given a large white canvas 'V' to lay out near where they set up their guns on Z Day. Wackett demanded that dropping aircraft land the ammo no further than one hundred yards from the white 'V,' and, in training, the RAF pilots were soon able to land their loads well within the one hundred yard zone. It would be a matter of repeating this accuracy on the morning of 4 July, but with the added dangers of enemy ground fire and attacking enemy fighters.

As darkness fell at the airfields, the aircraft were prepared with fuel, bombs and ammunition, parachute-equipped ammunition boxes were piled up in readiness, and pilots once more studied maps showing their area of operation.

*

At 6.00 that evening, accompanied by American medical orderlies, First Lieutenant Frank E. Schram of the US Medical Corps, who was attached to the 132nd Infantry, reported to Major B. C. Kennedy, the 15th Battalion's medical officer, at his Regimental Aid Post behind the front line. At 10.30, Kennedy, his doctors and orderlies, along with Schram and his party of five American orderlies and two squads of unarmed stretcher-bearers, moved up to join Lieutenant-Colonel McSharry and his staff at 15th Battalion headquarters. In the same way that pairs of NCOs had been allocated as runners to each platoon commander in the assault force – one Australian and one American runner to each Australian and American platoon – the stretcher-bearers were made up of Australians and Americans who would work together on the battlefield.

'We had twelve stretcher-bearers for each company,' said Schram, 'also one man in charge of each stretcher-bearing detail, which made three stretcher-bearing squads. Four Americans were assigned to each bearing section, and these were mixed or distributed with experienced Australians, so that each stretcher squad had at least one American and experienced Australians.'[121]

Because there was no medical facility in the front line, Lieutenant Schram and Major Kennedy had previously agreed with Colonel McSharry that the combined medical party would do a 'hop-over' with the assault troops when they advanced. That is, they would follow the attackers all the way to one of the 15th Battalion's primary objectives, Pear Trench. In the same way, McSharry was planning to follow along behind the four waves of assault troops to set up an advanced battalion HQ at Pear Trench. Once the Germans occupying that redoubt had been eliminated, the medical officers would set up an RAP there, substantially reducing the distance stretcher-bearers would have to travel to get the wounded into the doctors' hands. The medics would go over the top at the same time as the men of the assault force, and face the same dangers as they went into the attack – except their role would be to save lives, not take them.

*

At 11.00 pm, Australian and American intelligence officers and selected British troops from the Royal Engineers' Special Company began crawling out into No Man's Land, this time taking along white tape and wirecutters. The tape was to create the operation's jumping-off line, the wirecutters to cut large gaps in the Allied barbed entanglements that ran through No Man's Land in advance of their trenches. This wire had originally been put there to prevent the Germans from reaching the Allied front line.

There were occasional small gaps in the wire called 'sally ports'. These narrow gateways existed to permit the Australians to sally forth on their frequent raids across No Man's Land. For the upcoming assault, much larger gaps were required, and creation of those gaps now occupied the men with the wirecutters, who snipped slowly and quietly so that the Germans in their front-line trenches weren't alerted. Of course, thick German barbed wire also extended in front of their own trenches, but General Monash's preliminary artillery barrage was designed to eliminate that barrier by carving it up with high explosive shells.

*

As the intelligence officers and engineers went forward to do their preparatory work, in the 15th Battalion's trench line Ned Searle looked around the unfamiliar faces of the men of his section, and those of the Americans of the 132nd's G Company sharing the trench with them, and wondered how they would perform when the time came. It's likely he also wondered how many men he would have to kill before 4 July was over to earn him his VC.

Ned would never forget the first man he had ever knowingly killed, in the early hours of 7 August 1915. Ned had been at the forefront of the 15th Battalion's advance up the Gallipoli Peninsula's Hill 971 with fixed bayonets, in a surprise attack. 'I got first blood out of our company,' he had written home after the event, more in shock than in celebration. To preserve the element of surprise, the Australians had been ordered to remove the cutoffs from their rifles, so they couldn't fire. The Turks were to be despatched silently, by bayonet. As Ned pushed up the hill, he'd found a Turkish soldier popping up from a hole in the ground, an unseen enemy forward outpost directly in front of him.

Apparently, the Turk had been merely intending to stretch his legs. Seeing an Australian soldier bearing down on him, the astonished Turk brought up his Gewehr 98 rifle to fire. Ned, with his own Lee-Enfield still on his shoulder, grabbed the enemy weapon and started wrestling the Turk for it. Ned's mate Private Andy Belstead had then arrived on the scene and jabbed the struggling Turk with his bayonet. The wounded foe, letting go of his rifle, turned and ran. With a curse, and pulling his own bayonet-equipped rifle from his shoulder, Ned had set off after the fleeing man, who had to be stopped before he gave the alarm. 'And my bayonet was sharp,' Ned would say.[122]

Ned, a good runner, soon overtook the wounded Turk. When he did, he plunged his bayonet into the fleeing man's back, between the shoulder blades, felling him and killing him instantly, and silently. Ned had bayoneted more of the enemy since that day, especially in a trench called OG2 in 1917's Battle of Bullecourt. That trench had been occupied by a thousand Germans; within minutes, the Australian charge had left most of them dead or prisoners. During 3 July, Ned had sharpened his bayonet in expectation of having plenty more custom for it before long.

*

One of the men crawling out into No Man's Land from the 16th Battalion's lines to help lay the JOT was twenty-four-year-old, five-foot-seven tall, nine-stone (57 kilograms) Lance-Corporal Thomas 'Jack' Axford. Neither physically imposing nor loud-mouthed, Jack was not the sort of man who stood out in a crowd. Described as 'unexcitable' and 'softly spoken', he was the last person anyone would expect to do anything spectacular, even if he had occasionally shaped up in the ring as an amateur boxer in Kalgoorlie before the war, and more recently in khaki on 4th Division sports days.[123]

Born in South Australia to a Tasmanian father and a South Australian mother, Jack was a Catholic of Irish extraction who'd grown up at Coolgardie in Western Australia. Before the war, Axford, a teetotaller, had, ironically, worked as a labourer at the Boulder City Brewery. Enlisting in Kalgoorlie in July 1915, he'd arrived in Egypt after the Allied withdrawal from Gallipoli and had subsequently gone on to the Western Front with the 16th Battalion. Hospitalised in England in 1916 after the Battle of Mouquet Farm in France for 'shell shock', he had returned to his unit and been wounded in the knee at Gapaard Farm in Belgium in 1917. Since enlisting, Jack had been mentioned in despatches six times, and in May 1918 he was awarded the Military Medal for playing a gallant part in halting the 1918 German spring offensive. Quiet, inoffensive Lance-Corporal Axford was about to take part in his next battle, and win his next medal.

After helping lay the jumping-off tape and cut the barbed wire, Jack remained out in No Man's Land as a one-man patrol outside the 16th Battalion's section of the front line, keeping his ears pricked for enemy activity in the vicinity. The Germans were never as active as the Australians in regularly sending patrols to raid enemy lines; they didn't seem to have the stomach for it. But that didn't preclude the Germans attempting a raid on this particular night, or, perhaps alerted by unusual movement in the Australian lines, sending a patrol over to investigate. The last thing the Australians wanted was for a German party to discover the gaps they had cut in their own wire. That would tip Fritz off to the fact the Aussies were about to mount a fullscale attack. If necessary, to keep that secret safe, Jack Axford would kill any Germans who came his way in the darkness – silently, with the bayonet.

As the tape-layers and wire-snippers carefully went out to do their business in No Man's Land, a hot meal and hot tea were delivered to all the men in the trenches who would take part in the attack – a combined supper and breakfast. As they all knew, for some it would be their last meal, ever, and a number of Australians supplemented their food with a surreptitious tot of rum, to settle their nerves. Z Hour was just four hours and ten minutes away.

*

At Chateau Bertangles, all had gone quiet. Conversations had ended. Telephones had ceased to jangle, telegraph keys stood frozen. Once the operation began, they would all start to ring and tap again, with reports coming in every few minutes. For now, a tense silence prevailed. All the orders had been issued, all the preparations made. Some Corps HQ staff had put their heads down to get some sleep before the operation began. Others were too keyed up to sleep. Following dinner, Monash himself had lain down to get some rest, instructing his staff to wake him well before Z Hour.

'When once a commander's orders are issued, there is little left for him to do but watch and wait,' Monash wrote home to his wife.[124] Apart from the 136-point battle plan he had ordered General Maclagan to carry out, Monash had also given the battle's operational commander a very precise timeline for implementation of each element of the plan. 'Every individual unit must make its entry precisely at the proper moment, and play its phrase in the general harmony,' he said.[125] Plus, Monash had given Maclagan a time limit for the execution of the plan. He wanted all objectives secured within ninety minutes of the operation's commencement. It was a big ask. Never before in this war had so much Western Front ground been taken in so little time. Monash, confident his Australians and their American colleagues could pull it off, quickly slipped off to sleep.

*

Colonel Sanborn of the 131st Infantry was also grabbing some shuteye, in his case at his regimental HQ at Pierregot. During the day, he had led the remaining troops of both the 131st and 132nd on a 'terrain exercise' behind British trenches at Vaiden, trying to mimic the attack their countrymen would make the following morning, but in this case against a nonexistent enemy.

Sanborn's thoughts were on his boys now in the trenches with the Aussies as they counted down the hours to their first attack of the war. 'Fussy' Joe worried that his men would be going into action without the support of their usual comrades-in-arms of the 124th Machinegun Battalion, whose men General Read had held back at his HQ at Molliens-au-Bois. Sanborn also worried that his platoons would be going in with just a handful of the new Lewis gun automatic rifles, and even then their crews would have had barely a couple of days' training in their use. The colonel could only hope and pray that his boys gave a good account of themselves on their national day, and didn't let him or the United States down.[126]

*

The watches of Australian, British and American officers involved in the Hamel operation were synchronised twice leading up to Z Hour. The first time was at 9.00 pm on 3 July, the second at 2.10 am on 4 July, sixty minutes prior to Z Hour. As those watches ticked past midnight and American Independence Day arrived, Australians and Americans of the first wave of the assault force clambered from their trenches and slowly crawled out into No Man's Land for 100 metres, halting once they reached the jumping-off tape.

This move forward came as a relief to waiting Americans. Lieutenant-Colonel McSharry of the 15th Battalion would later report that the Yanks attached to his unit had occupied the front-line trenches 'with the same nervous expectancy exhibited by a thoroughbred before starting in on a race'. McSharry's own men remained outwardly calm, cool and collected. 'I was impressed,' he said, 'with the silent and orderly way in which our boys formed up on the taped line.'[127]

Over close to three hours, the troops went forward in stages. Once the first wave was in position, men of the next wave moved up, then the men of the third and fourth waves behind them. Out in No Man's Land, once Jack Axford knew his mates were at the JOT, he slithered back to join his 16th Battalion platoon for the assault. The last troops would be in position by 2.50. Behind their now-severed barbed wire, they lay, and waited.

Until Z Hour, talking and smoking were banned. If the Germans worked out they were out here in the open, their artillery and machineguns would zero in on them and cut them to pieces. This 'caused some anxiety' among the green American troops, Captain Gale of the 131st would say.[128] As it happened, an Australian 4th Brigade man lying at the jumping-off tape would be unlucky to be hit by a bullet from a German machinegun that fired randomly his way. Without fuss, or noise, he was dragged back for medical attention.

Among the 15th Battalion men at the tape, Sergeant Ned Searle wasn't anxious. When he was sober, Ned was the calmest, coolest of characters. Eighteen months earlier, beneath Hill 60 in Flanders, he'd been assigned to guard duty in an underground tunnel. Australians were tunnelling to plant a huge land mine beneath German lines. At the same time, the Germans were known to be tunnelling the other way, and Ned had instructions to remain silent and keep his ears pricked for the sounds of German digging. For the task, he'd even been provided with a metal listening trumpet to put against the tunnel wall.

Several hours into his shift, Ned, sitting on a crate and bored silly, had rolled himself a cigarette. Suddenly, a pick had come through the wall above his head. Still with the unlit cigarette in his mouth, Ned had slowly come to his feet. As he watched, the pick created a hole the size of a man's head. And through that hole Ned saw the face of a German soldier. In one hand, the German held a pick; in the other, a candle. In mutually debilitating shock, Ned and the German stared at each other. Then the Fritz made a move. Reaching through the hole in the tunnel wall with his candle, he lit Ned's cigarette. And then both men had run for their lives to alert their superiors.

Now, not for the first time, and with the men of his section around him, Ned lay waiting for the word to go into the attack and kill more Germans. He hoped one of them wasn't the man with the candle. Looking out into the night, he studied the landscape in front of him. Ahead lay his own barbed wire. Beyond that, the open ground rose a little toward Hamel town. Beyond that, Ned knew, over a little ridge, there was a depression, with the old trench system on the ridge on the far side of it. Up, down, then up again he would have to tramp across the Hamel Valley to reach that old trench system, the objective established by General Monash's blue line on the folded map in Ned's tunic pocket. Despite his calm, right now Ned could have done with a cigarette. And a beer.

As the Australians and Americans waited, the air temperature quickly dropped. The nearer 3.00 am came, an increasingly thick white fog rolled in from the Somme and began to hug the hollows on the battlefield. Fog was unusual for this time of year, but that didn't overly worry the Australian commanders. While it would mean the officers in charge of keeping the advancing units on track to their objectives via compasses would have their work cut out in the growing pea-souper, the fog would provide the attackers with even more cover and shroud their presence until they were right on top of German defenders.

General Monash was to himself paint an evocative portrait of the minutes leading up to a battle's launch. 'Company and platoon commanders, their whistles ready to hand, are nervously glancing at their luminous watches, waiting for minute after minute to go by, and giving a last look over their commands, ensuring that their runners are by their sides, their observers alert, and that the officers detailed to control direction have their compasses set and ready. Carrying parties shoulder their burdens, and adjust the straps. Pioneers grasp their picks and shovels. Engineers take up their stores of explosives and primers and fuses. Machine and Lewis gunners whisper for the last time to the carriers of their magazines and belt boxes to be sure and follow up. The Stokes Mortar carrier slings his heavy load, and his [loaders] fumble to see that their haversacks of cartridges are handy.'[129]

Monash also knew that behind the line, things were just as tense: 'Scores of telegraph operators sit by their instruments with their message forms and registers ready to hand, bracing themselves for the rush of signal traffic which will set in a few minutes later. Dozens of staff officers spread their maps in readiness, to record with coloured pencils the stream of expected information. In hundreds of pits, the guns are already run up, loaded and laid on their opening lines of fire. The sergeant is checking the range for the last time. The layer stands silently with the lanyard in his hand.'[130]

From behind the lines, the artillery would launch the battle, and it would be the artillery officers who gave the first command. 'The section officer, watch on wrist, counts the last seconds,' Monash wrote.

'"A minute to go . . . !"

'"Thirty seconds . . . !"

'"Ten seconds . . . !"

'"Fire!"'[131]

10.

The Hell of the Opening Barrage

'A real Fourth of July celebration.'
Unidentified American 132nd Infantry Regiment corporal

AT 3.00 THAT Thursday morning of 4 July, the Australian artillery began their now-routine eight-minute barrage of German positions in the Hamel salient. At 3.02, covered by the cacophony of the barrage, the fifty-eight tanks assigned to the operation began moving, rolling up from their village waiting places to a point a thousand metres west of the front line. Halting there at a prepared white line of their own, the armoured monsters again paused.

As they had done for weeks, in the German trenches, troops hurriedly strapped on their gas masks and scampered down into the dugouts that peppered their trench line. Some of these dugouts, like those at a quarry east of Pear Trench, were no more sophisticated than rabbit holes. Others were reinforced with wooden logs and sandbags. They all nonetheless provided protection against all but a direct hit. A few larger dugouts, especially those used for German battalion headquarters, were dug deep, had thick concrete walls and roofs, and were impervious to all but the very largest shells.

In these dugouts, the defenders would shelter until the deadly eight-minute bombardment had passed. As soon as it ended they would scramble back up to their machine-guns and trench mortars, just as they had been doing for the past weeks. The Germans in the Hamel salient thought this bombardment was merely a nuisance measure, and had no idea they were about to be on the receiving end of a major assault, or that many of them would be dead once the new day dawned.

And now came one of General Monash's little tricks, a stratagem he had employed with success several times before. As on all the preceding mornings, one shell in every eight in the bombardment contained smoke. For the past few weeks the remaining shells had contained a mixture of high explosive and gas, but on this morning the content had changed to smoke and high explosive. There were no gas shells. But the enemy didn't know this. Seeing the drifting smoke, Fritz was still expecting gas. 'He would, therefore, promptly don his gas mask,' said Monash, 'which would obscure his vision, hamper his freedom of action, and reduce his powers of resistance.'[132] That was the plan, anyway. It would remain to be seen if the Hun was fooled this time.

One young Illinois boy of the 132nd Infantry, lying on his stomach with his fellow American squad members out in No Man's Land and watching and listening to his first-ever artillery barrage from close range, was so astounded by the sensation it caused him to involuntarily catch his breath. Beside him, an equally staggered buddy jabbed him in the ribs and asked him what he thought of it. The boy found a nervous smile, and his breath. 'A real Fourth of July celebration,' he replied.[133]

Promptly at 3.08, the regular morning bombardment ended.

'The barrage passed like a storm, leaving behind perfect peace,' an unidentified Australian officer of the 15th Battalion would later tell English war correspondent Philip Gibbs.[134] For two minutes that peace prevailed, as out in No Man's Land, drifting smoke from smoke shells blended with the fog to create a swirling grey-white wall. In the German lines, troops were emerging from their dugouts to reoccupy the defences.

Then at Z Hour, 3.10, the main barrage began. Some 650 field-guns, howitzers and mortars behind the lines boomed and belched fire, smoke and death. Most were participating in the creeping barrage and aiming at the same line on the map out in No Man's Land, 200 metres in front of the waiting assault troops. But, as per the Monash plan, 160 big guns were aiming at the known positions of the 477 enemy artillery pieces in the sector, behind the German lines, to suppress their return fire.

At the same time, twenty heavy machineguns located on high ground north of the River Somme began firing at German positions in the salient, and mortar crews both north and south of the salient also began firing smoke cannisters onto the battleground to add to the smokescreen. As it turned out, this smokescreen element of Monash's battle plan proved unnecessary, because of the fog. That fog, the only surprise the Australian general was to receive that morning, had its advantages and disadvantages. 'This impeded observation and made guidance difficult, but it greatly enhanced the surprise,' Monash would say.[135]

In addition, shells exploding on the chalky ground raised dust that mixed with the fog and smoke. As a consequence, the previously rehearsed use of rifle grenades to mark targets for the tanks using white smoke proved unworkable. Smoke from the rifle grenades would blend in with, and be indistinguishable from, the fog, smoke and dust.

The Americans were right to be nervous about lying out in the open as the bombardment rained down in front of them. With their opening rounds, two field guns firing as part of the barrage on the right of the waiting 11th Brigade's position dropped short. Two shells fell onto men lying there in preparation for the attack. An Australian and an American officer at the JOT were both killed instantly, with another American officer wounded. This visibly unnerved some wide-eyed young Americans, but all held their positions.

In the centre of the line, Ned Searle and his men of D Company were lying at the tape on the extreme right of the 15th Battalion's position when shells fell short, onto A Company, which was over on the left of the 15th's formation. This killed twelve A Company men and wounded thirty, 'as well as rattling our men to some extent', said Lieutenant-Colonel McSharry.[136] Despite this, and perhaps conscious of the example they were expected to set for their new American comrades-in-arms, the men of the 15th held their nerve, and their ground. As the shells continued to drop, many soldiers silently prayed that they would live to see the sunrise.

Now, all along the 6.5-kilometre front, officers put metal

whistles to their lips, and blew hard – the shrill of the whistles was the signal for all assault troops to rise up and start advancing. As one, thousands of Australians and Americans pulled themselves to their feet and began moving forward at walking pace in four waves towards the falling shells. Sometimes in a line, sometimes in small groups, they stepped out with bayonets jutting from the ends of rifles, while Lewis gunners advanced with their machineguns on their shoulders. Unable to see more than a few metres ahead in the darkness and fog, the troops were guided by officers with compasses who would keep them on track to their objectives.

Overhead, invisible above the fog, Australian fighter aircraft of Number 3 Squadron droned by in pairs, so low it seemed the troops could reach up and touch their wings, as they headed for the German positions with their bombs and their bullets. Taking off from the airfield at Villers Bocage at 2.30 am, the RE8 aircraft had entered the battle precisely on schedule. Once over the German positions, these aircraft flew up and down their lines, dropping bombs and strafing the trenches with their machineguns.

The noise the aircraft made was deafening, and, as General Courage had hoped, combined with the sound of the artillery barrage, it drowned out the sound of the monsters of the 5th Tank Brigade as they resumed their advance, clanking and rumbling forward to the attack. The tanks, travelling at twice the speed of the infantry, were intended to catch up with the footsloggers no later than the ten-minute halt as the sun rose at 3.30, although Ned Searle and his mates would believe it when they saw it. In fact, some tanks would overtake the infantry as soon as 3.16 am. Others, however, getting lost in the darkness, fog and smoke, would fail to make their allotted rendezvous at all.

Just the same, artillery, infantry, aircraft and tanks all entered the carefully orchestrated battle at precisely the times allotted to them. This Hamel battle plan, General Monash's symphonic composition, was playing out as it had been scored, although the enthusiasm of some American players did prove a problem early on. 'The pace was slow,' Colonel Sanborn later noted of the steady eastward walk through the fog and smoke as, every three minutes, the barrage jumped another hundred yards ahead. Australians even lit cigarettes as they strolled to the attack.[137]

Keyed-up American troops were visibly impatient to get into action. 'They understood,' war correspondent Gibbs would write, 'that upon their few companies fighting as platoons among the Australians rested the honour of the United States in this historic episode.' General Bell had made no bones about it when addressing his men several days earlier: 'We shall be very disappointed if you do not fulfil the hopes and belief we have in you,' he'd said.[138] So now, a number of Americans, anxious to prove themselves, picked up the pace, pushing out ahead and taking them dangerously close to the friendly shells falling in their path.

Colonel Sanborn noted, 'The men were eager to advance and had to be cautioned several times to remain a sufficient distance behind the barrage.'[139] On the left of the advance, within the first three minutes several shells dropped short, immediately to the right of a Company E platoon, whose men were advancing ahead of the 43rd Battalion. This sent shrapnel scything through American ranks, cutting down the platoon commander Second Lieutenant Elmer Plummer and half a dozen enlisted men. Three of the wounded, squad leaders Sergeant James E. Krum and Corporal Andrew C. Schabinger, and Lewis gunner Private William F. Linskey, though all wounded in the right arm, picked themselves up and rejoined the advance. The members of this trio would play their appointed roles in the battle before seeking medical attention.

Around the wounded men, none of their green American comrades wavered. 'The morale of our troops on their first operation under shell fire in an attack was wonderful,' their company commander Captain Luke was to proudly observe. 'They went into action as if they had been there before.'[140] The other men wounded by this fire were left where they fell, to be collected by the stretcher-bearers following behind. This incident was lesson enough for the remaining men of Company E. Said Captain Luke, 'After the first "lift", our men kept well in the rear of the barrage, which was still short, and did not meet with the same thing again.'[141]

Driver Harry Dalziel, at the centre of the advance beside his 15th Battalion Lewis gun partner, with his two pistols and German dagger, and impressed by the smokescreen and barrage being laid down immediately ahead, heard Americans of the 132nd Infantry chanting. 'Win the war! Win the war!' they chorused as they went forward.[142]

Some of these 132nd Infantry men were also wounded by Allied artillery fire after pushing ahead in their enthusiasm. Medical officers Major Kennedy and Lieutenant Schram and their party came upon these injured men where they had fallen, and calmly set about helping them. 'We attended wounded men in No Man's Land while the barrage was going on,' said Schram matter-of-factly later.[143]

Despite the losses to Allied fire, the advance continued steadily, inexorably, towards the primary objectives.

11.

The Assault on the Left Flank

'Our men were timid at first in using the bayonet, but after they once drew blood it did not bother them in the least.'
Captain James Luke, Company E, US 131st Infantry

GERMAN GAS ALARMS could be heard ringing as the Australians and Americans advanced through the smoke, fog and dust and neared the first German trenches. The sound put smiles on attackers' faces: General Monash's little three-card trick with the gas shells had worked.

Three hundred metres into the advance, and after passing through gaps in the German wire, the 43rd Battalion and the 131st Infantry's Company E were the first units of the assault to come under machinegun fire. An Australian lieutenant was killed by a spray from unseen German Maxim MG08 heavy machineguns, firing blindly into the mist of fog and smoke from an advance post dug into the chalky ground. Several other 43rd Battalion men were wounded by the same weapons. Corporal Frank Shaw, a Lewis gunner with the 43rd, boldly standing tall as others hit the ground around him, fired his weapon from the hip as he advanced through a wheatfield. He quickly silenced three German machineguns operating from the outpost to one side of them.

As these left-flank troops pushed on, another heavy machinegun opened up from a nest immediately in front of them, with the gun's familiar deadly *thud-thud-thud*. From experience, the Australians knew that German machinegun detachments were made up of a dozen or so men led by an officer or senior NCO and manning a Maxim MG08 sitting on cradle-like legs and the equivalent of the British Vickers, plus several smaller machineguns which were like Lewis guns, on bipod or tripod legs. So, every MG nest posed multiple threats.

Having used all his ammunition against the previous outpost, Frank Shaw cast aside his Lewis gun, drew his pistol and ran towards the flash from the Maxim's muzzle in the gloom. As Shaw dashed forward, he was joined by Corporal H. G. Zyburt of the 131st Infantry's Company E. Side-by-side, the Australian and the American dropped into the German trench, then set about clearing it.

A German officer loomed in front of Shaw. Without hesitation the Australian shot the officer dead with his pistol. Tackled by another German soldier, Shaw went down. As the pair struggled, the German's coalscuttle helmet went flying. In the desperate wrestle that followed, Shaw smashed in his assailant's skull with the butt of his revolver, killing him. Meanwhile, Corporal Zyburt bayoneted all the remaining German occupants of the post. Shaw and Zyburt then took possession of the German machineguns in the post, and their ammunition.

A total of eight dead enemy soldiers were found in the trench once Shaw and Zyburt had finished their work. Their captured machineguns were handed over to the 'mopper upper' platoon coming behind, to join the large collection of German heavy weapons that would be taken by the assault troops in the battle. Said British war correspondent Philip Gibbs, 'Many of these were at once turned onto the enemy and fired all day with his own ammunition, as every Australian machinegunner is perfectly familiar with the handling of the German weapon.'[144] This was no accident; Australian commanders had made a point of having their gunners train with German machineguns.

Following Frank Shaw's example, several more Australian Lewis gunners wiped out more German machinegun nests in their path by firing from the hip, and the advance swept on. Reaching the mid-battlefield 'halt line' on their maps, the advancing troops briefly came to a stop. As planned, the barrage also abated, and equally as planned the first tanks rolled onto the scene in this pause, although not as many as expected. With tanks in support here and there, the infantry pushed through gaps in the enemy wire that had been created by the pulverising barrage, or gaps made by tanks squashing their way through wire. Still, most of the hard fighting would fall to the footsloggers.

To their surprise, the 42nd Battalion and the 131st Infantry's Company C took the first enemy trenches they encountered without opposition. 'Before reaching Hamel,' said Colonel Sanborn, 'the enemy's front and support lines [were] taken and mopped up, many prisoners and machineguns being taken.'[145] Scores of German soldiers tumbled out of their dugouts with hands held high and crying, 'Kamerad! Kamerad!' Meaning, 'Friend! Friend!'

As General Monash had hoped, these surrendering Germans were still wearing their gas masks; until they saw that the Australians and Americans were not, and realised they'd been fooled. Now, disarmed, they were bundled back to support troops behind the advance. The men of Captain Gale's Company C alone captured 150 Germans without a fight here, along with numbers of machineguns, three trench mortars and a British supply tank that had been in German hands.

The units on the left advanced a good 800 metres before enemy artillery began to respond to their attack. German troops in the trenches had been so surprised and over-whelmed by the infantry assault they had failed to call in artillery support. When the Australians and Americans saw red and green German flares finally burst above them in the gloom, fired by German units further back to indicate where their artillery should aim, they tensed for the howling arrival of shells.

The problem for the German artillery commanders was that, because of the fog and smoke, and now because their front-line troops had crumbled and no one remained to direct their fire, they were literally firing blind; they had no idea where their enemies were. As a result, this German counter bombardment landed on the old Australian front line well behind the advancing Australians and Americans, on open territory in front of the trenches, and on the support trenches behind them. At this point, those vacated trenches had yet to be occupied by support troops, so no Allied casualties resulted.

The number of enemy shells falling was also much less than had been expected. Later, Australian commanders would learn from aerial reconnaissance that a number of German artillery pieces had been knocked out by the operation's artillery barrages and aerial bombing. Panicked German artillery commanders also hurriedly withdrew many of their guns through fear of them being overrun by the surprise attack. Eventually, the remaining German gunners improved their aim, and their shells began to fall closer to the attackers. Even so, when the advance halted at the halfway mark to pause for ten minutes to allow the tanks to catch up, German shells continued to fall behind them. Pounding empty ground to the attackers' rear, exploding no closer than 200 metres away, these German shells also failed to cause any casualties.

Nearing the western edge of Hamel, the 43rd Battalion and Company E came under sustained machinegun fire from a well dug-in MG nest. American Lieutenant Symons, leading Company E's reserve platoon as it brought up the rear of the 43rd's advance, saw that the men ahead had been pinned down by these machineguns, and led his troops away, working around to one side and outflanking the Germans in the post unseen. When Symons rose up and led a charge on the machineguns from the flank, he was shot by a German and fell, wounded. But Symons' Australian runner Sergeant Frank M. Darke spontaneously took over command of the American platoon and led the charge into the trench. According to war correspondent Gibbs, some Americans yelled the war-cry 'Lusitania' as they charged, a reference to the April 1917 sinking of the American ship *Lusitania* by a German U-boat that had brought the United States into the war.

Sergeant Darke and his Yanks wiped out the defenders in this trench with bullet and bayonet, then stormed the series of dugouts along the trench. Australians had long experience in use of the bayonet. 'Our infantry are always vigorous bayonet fighters,' General Monash was to say, and they gave their American companions an efficient, cold-blooded example to follow on this day.[146] Captain Luke of the 131st would note, 'Our men were timid at first in using the bayonet, but after they once drew blood it did not bother them in the least.'[147]

When three Germans emerged from a dugout and made a run for it, they were shot down. Following the businesslike work by the Australian-led American platoon, the Australian and American attackers who had been pinned down rose up and continued to advance. Sergeant Darke then led the American platoon into Hamel, where they assisted in mopping up.

The 15th Battalion's War Diary would record that 'one party of thirty enemy were wiped out attempting to escape into Hamel'. Another party of thirty Germans fleeing from a strongpoint was 'also shot down by our Lewis Gun fire'. Half a dozen British tanks arrived in the early morning light to join the 43rd Battalion and Company E for the attack on Hamel town, emerging through the exploding shells and drifting smoke as Australian and British artillery pounded the town for ten minutes. When the attack went forward again, the first enemy dugouts encountered were found to have been deserted by their defenders, who were clearly terrified by the appearance of armour.

'When the barrage lifted from Hamel,' said Colonel Sanborn, 'our troops rushed in, mopping up machinegun

emplacements, houses, barns, factories, stores, dugouts, etc.'
There were also concrete bunkers in the town, one of which
contained a German battalion HQ, whilst another housed
an aid post. 'Most of the enemy in the village were found
in deep dugouts,' said Captain Gale, 'and easily surrendered.' A sergeant with Company C's intelligence section
single-handedly took the surrender of the German battalion
HQ staff, comprising four officers and twenty-three other
ranks.[148]

Here in Hamel, the Mark V tanks showed what they could
do. 'After the tanks got working there was good cooperation
between them and the infantry,' said Colonel Sanborn. These
tanks made for each dugout that was pointed out to them
by the Australians and Americans. Usually, but not always,
they pulverised them with shellfire. Sometimes they simply
drove over emplacements to destroy them. 'One entire line
of dugouts was crushed in by a single tank,' said Sanborn,
'which appeared to be a great surprise to the enemy, and prisoners taken seemed greatly afraid of them.'[149]

One American, herding prisoners from a dugout, appreciated how terrifying the tanks must be to the Germans, feeling
the ground shake as a tank passed a thousand metres away.
'The six tanks assigned to this battalion did very efficient
work,' said Sanborn's subordinate Captain Gale. 'Probably
their best work was in strengthening the morale of our troops,
as the tanks kept close up to the barrage and went after every
strongpoint that appeared.'[150]

On the extreme left of the assault, a tank turned up after
Australian troops had overwhelmed German trenches and
small dugouts at Notamel Wood to the north of Hamel, in

vicious hand-to-hand fighting against 'considerable resistance'. Too late to help at Notamel Wood, the tank turned
south and pushed into the ruined town itself. 'The tanks
worked splendidly,' said Company E's Captain Luke, 'except
one on our extreme right, which for some reason got stuck
in Hamel and had to back out. As this tank did so it lost its
bearings and fired on some of our own troops with cannister,
killing one officer and wounding one or two of our men.'[151]
The Americans also witnessed two tanks being put out of
action by hits from German artillery shells, which blew off
tracks, after which the crews bailed out.

When Company E's Sergeant Albert Erhardt and his
platoon were pinned down by the murderous fire of a German
machinegun on the outskirts of Hamel, Erhardt dashed out
into the open to the nearest tank and directed it against the
MG nest. Once the tank had done its work, Erhardt and his
men moved in and mopped up. The American troops were
still coming to terms with the Lewis Gun, but one American
in Hamel proved to be a quick learner. Company E's Private
William Linskey, who had been wounded in the shoulder by
friendly fire in the first minutes of the advance, continued on
to the primary target with his Lewis Gun and used it to great
effect in the clearing of Hamel.

Following the Monash plan, the 42nd Battalion and
Company C pulled back to the western outskirts of Hamel
and began digging new trenches to oppose the expected
enemy counterattack from the east. 'All the ground was
extremely hard, being made of chalk,' Captain Gale recorded.
German shells also occasionally fell around them as they dug.
Gale was particularly proud of one of his platoons, which

'showed great coolness in action in marking out and digging the trenches' while under fire.[152]

Once the 43rd and Company E had also played their part in clearing the town of Germans, sending prisoners back to the Australian Corps POW pens behind the lines – called 'bird cages' by the Australians – they too quite deliberately pulled back just to the west of Hamel and dug in. Despite the hard chalky ground, within an hour these troops had created trenches deep enough to protect them from all but direct artillery hits. Said Colonel Sanborn, 'The front covered by the 43rd Battalion, Australians, including troops of Company E, extended from the Somme River to a point opposite the left of Vaire Wood, about 2600 yards, or about a total of one man for every two yards of front.'[153]

This pull-back left Hamel deserted and silent. Not even a dog moved in the town now. It proved a wise move. At 6.10 am, enemy shells would begin to rain on Hamel. The shelling of the town would continue for several hours, with German commanders convinced that the Australians had occupied it. They wasted their shells. Not a single Australian or American casualty would result.

Also as part of General Monash's plan, Americans of the 108th Engineers attached to the assault for pioneer duty with picks and shovels quickly moved into the occupied territory. Ignoring enemy shells dropping close by, the Yanks began digging communications trenches from the new trenches the 42nd and 43rd were creating outside Hamel all the way back to the old front-line trenches. When Australian troops escorting hordes of German prisoners passed the toiling engineers, an American officer called out to the Aussies.

'Say, can't we lend you a hand?' he offered.

'Yes,' said another Yank, 'can't we be of any use to you?'

The Australian officer in charge of the prisoners nodded. 'Some of your lads might help us conduct the prisoners,' he suggested.

Mobbed by eager American engineers, the Aussie officer welcomed them into the escort detail. This allowed him to detach the majority of his own men from the escort and send them back to the new front line, ready to help their mates greet the expected enemy counterattack. According to war correspondent Philip Gibbs, 'No German prisoners have had such a strong and proud escort as that provided by the Americans, who had not the luck, as they thought it, to take part in the actual fighting with their comrades who had gone forward with the Australian infantry and tanks.'[154]

'A good number' of men from the 108th Engineers also worked spontaneously at the advanced dressing station at Pear Trench, giving the existing stretcher-bearers a hand and literally lightening their load. Inspired by this, Colonel Allen, commanding officer of the 108th Engineers, officially detailed fourteen of his men to assist as stretcher-bearers at the advanced dressing station that night. The engineers would return the night of 5 July to help with casualties stemming from enemy shelling and counterattacks. With casualties among stretcher-bearers themselves high, the American engineers also voluntarily helped locate and bury the dead of both sides where they had fallen. Australian and American dead were duly buried side-by-side in the Hamel Valley, within sight of Hamel, with their graves marked by wooden crosses bearing each man's name, rank and unit.[155]

One American stretcher-bearer serving with the 131st Infantry, Private Christopher Keane, improvised when it came to making up for lost comrades. After two stretcher-bearers working with him were killed by German shells, he coopted several German prisoners to carry wounded through the enemy fire to places of safety.

As the 42nd and 43rd Battalions and their American 131st Infantry companions dug in outside Hamel, the 44th Battalion, which had been advancing behind the 42nd and 43rd, divided as it came up to Hamel, with half its companies passing north of the town and half south of it. On the eastern side of Hamel the 44th reformed, then pushed on towards the ridge in the near distance, their final objective, climbing up the slope and crossing the road that slanted diagonally up it as they aimed for the old British trench line that ran along the top of the ridge.

One member of the 42nd Battalion who failed to fall back and dig in was Corporal Frank Shaw. Contrary to orders, the dauntless Lewis gunner passed through the town and kept advancing east, looking for more custom for his trusty weapon. In a quarry beyond Hamel, Shaw came across more German dugouts and another machinegun post, whose surviving occupants quickly threw up their hands after he sprayed their position with his Lewis Gun and killed several of their comrades.

Only now did Shaw return to the 42nd, bringing seventeen terrorised prisoners from the quarry, who were carrying their machineguns under the corporal's watchful eye. Shaw would be the only Australian enlisted man whom Colonel Joe Sanborn would mention by name in his postwar account of the battle. 'In all,' said the American, who was clearly impressed with the Australian, 'Shaw fired nine magazines throughout the operation, and proved the value of a Lewis Gun in the hands of a brave and determined man.'[156]

Meanwhile, as planned, a platoon of Americans from the 131st's Company C continued with the advance all the way up onto the ridge. 'A large number of German killed and wounded were found on top of the knoll and in the trenches,' said company commander Captain Gale. 'About one hundred Germans were found in these trenches who gave themselves up and were sent to the rear.' Captain Gale's past career as a police inspector would come to the fore when he reported after the battle: 'In the taking of German prisoners, a tendency was noted on the part of Australian troops of an entire disregard for the personal property rights of prisoners of war, they stripping them as a rule of anything of value. It is feared that probably some of our troops followed this along as an example.'[157]

The battling troops were also very conscious of the activity of Australian fighter aircraft above as the new day's warm sunshine burned off the fog and created a clear summer sky. 'The aeroplanes kept in constant and close touch with us all the time,' said Captain Gale, 'which also added to the morale of our troops.'[158] Once daylight arrived there was a constant threat of being strafed by the German aircraft of Baron Manfred von Richthofen's famous Flying Circus.

Richthofen, the 'Red Baron', an ace with eighty aerial 'kills' to his credit, had himself been shot down over Australian lines in April and killed. The Australians had buried him with full military honours, and General Monash had been given a piece of the wooden propellor from Richthofen's downed crimson fighter the 'Red Falcon' as a souvenir.

Nonetheless, the Red Baron's wing of four *jastas*, or squadrons, which, from 14 July would be commanded by a young Hermann Goering, who in years to come would be the creator of the World War Two Luftwaffe and second highest ranking Nazi after Adolf Hitler, was still very active and posed a real threat to the success of the Hamel operation. Consequently, the Australian pilots, returning to their Villers Bocage airfield in relays to refuel and rearm through the mid-morning before returning to the skies over Hamel, were doggedly efficient sentinels and protectors. 'They kept the area entirely clear during the engagement and for several hours afterward of enemy aircraft,' said Captain Gale.[159]

12.

The Assault in the Centre

*'All ranks of the tank crews were impressed by the superb
morale of the Australian troops.'*
Major-General John Fuller, British Tank Corps

LANCE-CORPORAL JACK AXFORD was advancing at the
forefront of the 16th Battalion, which had been tasked with
dealing with Vaire Wood and Hamel Wood, before, under
General Monash's battle plan, withdrawing to the old front
line to act as a reserve. Jack and members of his platoon got
through the German wire without any problem, but to one
side of them another platoon of the 16th was held up when it
found the artillery had failed to create breaks in the wire in
their path as planned. With the Australians bogged down at
the wire, German machineguns zeroed in on them, cutting
down a number of men including a company commander.

Seeing this, Jack Axford, who had cleared the wire,
diverted sideways and dashed in the direction of the trench
containing the offending machineguns. First tossing in his
two little pineapple-shaped grenades in quick succession, Jack

jumped in after them and bayoneted every German who stood in his way. Within seconds, little Jack Axford had killed ten Germans. Another six terrified Fritzes threw up their hands and surrendered to the lone Australian. Jack made his prisoners heave their machineguns over the trench's parapet, out into the open.

Then, poking his head over the parapet, Jack yelled to the stalled 16th Battalion platoon, 'Come on!'

The men of that platoon rose up and skirted to the flank to use the gap in the wire that Jack's platoon had utilised, then ran to jump into the trench with Jack. Handing his prisoners over to the new arrivals, Jack climbed out and hurried after his own platoon, which was continuing to advance.

As the 16th Battalion pushed toward Vaire Wood and Hamel Wood, and the 13th Battalion attacked on the south side of Vaire Wood, the 15th Battalion and the attached G Company of the 132nd Infantry advanced to the north of the woods. The 15th's A Company had been given the task of dealing with Pear Trench, supported by three tanks. Already depleted by the loss of forty-two men hit by friendly fire at the jumping-off tape, A Company was about to tackle the most difficult objective the assault force would face that day.

Not only did the trio of tanks assigned to Pear Trench fail to materialise, as the men of the 15th and the attached 132nd Infantry company reached this formidable redoubt they discovered that the defences, including the wire out front, were completely intact, having escaped the creeping barrage. Later, it would be found that all the shells aimed at Pear Trench had fallen immediately behind it. This enabled the enemy to emerge from their dugouts and man the extensive Pear Trench defences, albeit still wearing their gas masks.

As a result, all twenty-three German machineguns and several mortars in Pear Trench were undamaged, manned, and firing viciously at the attackers by the time the first wave reached the wire in front of them. Only a few sally ports offered a way through these wire entanglements, although some men succeeded in also scrambling through where the wire was thinnest. 'We had trouble getting through the wires,' Captain William J. Masoner of Company G would sourly complain, 'as the barrage had not torn them down, and the tanks did not arrive in time to destroy them.'[160]

'The enemy fought with his machineguns bravely,' said the 15th Battalion War Diary of the struggle at Pear Trench, 'and our casualties were fairly heavy at this point.' After passing through the wire, the Australians rushed the trench, 'the enemy putting up a spirited fight with machineguns and bombs. Our men dashed in with the bayonet and soon overcame the garrison of the front line.'

The 132nd's Captain George H. Mallon had been attached to Company G as an observer for the battle, and he saw comrades fall to these guns at Pear Trench. 'We lost heavily in front of two machineguns before they were silenced by troops attacking from the rear,' he said.[161] Once defenders in the trenches out front of Pear Trench were overcome, the 15th Battalion men had passed along its rear wings and down a sunken road behind it, to tackle strongpoints there, 'bombing and bayonetting the garrison who fought tenaciously', said the 15th Battalion War Diary.

Harry Dalziel's company commander Captain Ernest

Carter had ordered his Lewis gunners to fire their weapons from the hip, and in that stance Harry's Lewis Gun partner had just wiped out one German machinegun nest in the redoubt when another that opened up from one side cut him down. Without a moment's thought, Two-Gun Harry drew his revolvers then ran at the offending machinegun with a pistol in each hand. Hurdling the parapet and dropping into the trench, Harry blazed away, killing seven German machinegunners with his revolvers. Another German further along the trench got off a shot at him, hitting Harry in the right hand's index finger and knocking the pistol from his grip.[162]

With a howl of pain, Harry let go of the second revolver and instinctively grabbed his wounded hand. The German who'd shot him charged at him, but Harry reacted quickly, wrestling his attacker to the ground. Getting on top of the German, the Australian reached for the dagger on his belt, drew it, and struck. 'I lunged at him with my German dagger,' he later recalled, 'catching him right over the heart. His dying cry upset me, and I shivered at Pear Trench.'[163]

Soon, other Australians of Harry's company and Americans of Captain Masoner's company were surging into this section of Pear Trench around Harry, clearing it in fierce hand-to-hand combat. After years of war, the Australians had become accustomed to seeing enemy dead on the battlefield, but for the Americans, it came as a shock. Captain George Mallon looked around the carnage when he climbed into the secured Pear Trench, and shuddered. 'A great many Germans were killed at this point,' he would say. 'I counted forty in a very small sector.'[164]

After Harry Dalziel slipped his bloodied dagger back into its scabbard and reloaded and reholstered his pistols, he saw the 'moppers up' of the next wave of the assault arriving to collect German prisoners and machineguns around the captured redoubt. An officer, spotting Harry's bleeding hand, ordered him to go to the rear and have it attended to. Adrenaline was pulsing through the driver's veins by this time, and Two-Gun Harry was ready for more dices with death. But orders were orders, and, unhappily, Harry turned to obey the officer. He hadn't gone far when he spotted stretcher-bearers who were carrying wounded down into the trench line west of Pear Trench, and he made a beeline for them.

Lieutenant Schram, Major Kennedy and their medical party had followed the assault troops all the way to Pear Trench to set up their advanced dressing station close to the fighting. They had been hoping to find a suitable German dugout, equipped with lamps, but no such dugout had been liberated by the time they arrived, and already the stretcher-bearers were coming to them with dozens of wounded from the Pear Trench assault. So, Kennedy decided to use an open trench as their ADS. At least it was comparatively sheltered from enemy fire. They had several wheeled stretchers with them – gurneys, the Americans called them – and these became the doctors' operating tables.

'Cases were brought in rather fast,' Lieutenant Schram later reported, 'but we succeeded in dressing them and getting them out in rapid time.'[165] As soon as wounded men were assessed and dressed, they were put in the hands of stretcher-bearers once again, to be carried or escorted back more than 1.5 kilometres over open ground to the better facilities at the nearest Regimental Aid Post at the original front line.

From that RAP, serious cases could be evacuated to a Casualty Clearing Station by motor ambulance. There, doctors assisted by military nurses would carry out procedures in fully equipped operating theatres. Once wounded men were able to travel further, they would be loaded onto hospital trains at the CCS's own rail siding and evacuated to hospitals. Final recovery and recuperation would take place in England. To aid the CCS doctors, Lieutenant Schram had been trained to attach diagnosis tags to the tunic of each case, but Major Kennedy soon dissuaded him from that practice.

'They come in too fast,' said Kennedy with a shake of the head, as they worked quickly to stem bleeding and apply splints to limbs broken by bullets, blast and shrapnel. 'To use diagnosis tags would delay them getting out.'[166]

Before long, the numbers of walking wounded and men carried into the ADS threatened to overwhelm the doctors and their assistants. 'We had some difficulty getting rid of our dress cases,' Schram would report. 'They were not evacuated fast enough. We had difficulty for a while in obtaining sufficient stretchers.' Before long, their supply of splints also ran out, so the doctors resorted to using rifles as splints, strapping them onto shattered limbs. Schram soon found that the first-aid kits the Americans had come to the front with were too small and inadequately equipped. And unlike the Australian doctors, Schram had no painkiller to give the more seriously wounded men, and he made a mental note to acquire morphine from a hospital before he went into a combat zone again.

To speed things up, Major Kennedy after a while was able to have a relay post set up halfway back, so that increasingly weary Australian and American stretcher-bearer teams could hand their cases over to fresh stretcher-bearers for the carry back to the RAP, then themselves return to the ADS for more 'customers'. Kennedy also sent back for more splints and bandages.

It was to this overworked Pear Trench ADS that Two-Gun Harry Dalziel took himself for attention. He didn't get as far as Doctors Kennedy or Schram. Australian stretcher-bearer Private James Shearer bandaged Harry's hand and urged him to take himself back to the RAP, but Harry wasn't interested in leaving the battle. As soon as Shearer had patched him up, Two-Gun Harry scampered to rejoin the 15th Battalion's A Company as they continued their advance.[167]

*

While Pear Trench was still being subdued by A Company, the rest of the 15th Battalion had pushed on by it. At Vaire Trench, near Vaire Wood, D Company encountered heavy machinegun fire that sent the men of the company to ground and halted the advance. As the gun turned towards new targets, Sergeant Ned Searle knew that it was time to make his bid for a VC.

'Come on, you blokes!' Ned bellowed as he came to his feet with rifle at the ready.

Hoping that, behind him, the men of his platoon were also rising up to join him in rushing the gun, and running as fast as his legs would carry him, Ned dashed towards the trench housing the machinegun. The closer he came to the Germans he realised there was more than one machinegun in the post. Apart from the heavy Maxim, three light machineguns were now also in operation, chattering away. Reaching the lip of the trench, Ned threw himself to the ground. With the main gun juddering lethally just a metre or two from his head, Ned took out two hand grenades. In quick succession he pulled the pins, lobbed the grenades over the parapet, then ducked back down. From pin-pull to detonation there was a pause of seven seconds. As Ned waited, it seemed like seven agonising minutes. Finally, two dull explosions. Followed by cries of pain and alarm. The machineguns fell silent.

Up Ned rose again. Hurdling the parapet, he dropped into the middle of the smoking machinegun nest. A figure in field grey lunged at him. Ned sidestepped and plunged his bayonet into the man. As Ned withdrew his blade, another German came at him. Ned expertly despatched him with his bayonet, too. Eleven remaining German soldiers of the 55th Regiment, 13th Infantry Division, including a junior officer, all with gas masks on, threw up their hands in terror, and surrendered.

'Kamerad! Kamerad!' they cried, as dead comrades lay around them with their blood splattered over the chalk.

The members of Ned's section dropped into the trench to join him, and soon scores more Australians were pouring into the trench and securing it. Whilst his men covered the surrendered Germans, who sheepishly removed their gas masks, Ned personally searched all of them. From the officer, a square-faced, narrow-shouldered lieutenant, he removed a long-barrelled Luger artillery pistol in its holster, strapping it around his waist. 'Larrikin' Ned also tried on the officer's peaked cap, but the German had a big head and the cap was too large for the Australian.

Deciding that the officer was about his size and that his smart German Army tunic would look good on him in the bar of the Westbury Arms pub when he got back home, Ned then ordered the German to disrobe. The lieutenant protested that this was contrary to the provisions of the Geneva Convention, but a nudge from Ned's bayonet told him it was required by the provisions of the Searle Convention, and he removed the tunic and handed it to the Australian sergeant.

From another German, Ned removed a flat enlisted man's cap that fitted him perfectly. And in the tunic pocket of another quaking prisoner he found a photograph of the entire machinegun detachment, the living and the dead, posing with their machineguns as they looked, unsmiling, at the photographer. Ned would keep that memento for the rest of his days. Ned made his prisoners carry their four machineguns, and ammunition, as he and his men handed them over to the moppers-up of the next wave.

Captain Bradley trotted by, calling his congratulations to Ned for a job well done. As Ned hoped, following the battle Bradley would submit a recommendation to Colonel McSharry that Ned be decorated for 'conspicuous gallantry and devotion to duty'. But for now, as soon as they'd handed over their prisoners to moppers-up, Ned and his men rejoined the push east.

*

Harry Dalziel caught up with his A Company mates east of Pear Trench. His wound was still leaking blood through and around his hasty bandage when he found his comrades, but, undeterred, he continued the advance as his platoon came to a deep concrete dugout. Unlike at Pear Trench, the artillery bombardment had wreaked havoc here. 'We found Huns dead in all directions,' Harry would later say. 'Up in trees, under duckboards, in shell holes, everywhere.'

Standing at the top of the concrete steps leading down into the bunker, the platoon's number one Lewis gunner fired down into it with gun on his hip. This generated desperate cries of 'Kamerad!' from below, and moments later unarmed Germans began streaming up the steps. 'The poor Huns came up with their hands above their heads,' Harry would say. 'I felt like a warlord with my two pistols pointing at them and one dagger on my belt.'

To Harry's amazement, in a bid to buy their lives the Germans offered their Australian captors their gold and silver watches as they were roughly searched for weapons. Dalziel didn't take any of the watches on offer, but some other Australians would. 'We sent them off with their beautiful watches to the "moppers-up",' said Harry. 'This was a grand experience for me and I relished every minute of it,' he confessed. But Two-Gun Harry's battle was not yet over. Not by a long shot.[168]

*

Twenty-one-year-old Corporal Albert C. Painsipp of the 132nd's Company A had just gone through a gap in the

German wire in advance of the trees of Vaire Wood when a machinegun in a wheatfield opened up on him. An armour-piercing bullet slammed into the American's thigh, spinning him around and knocking him down. Hauling himself back to his feet, Painsipp staggered towards the trench containing the machinegun. The gunner, thinking he'd killed Painsipp, had traversed his weapon to fire at other targets. Now, seeing him coming afresh, the gunner desperately swung the gun back to cut him down.

Dropping his rifle and lunging for the barrel of the gun with both hands to save himself, Painsipp tried to upset the grim grey Maxim, but it was too heavy and the gun's two-man crew frantically resisted his efforts. Letting go of the hot barrel, Painsipp dropped back down below the parapet. Here, the machinegun couldn't incline far enough to get him. But he knew he would die here if he didn't act fast. The Americans had little experience of Mills Bombs, and few made effective use of them during the Battle of Hamel. In contrast, Corporal Painsipp knew that the Mills Bomb in the pouch on his chest was his only chance. Dragging out the grenade, Painsipp yanked the pin and tossed it into the trench. The detonation silenced the gun.

Retrieving his rifle and picking himself up, Painsipp dropped into the trench with his bayonet at the ready. He found the grenade had killed four occupants of the post. A fifth German was running off along the trench's duck-boarded floor, away from him. As the corporal limped after the escaping German, the enemy soldier disappeared down steps into a dugout. Without hesitation, Painsipp went down the steps after him, with rifle levelled. It was pitch dark down here, and out of the darkness Painsipp's quarry leapt at him. But Painsipp was handy with the bayonet; he rammed the blade into his assailant, killing him.

Finding the dugout empty apart from the now-dead man, Painsipp turned and climbed back up into the daylight. Just as he was emerging, another German came at him with a bayonet. But he only caught Painsipp in the arm. It was a fatal error, for the German. Painsipp countered, plunging his own bayonet into his attacker's chest. The man slid to the trench floor. Still, Painsipp's ordeal wasn't over. Yet another German rushed at him with bayonet levelled. Knocking the German's blade aside so that it only scratched him, Painsipp countered with a lethal blow of his own. As this latest assailant sagged, dead, to the ground, Painsipp withdrew his bloodied bayonet. By rights, the American should have been dead four times over.

From behind him, Painsipp heard the judder of a machine-gun firing. Yet another German had taken over the gun that Painsipp had silenced with the grenade, and, unaware of the American's presence, was kneeling behind it, firing at the advancing Australians and Americans outside the trench. Lifting his rifle and taking aim, Painsipp pulled the trigger, plugging this latest gunner. The German fell away, dead, and again the machinegun went silent.

Now that he had cleared the nest and removed the last threat, Painsipp's strength deserted him, and he sagged to the trench's floor. Sitting with his back against the chalk wall, surrounded by dead Germans and with a trio of wounds, Painsipp was bleeding heavily and knew he could go no further. Looking around, he saw a piece of white cloth lying within reach; perhaps one of the Germans had been preparing to surrender. Tying the rag to the end of his rifle, he held up the weapon and slowly, painfully, waved it back and forth to attract the attention of stretcher-bearers.

*

A number of 132nd Infantry men overcame their timidity with the bayonet after they saw one of their popular Company G comrades, Private Henry F. Engelhardt, a twenty-seven-year-old draftee and former foundryman from Alton, Illinois, killed at the end of a German bayonet in the trenches.

Elsewhere, Americans saw a German pretending to be wounded raising his hands in surrender and beckoning an American stretcher-bearer, only for the German to skewer the stretcher-bearer with a bayonet when he came up to help him. 'He was treacherously murdered!' was the story that swept through American ranks. Now, anger and a lust for revenge drove American bayonets into German breasts, and any thoughts of mercy were forgotten.[169]

*

A baby-faced but earnest corporal of the 132nd's G Company had pushed through Vaire Wood, firing at fleeting targets as he went, and was advancing against the heavily-defended German trench line beyond Hamel town. The corporal had led twenty-four Americans into combat, and, the night before they came into the line, all had formally vowed to inflict as much damage on the Germans as possible this day, then, like boys in the schoolyard, spitting on their palms and shaking hands in confirmation of their oath.

The corporal was unscathed and had avoided any life and death scenarios up to this point, when two Germans came running towards him from a German post with their hands held high and yelling 'Kamerad!' Not knowing what this meant, the corporal raised his rifle to shoot.

'Don't touch them!' called one of his officers from nearby.

The corporal turned the German pair over to troops coming along behind, and kept advancing, all the time with his finger on his rifle's trigger. From out of nowhere, a bullet fired by an unseen rifleman hit him. The youngster stumbled on a few more steps, then, as the realisation hit him that he'd been wounded, he dropped to his knees. To finish off the corporal, a German charged him with rifle and bayonet. Instinctively, the American raised his rifle and fired. The German dropped, sprawling on his face in front of the corporal, and didn't move again.

Moments later, a second German, bareheaded and yelling, came at the American with a bayonet lowered. The baby-faced corporal pulled his trigger again, only to find he was out of ammunition. In the flash of a second, as the German bore down on him, the youth came to a realisation. 'I knew I had to get up and fight,' he would later say. Rising back to his feet, the corporal brought up his rifle. As he had been trained, he turned the German's blade aside with his own. In the same fluid motion, he brought the butt of his rifle around, and, as the German's momentum carried him past, the corporal cracked the back of the man's skull and the Boche went down, and stayed down. Somehow, the corporal had survived.[170]

'We kept on advancing,' said the corporal's commander, Captain Masoner. Over this trench line and up the slope towards the trenches on the ridge that represented their final objective they continued.[171] When the attacking forces that were now pushing on beyond Vaire and Hamel Woods reached that trench line up on the ridge, they found them heavily defended by waiting Germans. More machineguns spat fire in their direction.

But now tanks appeared and growled relentlessly up the slope, passing the climbing troops to lead the attack at several places along the line. The Germans here were in for a tough time. 'It was necessary for the tanks to go forward mopping up some trenches and strong points,' said Colonel Abel Davis, the 132nd Infantry's CO, 'and proved of great value in neutralising the enemy strong points.'[172]

Wherever and whenever the tanks turned up, the attackers put them to good use. After tackling the German trenches in front of Vaire and Hamel Woods, Ned Searle and his comrades of the 15th Battalion's D Company were on the extreme right of their battalion's advance to the ridge. Three British tanks helped the 15th here. One was soon knocked out by German fire. According to Lieutenant-Colonel McSharry, the 15th's CO, another tank was 'not very keen', but the third was 'gallantly handled, and saved us a great number of casualties at the final objective'.

At that final objective, the central portion of the blue line trenches on the ridge, 'the enemy made a short stand', McSharry said, 'until our men rushed the position and cleaned it up with the assistance of a tank, taking three heavy machineguns and twenty-seven light machineguns'. With the help of that tank, D Company was the first 15th Battalion company to secure its final objective.[173]

'Our tanks served us very well,' said Captain Masoner, 'going close to the enemy line and destroying their machine-gun emplacements using armour-piercing shells. One of our lieutenants and several of our men discovered a machinegun position and with the aid of a tank took six prisoners and destroyed the machinegun.' To attract the attention of the tank's commander, the American lieutenant had rung the bell on the tank's rear, just as he had been earlier briefed to do.[174]

The Tank Corps would come out of this battle, the first exhibition under combat conditions of the Mark V's awesome capabilities against infantry in fixed positions, full of admiration for the Aussie infantry they fought alongside at Hamel. Said the Tank Corps' Major-General Fuller: 'All ranks of the tank crews operating were impressed by the superb morale of the Australian troops, who never considered that the presence of the tanks exonerated them from fighting, and who took instant advantage of any opportunity created by the tanks.'[175]

Right along the 5.6-kilometre front of the assault, the final objective, General Monash's blue line on the bare expanse of Hamel ridge, was being reached, and taken, in fierce, no-holds-barred fighting.

13.

The Consolidation, Morning of the Fourth of July

'It was the best of shooting there for a while.'
Driver Harry Dalziel, A Company, Australian
15th Battalion

AT CHATEAU BERTANGLES, General Monash and his staff nervously waited through the 3.30 sunrise for news of the attack's progress. The Australian brigades had sent forward HQ parties in the wake of the infantry advance, and, less than thirty minutes after the assault had commenced at 3.10, these parties had established brigade forward stations in the former German front line. From there, signallers trailing telephone lines and using a combination of telegraph, radio, carrier pigeons and runners fed up-to-date information on the current state of the operation back to brigade HQ. Regular updates were then telegraphed through to General Maclagan's operational HQ, which immediately relayed them to General Monash at Corps HQ at Bertangles.

Even before these brigade forward HQs were up and

running, the reports were coming in thick and fast. At 3.20, the 6th Brigade advised that the 21st Battalion, which was advancing on the right flank of the assault, was meeting light opposition as it proceeded as planned, and was sending back its first German prisoner. In the centre of the assault, 4th Brigade HQ was receiving a trickle of prisoners back at the old front line. It reported: '15th Battalion had stiff fight for Pear Trench and carried it inflicting heavy casualties.' At 3.35, 4th Brigade further advised: '16th Battalion reports enemy front line passed and everything going well. Prisoners on their way back in large numbers.' On the left, the 11th Brigade reported that the 42nd and 43rd Battalions were taking large numbers of prisoners, who were surrendering in droves.

By 3.45, General Monash knew that everything was going precisely to plan, and to schedule, with all three brigades across the full front of the assault achieving their primary objectives. By that time, reports were coming in of hundreds of German prisoners being taken, along with the identities of the prisoners' units. Early indications were that the 11th Brigade on the northern flank of the advance and the 6th Brigade on the southern flank were having a relatively easy time of it, with Hamel itself already secured, while the 4th Brigade in the centre was facing fiercer resistance because of a failure of the barrage to hit the wire and emplacements at some targets, and the non-appearance of allotted tanks. The final objective, Monash's blue line, still remained to be secured.

As Monash waited for more news of the advance and to learn what countermeasures the Germans might be launching, he had a few means of taking his mind off things. One was the Corps HQ pet, a German messenger dog captured by Australian troops in May. 'He is a beautiful Alsatian wolf-hound and is very friendly,' Monash wrote to a young girl back in Australia who had penned him a fan letter. 'He has learned to understand English, and is very faithful to us, and we all pat him.'[176]

Another Monash pastime was sketching. 'I find this occupation keeps my nerves cool and steady,' he told his wife. And whilst he waited for his 4 July operation to pan out, he sketched a man's head, from memory. 'The head is that of a typical French poilu,' he wrote to his wife, to whom he would send the drawing. 'In fact that of the motor driver who yesterday drove Mr. Hughes from here to the Versailles conference.'[177]

Monash completed his sketch of the French driver at 5.00 am. By that stage, the general knew he had a crushing victory on his hands. On the right, the 6th Brigade reported mission accomplished at 4.20. Ten minutes later, at 4.30, the 4th Brigade was reporting its final objective in the centre gained. At 4.43 am the 11th Brigade advised that all objectives on the left had been seized.

The 6th Brigade, the first to achieve the final objective, had in fact been halted in its tracks when it reached the last obstacle, meeting stubborn resistance from machinegun nests on the ridge manned by Germans who were clearly prepared to fight to the last gasp. Their wish was duly met. Every battalion in the assault was equipped with two Stokes light mortars. The 6th Brigade's light mortar teams, each armed with thirty-two mortar bombs, were brought up. Proving deadly accurate, they swiftly took out German posts holding up the advance. The 6th Brigade's troops had then surged into the enemy trenches and gained the ridge.

Monash had set an ambitious target when he'd required that all enemy territory in the Hamel Valley and all specific primary and final objectives be seized within ninety minutes of Zero Hour. This was in fact achieved in ninety-three minutes – a stunning achievement in any circumstance, but in this war, where Allied gains were measured in days and a few yards, not in minutes and miles, it was downright unheard of. 'The attack was a complete surprise, and swept without check across the whole of the doomed territory,' Monash was to report. 'It gave us possession of the whole of the Hamel Valley, and landed us on the forward or eastern slope of the last ridge, from which the enemy had been able to overlook any of the territory held by us.'[178]

Monash also received pleasing information from 15th Brigade HQ to the north. This was the brigade tasked with undertaking diversions. One diversion was a dummy attack, another a raid on enemy trenches, the third an advance in the Ancre Valley, opposite Dernancourt. The raid had taken the designated trenches, and the Ancre attack had also been a complete success, with all objectives gained and held, against limited opposition. The successful diversions had actually moved the front line at the Ancre several hundred metres east. From the south, too, came the news that troops of the Australian 2nd Division had advanced their front a short distance to join up with the extreme right of the newly gained blue line trenches. The indications were that the German Second Army, which held the enemy front line for more than fifteen kilometres from the Ancre to opposite

Villers-Bretonneux, was reeling in disarray in the face of the Australian/American attacks.

At 5.25 am, the 4th Brigade advised: 'All objectives reported taken and consolidation proceeding well. Tanks commence to move back.'[179] War correspondent Philip Gibbs, who was based at the 15th Battalion's advanced HQ, watched the tanks return. He would write: 'Australian soldiers who were lightly wounded came riding happily back on the tops of the tanks, of whom they are now hero-worshippers because of their splendid share in the success of the day.'[180] Some American wounded were evacuated in the same manner. It was a rough and precarious ride up there on top of the Mark Vs, like riding an elephant bareback, and Major Kennedy at the Pear Trench ADS made a note not to allow any wounded men with fractures to be carried on tanks.

As it turned out, the infantrymen's fear prior to the battle that tanks would run over their wounded lying on the ground never came to anything; there was not a single instance of this happening. Back at the old front line, wounded brought in by both the tanks and by stretcher-bearers were quickly evacuated to hospitals despite a shortage of motor ambulances for the task.

Five tanks failed to return. These had all been knocked out by German shells during the assault and abandoned by their crews. General Monash, when he wrote about the battle, would put the number of knocked-out tanks at just three – a number passed on to him by subordinates. Major-General Fuller of the Tank Corps, in his account of the battle, would affirm the number was five, but even so these losses were considered negligible. What was more, the Tank

Corps immediately implemented plans to recover the abandoned monsters.

Despite the successes since Zero Hour, the Battle of Hamel was far from over. Now, the Australians and Americans would have to weather the storm of the expected fierce German counterattack, which was 'sure to come', according to the chief of staff of the American 33rd Division, Colonel William K. Naylor.[181] Only once counterattacks had been beaten off and the hold on the Hamel salient had been consolidated could the assault be proclaimed a complete success.

No Australian soldier would ever forget the First Battle of Bullecourt, where Ned Searle and his mates had taken their objective, despite the failure of the tanks, only to be driven out of the German trenches they had taken, when the enemy counterattacked and the British Army had failed to support them. In this case, Monash had every intention of supporting his men, and had taken detailed precautions to ensure they were prepared for whatever the other side threw at them.

*

From the blue line trenches on the ridge above Hamel, Australian officers with field-glasses could see numerous deserted German artillery pieces in the distance as Australian and British shells fell among them. Until ninety-three minutes earlier, those field guns had been well behind the German front line. Now, they were in No Man's Land. Some had been damaged or destroyed by Number 3 Squadron and the Allied bombardment, while others had been abandoned by gun crews who had fled in the face of the assault. Some Australian officers sent messages back to their HQs asking permission to continue the advance as far as those guns. But overenthusiasm could result in extending the gains, and the front line, too far, making both vulnerable. Orders came back to stick to the operational plan. The attackers were to stay where they were, and consolidate their positions.

'Dig in!' the officers at the blue line ordered.

General Monash expected that, once the Germans had overcome the shock and surprise of the Hamel assault, their commanders in the rear would pour shells onto the blue line trenches on the ridge that had been lost to the attackers. Therefore, as part of the operational plan, the Australians and Americans now occupying these trenches were ordered to make them deeper, and safer, and to also dig small posts out in front of the blue line trenches. They set about this work with vigour.

Digging in at the centre of the line on the ridge were the 15th Battalion and the 132nd's Company G. 'We reached our objective about 4.30 am,' said Company G's Captain Masoner, 'and started to dig, our barrage falling behind the enemy's lines for another fifteen minutes. As soon as our barrage stopped, their snipers became very active. They also brought several machineguns into action. As our men did not have sufficient cover at this time, we suffered several casualties.' This only made the digging more energetic.[182]

'It was found on reaching the final objective,' said the 15th Battalion's Lieutenant-Colonel McSharry, 'that the enemy were in strong force out in front, so, whilst the rest of the line dug in and consolidated, small parties and Lewis Gun teams pushed well out . . . inflicting extremely heavy casualties on the enemy.'[183]

Two-Gun Harry Dalziel was one of those Lewis gunners who went out in front to create advanced posts. By this time, with several other Lewis gunners now manning captured German heavy machineguns, Harry had taken charge of one of A Company's Lewis Guns – he nicknamed it Tilly Lewis. Alone, Harry carried Tilly twenty paces in advance of the captured German trenches, then dug himself in. Once he'd made a hole large enough to lie in, he took the three sandbags strapped around his legs, filled them with chalky soil he'd dug, then used them to create a gun platform for Tilly. Harry never did explain where the gun's name came from. He'd probably known a Tilly Lewis back home.

Spotting movement at a German communication trench about 300 metres further east, one that had been partly collapsed by a shell or bomb, Harry took aim with his Lewis Gun. Sure enough, he saw a party of Germans emerge from that trench and run towards another that appeared equally damaged. Firing short, precise bursts, he cut the running men down in the open. 'It was the best of shooting there for a while,' he would later remark. The turkey shoot came to an abrupt end when he ran out of ammunition.[184]

Cursing, Harry decided that he would have to go in search of more ammo. He had been briefed at the outset that British carrier tanks would drop boxes of Lewis Gun ammunition in the open down behind the ridge. So, Harry rose up and began a crouching run back to the trench line. As he ran, a German machinegun somewhere a long way behind him opened up. After tumbling into the trench with bullets kicking up the earth close by, Harry checked that none had hit him. With a grin to the Australian infantrymen around him in the trench, he pointed to two spent German machinegun rounds that had lodged in the puttee circling the lower part of one leg.

'A near miss,' he philosophically observed.

Finding his way out of the trench, Harry crawled on hands and knees until he was over the ridgeline, dodging frequent German fire that came his way. 'A charmed life,' he said to himself, as, coming to his feet, he tramped down the slope looking for one of the promised dumps of ammunition. Sure enough, about 250 metres below the ridge, he came across ammunition boxes scattered haphazardly about on the ground. A carrier tank had brought its 4.5 ton load of ammo to this spot.

'Merci, monsieur,' said Two-Gun Harry to the driver of the long-vanished tank.

As there had been no troops around to unload it, the crew had been forced to get out and do the unloading themselves. They'd wasted no time in dumping the ammo before clambering back into the protection of their cab and heading the tank back the way they'd come.

Harry grabbed the first ammunition box he came to. With this on his shoulder, he set off back up the hill. After he crested the ridge and cleared the trenches, Germans poured fire his way. 'They were throwing everything at me from the needle to the elephant,' he would later recall. A mortar bomb burst behind him. A 7.92 mm round hummed by his ear, passing between the ammunition box on his shoulder and his head. Stumbling forward, he fell into the shelter of an old shell crater, only to find it full of water. Soaked as well as exhausted now, he removed his belt and tied it around the ammunition box, using it to drag the box behind him as he splashed out of the watery crater, then wormed his way out onto the flat ground beyond it. 'I crawled as I have never crawled before.'

Ahead lay his destination, the hole in the ground with Tilly still in position where he'd left her. He tumbled into his little nest. Then, keeping his head down, he set about opening the ammunition box to rearm his Lewis Gun. When he got it open, he cursed aloud. The box contained grenades, not bullets for hungry Tilly. 'Those German hearts would feel sore if I didn't provide them with more ammunition,' he said to himself, and again dragging the ammunition box after him, he turned around and crawled back to the trench line. Dropping back down into a trench with his A Company mates, he gave them the grenades to share out, then retrieved his belt, exited the trench, and crawled back over the ridge in search of a box of bullets.

Back on his feet below the ridge, Harry retraced his steps to the ammunition dump. This time, he took care to read the letters painted on the outside of the boxes he came upon, to find one whose contents were clearly rounds suitable for a Lewis Gun. Having satisfied himself that he had chosen correctly this time, he shouldered the ammunition box and made his way back up to the ridge and the 15th Battalion position.[185]

While Dalziel was away, Lieutenant Harry Yagle, leader of one of the 132nd's G Company platoons, saw that the Germans had succeeded in pushing up with a machinegun and siting it in a sunken road about 200 metres east of the blue line trenches. Getting together with his senior sergeant Frank A. Kojane and two Australians from the 15th Battalion, Yagle led the quartet in rushing the position. They captured the gun and the eight Germans with it, bringing the lot back to the blue line trenches.

As their prisoners were sent to the POW pen in the rear, Yagle and his companions returned their attention to digging in, as two Australian fighter aircraft flew low over the trenches of the new front line looking for German targets to strafe. 'Our aircraft were very active in the morning,' said Captain Masoner, commander of the 132nd's Company G and Lieutenant Yagle's immediate superior, 'dropping bombs on some of the enemy positions, also bringing ammunition and wire to our lines, dropping them by means of parachute.'[186]

The British aircraft of the RAF's Number 9 Squadron had the most dangerous mission of the morning, loaded down with ammunition boxes and dawdling in over the battlefield to make their drops. Boldly coming in low, they accurately parachuted their ammunition for the Vickers machineguns towards the Vs laid out on the ground by the Australians of the 4th Machinegun Battalion. 'The air-pilots were able to drop this ammunition from a height of at least 1000 feet to well within 100 yards of the appointed spot,' General Monash was to say. 'In this way, at least 100,000 rounds were success-fully distributed during this battle.'[187]

Australian and British aircraft had been active since before dawn, with the RAF planes flying from their base at Argenvilliers to the AFC's airfield at Villers Bocage to load up with the ammunition boxes they were to parachute to the advancing troops in multiple missions. High above the battlefield, Australian aircraft of the AFC's Number 3 Squadron circled continually, on the lookout for enemy fighters and ready to dive on them as soon as they went after the British RE8s. Enemy reconnaissance aircraft appeared over the battlefield at 8.00 am, but were quickly driven off by the Australian fighters.

The first air casualty came a little over an hour later, when one British plane was hit, not by enemy fire, but, according to several accounts, by friendly artillery fire aimed at German artillery positions and reserve lines beyond the ridge. Shortly after 9.00 am, troops on the ground watched as this stricken Royal Air Force RE8 plummeted nose first to the ground, still with its second load of the day in place and with partially open parachutes streaming from beneath each lower wing. The fighter fell in the middle of the recently gained territory, and stretcher-bearers soon hurried to the scene of the crash, which had shaken the aircraft apart. The RE8's twenty-two-year-old British pilot Henry Rietie and his observer were found to be dead.

At 10.00 am, the German air force put thirty-five fighters of differing types into the air over the Hamel Valley, seriously outnumbering the Australian fighters on patrol. As diving, weaving dogfights between fighters took place in the hazy summer sky, a number of German planes evaded the Australian covering force and went onto the attack. Some German fighters came down low and bombed and strafed the Australians and Americans in their newly secured trenches. Other German aircraft went after the vulnerable, low-flying drop planes.

The pilot of one British plane was badly wounded by a German attacker, but he managed to nurse his aircraft back to Villers Bocage and land. Another RAF fighter, on its second run of the morning and piloted by Lieutenant S. F. Harris, was shot down just south of Hamel by German pilot Leutnant Martin Dehmesch of the German air force's Jasta 58. Troops rushing to the scene of the mangled wreck found Harris dead. But his observer, Lieutenant D. E. Bell, an American serving with the RAF, was still alive, although seriously injured. Bell was carried to the nearest dressing station, the one at Pear Trench. There, Bell was tended by fellow American Lieutenant Schram. Despite Schram's best efforts, the American airman couldn't be saved.

For a full thirty minutes the Germans held supremacy of the air over the battlefield, as numerous enemy planes got by their outnumbered opponents and combined with German artillery to make things difficult for the men on the ground. 'At every opportunity,' said Captain Masoner, 'the German planes, flying very low, would fire into our trenches.' Bombing from the air was then a very imprecise art, and as long as the Americans and Australians kept their heads down in the trenches they were safe from everything bar a direct hit. Inevitably, some German pilots got lucky with their bombs, 'one of which was dropped into our trench and killed four men', Captain Masoner would note.[188]

To counter this, the AFC put every available Number 3 Squadron aircraft into the air, and by 10.30 the squadron had driven off the Germans. In the final melee, Australian pilots shot down two German planes, without loss to their own squadron. The vigilant Australian fighters would control the air here for the remainder of 4 July and all the next day, ensuring that the German air force no longer had any influence on the outcome of the ongoing battle.

*

During the morning, as digging in and the laying of wire continued on the ridge, German snipers taking careful potshots continued to harass the Australians and Americans. Out in front of the 13th Battalion's blue line trenches, which were to the left of the 15th Battalion's position, one brave American stretcher-bearer with the 132nd Infantry, who was striving to reach a wounded man in No Man's Land while carrying a white flag, was shot down and killed by a sniper. To put a stop to this, Private Harry Shelly of the 132nd and an Australian from the 13th Battalion teamed up. Crawling out of their advanced post, the pair made their way unseen to the enemy sniping post, where they captured all eight occupants without a fight. They made their prisoners crawl back to the blue line trenches with them.

On the right of the line, the 21st Battalion found an easier answer to snipers. Their Stokes mortar teams proved so accurate, they were able to drop mortar bombs right onto sniper positions, silencing one after another.

*

That morning, too, official Australian photographer Captain Hubert Wilkins had permission from General Monash to go forward and take photographs in the newly occupied territory

166

in the valley behind the blue line trenches. Among his shots, he photographed Australian and American dead lying together on flat ground at the foot of Hamel Ridge, German dead at Pear Trench and at the quarry, and Australian stretcher-bearers carrying wounded past the wreck of one of the two British aircraft shot down that morning.

Wilkins also captured on film a group of smiling Australian and American infantrymen of the 42nd Battalion and the 131st's Company C, including a Lewis Gun team, who were cheerfully sharing a hole scratched in the flat, chalky terrain outside Hamel and awaiting the anticipated German counterattack. These Aussies and Yanks formed part of the second line of defence, with the task of stopping the enemy if their counterattack overwhelmed the Australians and Americans dug in along the ridge further east.

Throughout the regained Hamel salient that morning, the troops of the assault force sat through the nail-biting wait for the German Army to throw everything at them in an attempt to dislodge the invaders. As Americans laid bets on when the counterattack would come, the experienced Australians would have told them that, if it were them, they would wait for dark before they counterattacked. They all knew that, behind the lines, Fritz was hurriedly moving thousands of men and hundreds of artillery pieces up from reserve positions kilometres away to try to dislodge them.

Similarly, during the day, while preparing to mount his counterattacks, the enemy attempted to recover damaged and abandoned German artillery pieces that were sitting out in No Man's Land, sending horse teams to haul them off. The attempt was in full view of the Australians on the ridge, who called in artillery fire to discourage Fritz from recovering their guns. 'When he sent up horses to try to drag them away,' said Philip Gibbs, 'they were scattered by our fire and failed in the attempt.'[189]

This would not prevent the inevitable storm. Everyone, on both sides, was aware that a German Army counterstrike was not a matter of 'if', but 'when'.

14.

The Reaction of General Pershing

'It was therefore somewhat of a surprise.'
General John J. Pershing, American Commander-in-Chief

AT HIS CHAUMONT headquarters that morning, General John Pershing received a shock. As far as Black Jack was concerned, all American troops had been withdrawn from the Hamel operation, as per his order of 3 July. 'It was therefore somewhat of a surprise to learn on the following day,' Pershing would later say, 'that four companies of the 33rd Division had taken part in the attack.'[190]

Who informed the American commander-in-chief of this is not clear, but an enraged Pershing immediately demanded an explanation from General Read of his II Corps. In response, Read stuck to the story given to him by Lawrence of British GHQ – that Field-Marshal Haig could not be reached in time to order the withdrawal of the last four companies. As far as Pershing was concerned, this didn't cut it. He had given an order to American officers, and he expected those American officers to move heaven and earth to carry out those orders, irrespective of what the British said.

General Pershing would never forgive the British for deceiving him over the Hamel affair. When he later wrote his memoirs he would make scant mention of the Battle of Hamel, and certainly didn't refer to it by name. Instead, he passed it off as an 'incident', and a minor one at that. 'The incident,' he wrote, 'though relatively unimportant in itself, showed clearly the disposition of the British to assume control of our units, the very thing I had made such strong efforts and had imposed so many conditions to prevent. Its immediate effect was to cause me to make instructions so positive that nothing of the kind could occur again.'[191]

Pershing would also make sure that official AEF accounts only referred to the operation as a 'local engagement', not as a battle. To have given any greater importance to it would have required Pershing to admit that the first American offensive action of World War One was under Australian command and as part of a British army. The Hamel affair would strain relations between Pershing and Field-Marshal Haig, and caused Pershing to immediately demand the return to his command of his 33rd Division and four other American divisions currently training with the British Army, to become part of the American First Army he was trying to create. Haig would continue to drag his feet.

Meanwhile, on the morning of 4 July, word passed from General Read to General Bell of the 33rd Division, and from Bell to Brigadier-General Paul A. Wolf, commander of the 66th Brigade, who was the direct superior of Colonel Sanborn and Colonel Davis of the 131st and 132nd Infantry

Regiments, that General Pershing wanted blood. Sanborn and Davis were sent orders to withdraw the last four companies from the front at once and march them to 66th Brigade HQ.

But the 131st and 132nd weren't going anywhere. Still very much involved in the consolidation of the Hamel salient gains, and preparing to fight off an expected German counterattack, their four companies had more fighting, and dying, to do.

15.

The Afternoon of the Fourth of July

'One of my corporals and an Australian went over to the
enemy line, killed a German officer, and brought back
two prisoners and a machinegun.'
Captain William J. Masoner, Company G,
US 132nd Infantry

SERGEANT NED SEARLE was feeling pretty pleased with
himself as he sat in a blue line trench on the ridge and lunched
on bully beef from a tin. His company had starred in the
victorious advance to the blue line. His company commander,
Captain Ern Bradley, would be decorated for his gutsy part in
the successful assault, and for ensuring that D Company was
first to reach the operation's final objective in the centre. As
for Ned, he had hopes of a VC.

During the morning, the 15th Battalion strung barbed
wire out in front of its part of the line. Some old German
wire was employed, but most of it had been brought up by
one of the carrier tanks. 'Enemy machineguns and snipers
were active all day,' Ned Searle's CO Lieutenant-Colonel

172

McSharry reported, 'and his heavy and light artillery shelled the captured area indiscriminately, but our casualties after reaching the final objective were light. A great deal of enemy movement was observed during the day, and our Lewis gunners with their own and many captured German machineguns inflicted very heavy casualties on the closely packed groups of enemy moving about and re-establishing their line out front.'[192]

By the warm afternoon, a German machinegun came into operation not far to the east of the 15th Battalion's part of the line and proceeded to harass Australian positions. As 2.00 pm approached, an unidentified Australian NCO led eight men of his platoon on an attack on the German post. They exited their trench when the machinegun was aiming elsewhere. With bayonets fixed, the Australians made a slow, crawling, weaving advance across No Man's Land, outflanking the enemy position. Dropping into the post, the attackers killed five Germans and captured eight, making their prisoners bring their machinegun and ammunition back to the new Australian front line with them. As the captives were sent to the rear, their captured German machinegun was turned on its previous owners by the 15th Battalion.[193]

Inspired by this act, a pair of multinational copycats decided to go after another German machinegun that was lashing the trenches being held by Australians and a platoon of the 132nd's G Company. Said company commander Captain Masoner: 'In the afternoon one of my corporals and an Australian went over to the enemy line, killed a German officer, and brought back two prisoners and a machinegun.' The American corporal involved was John De Smidt. His

Australian accomplice was not named. The pair crept all the way to the target, then back again. A medal citation would soon be on Masoner's agenda, and as a result Corporal De Smidt would receive both an American decoration and the British Distinguished Conduct Medal.[194]

These latest prisoners brought in by De Smidt and his Australian buddy, were, like Ned Searle's prisoners, hustled back through the lines by support troops and American engineers, to join the more than 1500 German captives already netted in the operation. Throughout the day, war correspondent Philip Gibbs, who wasn't permitted to go any further forward than the 15th Battalion's advance HQ, saw German prisoners coming in and listened intently as Australian and American intelligence officers questioned them before they were sent back to the bird cage in the rear.

'The prisoners I saw today under guard by the Australians had no idea how many American soldiers there are in France,' Gibbs noted, 'and were astonished to meet some of them in this last battle. They believe that we exaggerate the numbers grotesquely in order to scare them, and they have been utterly deceived by their rulers.'[195]

Not only were the Australian and American intelligence officers keen to learn about the prisoners' units and movements, they also wanted to gauge the morale of the German troops in the trenches opposite, after close to four years of war. German-speaking Australian soldier Sydney B. Young overheard an American questioning one German.

'Do you think Germany is winning the war?' the American asked.

'Yes,' the German infantryman replied. 'God is with us.'

'That's nothing,' the American came back, 'the Australians are with us.'[196]

Gibbs was in turn surprised by the physical stature and good morale of these soldiers of the Kaiser who had been defeated by the Australians and Americans. They were fit young men, not boys, and looked well fed. They were not second-class soldiers.

'These Germans, now in our hands after the brilliant attack by the Australians with these American companies, impressed me certainly as being among the best quality of men I have yet seen taken on our front,' Gibbs wrote in a press despatch. 'Rhinelanders, Brandenburgers, and Westphalians, they were tall men in the prime of young manhood, and obviously well nourished. They said themselves to our officers that, though their rations have deteriorated since the early days of the war – and one man spoke with the authority of four years' service – they are not all bad, as, whatever happens about food in Germany, the soldiers are provided first with enough to keep up their strength.'[197]

Gibbs was also surprised that the Germans maintained their discipline after capture. 'They were tired and spent after their battle, and lay about on the grass sleeping in every attitude of extreme weariness, but their discipline is still so good, even on our side of the lines, that when an Australian sergeant gave an order in their own tongue – he knows it perfectly, having been a student for four years at Charlottenburg – the *feldwebel*, or German sergeant-major, sprang up at attention as though a bell had been rung in his ear, and the other men rapidly obeyed the command to fetch their rations.'[198]

As Gibbs' first priority was to document the perfor-
mance of the American troops in the Battle of Hamel, he
went looking for Yanks to interview. Learning that the four
American companies were still up in the line with their
Australian comrades in arms, he went to the Regimental
Aid Post in search of wounded Americans who could relate
their experiences about the AEF's first offensive operation.
There in the RAP, Gibbs came across the boy-faced 132nd
Infantry corporal who, despite his wound, had stood up
to 'fight like a man' and won the duel with the German
bayonet-charging him by cracking his skull. The corporal
had no problem with killing Germans, he told Gibbs. 'They
are bad men, and death is a just punishment for all they
have done.'[199]

Gibbs also found Corporal Albert Painsipp in the RAP,
undergoing treatment for his multiple wounds. With Gibbs
scribbling in shorthand in his notebook, Painsipp recounted
his battle in a German dugout near Vaire Wood. 'He had
an astounding series of episodes,' Gibbs would write, 'in
which it was his life or the enemy's.' Painsipp explained to
the newsman how he had received three wounds and killed
seven Germans.

'That's two Boches for each wound, and one over,' Painsipp
added. In the end, as he had hoped, stretcher-bearers had
spotted the white cloth he waved at the end of his rifle, and
had come to his aid.

From the American wounded, Philip Gibbs also gained
an appreciation of their determination to fight well in their
first battle, to impress their countrymen, to impress the
Australians they fought beside, and to punish the Germans.

'The American soldiers have come over here with such a stern spirit,' Gibbs wrote that same day, 'and with no kind of forgiveness in their hearts for the men who have caused all this misery.'[200]

*

On the battlefield, American and Australian company commanders despatched carrying parties, sending them down to the dumps in Hamel Valley. The carrier tanks had done such a good job that only fifty men from a labour battalion had been needed to carry extra supplies up to the dumps from the rear. In the AIF, these labour battalions were generally made up of Chinese Australians, who, despite the fact they had volunteered for active service, were relegated to noncombat roles. Even General Monash referred to them as 'coolies'. At the dumps below the ridge, the parties of infantrymen sent down from the blue line trenches collected ammunition, water, food and wire, before lugging it all back up to the trenches.

Captain Gale of the 131st's C Company was impressed by the Australians' efficient organisation for getting food and hot drinks to their men in the new front line: 'The system of messing of the troops in the advanced positions was very good,' he would report, 'hot tea being provided twice each night, and in some of the trenches which were accessible, during the daytime.'[201]

*

At Bertangles, General Monash spoke that afternoon by telephone with General Rawlinson at British Third Army HQ. Since early morning, Monash had been keeping Rawlinson apprised of the progress of the assault, and both Rawlinson and Field-Marshal Haig were elated with the stunning success of the operation. Earlier in the day, Haig had sent Rawlinson a telegram, which Rawlinson had passed on to Monash and American commander General Bell:

> Will you please convey to Lt. Gen. Sir J. Monash and all ranks under his command including the tanks and the detachment of the 33rd American Division my warm congratulations on the success which attended the operation carried out this morning and on the skill and gallantry with which it was conducted.[202]

Monash had passed this telegram along to Prime Minister Hughes at Versailles, together with the news that in the early hours of that morning the Hamel operation he had seen in preparation the previous day had met its objectives within ninety-three minutes of commencement. Hughes excitedly shared these tidings with the other prime ministers at the conference: Lloyd George from Britain, William Massey of New Zealand, South Africa's Louis Botha, Canada's Sir Robert Borden and William Lloyd of Newfoundland, which was then a separate country. Hughes instantly became the centre of attention as he regaled them with news of the first Allied offensive victory on the Western Front in months. On behalf of his prime ministerial colleagues and himself, Hughes sent Monash a congratulatory telegram. Meanwhile, France's Prime Minister, Georges Clemenceau, announced that he would visit General Monash and his brave Australians at the earliest opportunity.

Hosting another visit from a politician was the last thing Monash relished. Already, he was thinking about his next battle. As he told General Rawlinson on the afternoon of 4 July, having wrong-footed the Germans he wanted to exploit the situation with 'another blow on an even larger scale' against the shocked enemy. 'His whole front from the Ancre to Villers-Bretonneux has become unstable, and is reeling from the blow,' he explained to Rawlinson.[203]

Only the fact that Monash had just one division in reserve discouraged him from immediately launching an even larger attack without reference to his army commander. So, he asked Rawlinson to either give him more British troops to narrow the front he had to defend, thus freeing up more Australian troops, or release the Australian First Division from Hazebrouck to join the Australian Corps, or both. But Rawlinson would agree to neither measure.

So, that afternoon of 4 July, Monash issued instructions to all Australian Corps divisional commanders: 'Commence most vigorous offensive patrolling all along the Corps front, with a view not merely to prevent the enemy from re-establishing an organised defensive system, but also ourselves to penetrate the enemy's ground by the establishment therein of isolated posts, as a nucleus for subsequent more effective occupation.'[204]

Monash was determined to launch his 'blow on an even larger scale' within weeks, but for the moment he returned his attention to the Australian Corps' wait for the immediate German response to its Fourth of July party.

16.

The German Counterattacks
That Night

'To my sorrow they were advancing again, coming on in
hordes about five hundred yards away.'
Driver Henry Dalziel, A Company, Australian
15th Battalion

AT 3.00 PM on 4 July, the Germans began to heavily
shell Hamel and the new Allied front line along the ridge
east of the town. From the blue line trenches all the way to
General Monash's headquarters at Bertangles, Australian
and American officers and men tensed in expectation of
the German infantry making their counterattack. But this
bombardment was not a prelude to an assault, just a fill-in as
the Germans strove to muster the resources for a later major
counter-blow. The barrage passed. Sporadic German shelling
and machinegun fire continued through the afternoon and
into the evening, but no infantry attack materialised.

The first of the German counterattacks finally came
at dusk, a little before 10.00 pm, against the centre of the

ABOVE LEFT: Lieutenant-General Sir John Monash, commander of the Australian Corps and brilliant architect of the Battle of Hamel victory. *AWM A02697*
ABOVE RIGHT: Field-Marshal Sir Douglas Haig, controversial British commander-in-chief, who believed in General Monash and was banking on his Battle of Hamel plan delivering the Allies a much needed victory. *AWM A03713*
BELOW: General Sir Henry Rawlinson, Monash's British direct superior, who would take credit for putting the Americans and Australians together. *AWM E03898*

ABOVE LEFT: Company Sergeant-Major Ned Searle, 15th Battalion AIF, who set out to win a Victoria Cross in the Battle of Hamel. *Courtesy of Craig Searle*

ABOVE RIGHT: Corporal Thomas Pope, the Chicago boy who won the US Army's first Medal of Honor of World War One in the Battle of Hamel. *Pritzker Military Museum & Library*

BELOW LEFT: Jack Axford, 16th Battalion AIF, one of the Australian heroes at Hamel. *AWM P02939.030*

BELOW RIGHT: Henry Dalziel, 15th Battalion AIF, who became better known as 'Two-Gun Harry' as a result of the Battle of Hamel. *AWM H15992A*

ABOVE LEFT: General John J. Pershing, commander-in-chief, American Expeditionary Forces, who forbade his men from going into battle with the Australians, and was furious when they did. *US Library of Congress*

ABOVE RIGHT: General George Bell Jr, commander, US 33rd Division, who was determined that his American troops go into battle to learn from the Australians. *Pritzker Military Museum & Library*

BELOW: Here being decorated in the field, Joseph Sanborn, commander, US 131st Infantry, the diminutive colonel who led his men when they fought alongside the Australians. *Pritzker Military Museum & Library*

Australian PM Billy Hughes, with war correspondent Keith Murdoch, on his disruptive visit to Australian Corps troops, 3 July 1918, the day before the Battle of Hamel. *AWM E02650*

As the battle continues to rage, Australian stretcher-bearers carry a wounded man past the wreck of one of the British RE8 fighter aircraft brought down outside Hamel, 4 July 1918. *AWM E04888*

Australians of the 43rd Battalion and Americans of Company E, 131st Infantry, share a trench as they await the German counterattack during the Battle of Hamel, 4 July 1918. *AWM E02690*

On the outskirts of ruined Hamel, Australian troops with one of the British tanks knocked out in the battle. *AWM E03843*

The German machinegun detachment destroyed by Ned Searle at the Battle of Hamel. Ned took this photograph from one of the Germans in the picture. *Courtesy of Craig Searle*

Just hours after the Hamel battle, German prisoners are escorted to the 'bird cage' by Australian pioneer battalion troops. *AWM E02634*

ABOVE LEFT: On his visit to Australian Corps, 7 July 1918, to congratulate the Australians on their Hamel victory, French Prime Minister Georges Clemenceau with 4th Division commander General Ewen Sinclair-Maclagan and corps commander General Monash. *AWM E02527*

ABOVE RIGHT: Australian and American troops photographed with German heavy weapons captured during the Battle of Hamel. *AWM E03393*

BELOW: Just weeks after the Hamel battle, the band of the US 132nd Infantry with Australian troops at the 4th Brigade sports day held at Querrieu. *AWM E02836*

King George V knights General Monash on the steps of Chateau Bertangles, August 1918, with a borrowed sword. *AWM E02964*

General Monash presents medals to Australian troops for their Battle of Hamel exploits. *AWM E02758*

Australian/American line, accompanied by a fresh bombardment of the trenches and of Hamel town. German aircraft also returned to the Hamel battlefield, to bomb Pear Trench, which German commanders were convinced contained an Australian forward command post. In fact, just as Hamel had been evacuated, as part of General Monash's plan Pear Trench had also been abandoned apart from the advanced dressing station, with the Australian and American infantry stationed in this area hunkered down in their new trenches nearby. Lieutenant-Colonel McSharry did have his 15th Battalion advanced HQ in the vicinity, but in a dugout in the trenches west of Pear Trench.

Apparently the German commanders thought the Australians and Americans would be drawn to the protection offered by the dugouts and bunkers in Hamel and Pear Trench, never crediting these troops with the capacity or grit to willingly occupy open trenches during extended bombardments. Had they known they were facing elite Australian troops they may have thought differently, but it appears that at least some Germans in this sector thought that they were only up against French troops south of the Somme, because when they surrendered they called out in fractured French to their captors. As a consequence of this flawed German thinking, there were no Australian or American casualties at either Pear Trench or Hamel from the nighttime bombing or shelling, and the enemy wasted many bombs and shells on the unoccupied positions.

The first German infantry counterassault came at the middle of the Australian line, at the blue line trenches held by the 13th and 15th Battalions and their American 132nd

Infantry cohorts. The part of the line held by the 13th received particularly intense attention, as German troops charged forward *en masse* with their artillery continuing to drop explosive and smoke shells on the blue line. German troops advanced into a hail of welcoming lead, from Australian and American machineguns and from German machineguns now in Australian hands. 'We reaped the benefit of having schooled our NCOs and Lewis gunners in the use of the German machinegun,' said Lieutenant-Colonel McSharry of the 15th Battalion.[205]

By this stage, the 15th's Two-Gun Harry Dalziel had returned to his new friend Tilly Lewis, in the post he had hollowed out for her in advance of the blue line. Before leaving the main trench, he had filled several panniers, or magazines, with Lewis Gun rounds from the ammunition box he'd brought up from the valley. The rest of the ammunition had been shared out among his comrades in the blue line trench. Ever since reloading his Lewis Gun, Harry had been waiting.

He had hoped the Germans had cleared out for good, but he was in for a fresh fight that night. 'To my sorrow they were advancing again, coming on in hordes about five hundred yards away,' he would recall. A few German shells were dropping around him and smoke was drifting in clouds, obscuring his view and his aim. Lying behind his gun, Harry let off carefully aimed bursts in the direction of the Germans to his left, emptying a magazine at them and taking a heavy toll.[206]

At 10.10 pm, a flare rose up into the night sky from the 13th Battalion's trenches. This was an 'SOS', a signal to Australian artillery observers that the battalion was under intense pressure from German infantry, and calling in an artillery bombardment on the territory immediately in front of its line. Already, the Germans had overrun a 13th Battalion forward post, capturing five Australians and two Americans there. The Boche were pressing the other forward posts all along the line. Soon, the sounds of Australian shells bursting in No Man's Land joined the cacophony of machineguns firing from the trenches.

Harry Dalziel had removed one empty pannier from his Lewis Gun and was reaching for a full one when, from out of the smoke in front of him, a fresh-faced boy in a coal-scuttle helmet came running toward him with hands held high. Harry reckoned the youth was no more than fifteen or sixteen years of age, and he was bleeding from a wound.

'Merci, comrade!' cried the boy, with fear in his voice and in his eyes. 'Merci!'

Harry immediately felt for the boy. This was no war for children. But just as he was thinking about making him a prisoner, from behind Harry two burly Americans came rushing at the boy with their bayonets levelled.

'Stop!' Harry yelled. With his Lewis Gun empty, he quickly drew his pistols. Pointing the revolvers at the Yanks, he bellowed, 'Don't move, or I'll blow your bloody heads off!'

The shocked Americans froze, protesting, 'But . . .'

'Take this little German back to the captain,' Harry commanded. 'Possibly, he may get some information from him.'

Glaring at Harry, the Americans took the German boy by the arm and hustled him back to the blue line trenches. Once they departed, Harry resumed firing at German attackers and emptied his second magazine. Determined to secure more ammunition, Harry left Tilly in her nest, crawled back to the main trenches, and from there hurried down from the ridge. In the darkness and smoke he lost his way. He found himself at Pear Trench, and the dressing station he'd visited earlier in the day.

In the dressing station, Harry saw a mature German soldier on a stretcher; his foot had been blown off. Close by, Harry spotted the two Americans to whom he'd handed over the boy. They had the boy with them, and he was having his wound attended to. On seeing Harry, one of the Americans had a conversation with the man who had lost his foot, then came over to the Australian.

'Buddy, this German soldier wants to speak to you,' said the American, nodding to the older German on the stretcher.

When Harry went to the German, the fellow looked up at him and said, in halting English, 'Comrade, you have saved my son.'

In amazement, Harry looked at the man without a foot, and then at the youth whose life he had spared earlier, and real-ised they were father and son. The father reached up and shook Harry by the hand. Hardly able to credit the coincidence, Harry departed, and found his way to the ammunition dump. Loaded up with another box full of bullets, he set off back up to the ridge. 'Crawling and puffing and dodging shells, and falling into shell holes, I managed to get back,' he later said.

In the 15th Battalion trenches, with his mates firing all around them, Harry calmly filled two more magazines, then crawled back out with them to reacquaint himself with Tilly Lewis. By this stage, his feet were sore and his head ached, 'as if there were two or three heads on my shoulders'. The German assault had stalled out in front of the blue line trenches. 'But the sniper fire still kept popping away,' said Harry. Several bullets hummed past his head, so he hunched down even closer to the Lewis Gun as he resumed firing. Finding that his right hand had stiffened up from his earlier wound and was almost useless, he changed the Lewis Gun's cocking handle over to the left side.

Again he ran out of ammunition, so again he began to crawl back to the main trench with an empty magazine for more. His head was aching so terribly that he found himself rolling about in agony, but he reached the trench, filled the magazine, then crawled back to Tilly. Fitting the latest magazine, he poured lead towards the Germans, who were now retreating. His head had become a sea of pain, and he found that blood was running down the left side of his face from a wound near the temple. 'They had hit me at last. My despatch, overseas to Blighty or my last resting place, was over.' Two-Gun Harry passed out.[207]

Much later that night, Harry Dalziel was found, unmoving, by American engineers collecting the dead for burial. They thought that Harry was a corpse, until he opened his eyes. He was carried down to the Pear Trench ADS. It was the American doctor, Lieutenant Schram, who attended him. Schram found that a German bullet had exposed Harry's brain on the left side of the skull. Carefully, he bandaged up the ugly wound. But Schram gave Two-Gun Harry no chance of survival as he was carried off to the RAP and evacuation to hospital.

*

In front of the 13th Battalion's position, the German platoon that captured the advanced post was still in possession of it. The savage Australian barrage that was now falling behind these German troops, inclusive of poison gas blowing east, meant they were cut off and couldn't fall back to regroup as the remaining German attackers had done in the face of fierce Australian and American resistance.

As 11.00 pm approached, a 13th Battalion squad and a Company A squad scuttled out into the darkness to retake the position. Approaching it from different directions, the Australians and Americans swarmed into the post, capturing fifty Germans and reoccupying it. Here in the centre, the counterattack had been halted, and would not be renewed. After a time, the Australian barrage ended, and German shelling slackened, only becoming occasional.

*

Shortly before midnight, German Second Army commander General Georg von der Marwitz launched his next counter-attack, this time aimed at the left of the Australian-American line.

Corporal Tom Pope's first platoon with Company E, 131st Infantry had a relatively easy time of the assault that day as it participated in the 43rd Battalion's advance, and had been the only American platoon not to lose a single man. As a result, and hearing stories of the heroic deeds of fellow Company E men such as Sergeant Erhardt and Corporal Zyburt, many in the first platoon were chafing for a chance to show their worth before the operation ended.

None more so than platoon commander Lieutenant Albert Clissold.

As shells rained down and hundreds of German troops came storming through the night, Clissold and his men would have their opportunity to shine. 'The enemy made a vigorous counterattack on a small front, approximately three hundred yards,' Colonel Sanborn of the 131st would later write, 'succeeding in capturing eighty yards of the front line trench with five Australians and two of our men.'[208]

A German party of platoon strength with a heavy machinegun and two light machineguns now occupied this stretch of the blue line trenches, where the seven Allied prisoners also remained. The Germans had additionally driven Americans out of a post in advance of the blue line and occupied it themselves. This cleft in the blue line could not be permitted to remain if the operation's seizure of Hamel ridge was to be a *fait accompli*. Even as two companies from an Australian reserve battalion were being rushed up to the ridge to reinforce the front line here, plans for rapid offensive action were laid. Before the Germans could either consolidate this gain or withdraw with their seven prisoners, 43rd Battalion HQ issued orders for an immediate counterattack by one of its platoons and one of the American platoons, to restore the position.

It was Lieutenant Clissold's first platoon that was chosen to hold up the American end of this attack. As Clissold consulted with his Australian counterpart, they agreed that the best plan was for each platoon to approach the now enemy-held piece of trench from a different direction. The Australians would flank left, the Americans would flank right. As the now German post east of the line stood in the way of Clissold's line of attack, his platoon would first have to deal with that. So, Clissold called for a volunteer to lead a grenade attack on the post – someone who had shown proficiency with Mills Bombs.

Corporal Raymond H. Powell put up his hand, so Clissold gave Powell and his squad a supply of grenades and the job of retaking the post. German shells were pounding down all around them. Ignoring these, Powell and his squad slipped from their trench and crawled across the open ground to the post without being seen by the Germans inside, who had their heads down during the bombardment. Just metres from their objective, Powell began heaving one grenade after another into the post. Once they had exploded, Powell came to his feet and launched himself into the post with his rifle ready, followed by his squad members.

A minute later, Powell was signalling to Lieutenant Clissold, waving him forward. All the Germans in the post were dead, killed by the grenades. Clissold led his men out into the night. Amid the darkness, exploding shells and drifting smoke, it was difficult to tell exactly where the enemy machinegun was in the blue line trenches. Unaware that the post behind them had just been retaken by the Americans, the German machinegunners had their backs to Clissold and his men as they fired at Americans and Australians west of them. Only the flash from the Maxim's muzzle would give away its exact location.

'I see it!' exclaimed Corporal Tom Pope. Rising up from the ground and waving the men of his squad to stay low, Tom set off at a sprint towards the Maxim and its unwitting crew.

Jumping into the trench behind the Germans, he bayoneted the gunner and then the loader. Then, climbing to stand astride the gun, totally in the open and exposed, Tom shot every German who approached along this section of trench.

Inspired by Tom Pope, the rest of his platoon and the Australian platoon came running, jumping down into the trench and retaking it, killing some Germans and disarming others who threw up their hands. Four German officers, fifty-three of their men and three machineguns were captured within minutes. The lost portion of the blue line trench had been regained. Never again would German troops occupy these trenches along the ridge east of Hamel.[209]

*

A third German counterattack was launched against the 6th Brigade on the right, 'using the many old trenches in the vicinity of our front line', the 6th Brigade would report. The enemy 'was only ejected and driven off using bombs', which went close to cleaning the defenders out of grenades. As a result, the 6th Brigade recommended that in future Australian infantrymen each be equipped with four grenades instead of two.[210]

This turned out to be the final German attempt to wrest victory from the Australians and Americans in the Battle of Hamel. To add insult to injury, at 3.00 am, just before dawn, the 13th Battalion sent a patrol from their trenches in the centre of the line which silently penetrated deep into German territory to the east. Surprising a German outpost, the patrol returned to the new Allied front line with twenty more Boche prisoners. Come the morning, their German commander would be scratching his head over their disappearance.

At 3.30 am on 5 July, the sun began to rise, heralding a clear, pleasant summer day in Picardy. All through that day, the Australian and American troops held their newly gained front-line trenches in the face of sporadic German artillery and machinegun fire. But the enemy seemed to have accepted that the Hamel salient had been lost, for no more troops were seen to be massing for counterattack. As a comparative quiet fell along the front line, preparations were made to implement the final elements of General Monash's operational plan: the withdrawal, replacement and resting of the troops who'd made the assault. This was scheduled to take place in stages along the new front line under cover of darkness that night of 5 July.

*

At Chateau Bertangles, 5 July dragged by as General Monash waited for nightfall and the news that his men had been relieved and the front line was secure. To help fill the time, he wrote again to his wife in Melbourne, telling her about Field-Marshal Haig's visit of 2 July, and of Prime Minister Hughes' 3 July interruption. Having sent Vic a telegram the previous day informing her that his latest offensive had been a success, he now also told her a little more about the Hamel victory.

'As cabled,' he wrote, '[it] was a brilliant success. No fighting operation that the corps has ever undertaken has been more brilliantly, cleanly and perfectly carried through, without the slightest hitch.' Knowing that it would take some weeks for the letter to reach his wife, he added, 'You will have learned all about it from the papers long before now. I send you herewith the original telegram of congratulations received from the Prime Minister, the Commander-in-Chief, and the Army Commander.'[211]

*

As the sun set, the men in the blue line trenches gathered up their bits and pieces as they prepared to make way for their replacements. It turned out that the Germans had other ideas. Having lost their foothold in the ridge trenches, that night of 5–6 July the Germans began what Colonel Joe Sanborn described as 'a savage strafe', pounding the new Australian-American front line with artillery fire.[212] The Australian battalions and their accompanying American companies scheduled to be pulled back that night were forced to hug their trenches, with the bombardment proving so fierce it wasn't safe to move a centimetre. The swap was postponed.

The wind having changed, blowing now from the east, the German gunners added poison gas shells to the smoke and high explosive shells they were sending over. This was the Americans' first experience of being on the receiving end of a gas attack. They had trained for it. Colonel Sanborn said of that training, 'The soldiers began to realise that their gas masks were their best friends. One private expressed the sentiment of all his comrades by stencilling on his mask the words, "I need thee every hour"; another, "In thee I trust."'[213]

Despite this, some men of Sanborn's regiment were unprepared for the real thing when it came. On the left of the new front line, thinking it was merely smoke that was drifting into their trenches, thirty-four men from the 131st Infantry failed to get their gas masks on in time. Their eyes burning, their lungs on fire, they were blinded and struggling for breath.

Stretcher-bearers wearing gas masks could only get to the gas-affected men once the enemy barrage lifted. Carried back to the ADS and then the RAP, the thirty-four would be evacuated via a Casualty Clearing Station to a hospital at Glorieux, and then to England. They would play no further part in the war. One of these gassed men was Corporal Tom Pope; his combat career had lasted less than forty-eight hours. Finally, after midnight on 6 July, the German bombardment lifted, and in the early morning hours the delayed Australian/American withdrawal and replacement process began by stages.

That night of 5–6 July, too, the Tank Corps sent carrier tanks out to drag the five knocked-out Mark Vs back to British workshops behind the lines. All five were recovered. They would subsequently be repaired, and be back in action within weeks. Meanwhile, the Tank Corps was cock-a-hoop about the battle and its outcome. Despite the failure of some of the 5th Tank Brigade's machines to reach their objectives and the lack of enthusiasm displayed by one or two tank crews, overall, and particularly in its work with the Australian 4th Division, the Tank Corps had shown for the first time in history that tanks and determined infantry working together against trenches and fixed emplacements comprised a frighteningly effective weapon of war. Knowing that the future face of warfare had been defined by this operation, the Tank Corps' Major-General Fuller would subsequently speak of 'the dramatic coup-de-main accomplished on July 4 by the 4th Australian Division and 5th Tank Brigade in the Battle of Hamel'.[214]

With the enemy fought to a standstill and Australian and American assault troops and disabled tanks coming out of the line, the Battle of Hamel was officially over. Its repercussions were about to begin.

17.

The Immediate Repercussions

'Sanborn's men won admiration of Australians. Made
good with Haig's hardest fighters in first battle.'
Chicago Tribune headline, 1918

AFTER DAWN ON 6 July, with all now quiet on their front,
the Australian battalions that had fought and won the Battle
of Hamel, together with their American colleagues, were
progressively replaced in the front-line trenches by companies from other Australian battalions, and moved back west
to the reserve positions in the old front line. In the centre,
for example, the 15th Battalion was replaced by the 49th
Battalion and pulled back to the support trenches in the old
front line, with the 13th Battalion and two companies of the
14th immediately in front of it.

The 15th's commander Lieutenant-Colonel McSharry
was well pleased with his boys' work. 'The success of the
operation,' he remarked, 'was due to the fine leadership of
platoon commanders and the superb dash and daring of the
men themselves, who dealt with any situation that presented

itself on their own initiative. The gallantry displayed both individually and collectively was quite up to the Australian standard.'[215] McSharry would soon be submitting recommendations for gallantry awards for his men's deeds in the Battle of Hamel. As Ned Searle hoped, one of the decorations destined for the 15th Battalion was the unit's first Victoria Cross.

McSharry was also recommending British gallantry awards for a number of Americans who had fought as part of his battalion in the battle. 'The Americans attached to us deserve special mention for their part in the operation,' he declared. 'They behaved magnificently, but were rather anxious to get too close to our barrage – a common fault with new troops. There is not the slightest doubt that they possess all the qualities required to make first rate fighting troops.'[216]

Only now were the American companies that had participated in the battle able to obey General Pershing's order to withdraw. It meant a fond and sometimes emotional farewell for Australians and Americans. Although they had only been comrades-in-arms for several days, they had forged a fraternal bond in blood. As the Americans of the 131st Infantry parted with the Australians of the 11th Brigade, an Aussie called out to them.

'You'll do us, Yanks,' he said, 'but you're a bit rough!'[217]

This put a smile on American faces that was still there when a proud Colonel Sanborn met his men of Companies C and E on the road as they marched the nine kilometres from the front to 66th Brigade and 33rd Division headquarters, the Chateau Molliens at Molliens-au-Bois. Captain Gale, the former police inspector now commanding the 131st's

Company C, enthusiastically reported to Sanborn, 'More real good was done to this company by this small operation with the Australians than could have been accomplished in months of training behind the lines.'[218]

Company E's commander Captain Luke was equally enthusiastic, if a little more concise, with his report: 'I can say that the show was a complete success.'[219]

Sanborn marched with his men to Chateau Molliens. When the troops arrived there at 9.00 am, he reported to his brigade commander, Brigadier-General Wolf, and advised that the Battle of Hamel had been a stunning victory in which his troops had more than proved themselves.

Wolf had not been a party to the sleight-of-hand pulled by his own superiors General Read and General Bell in order to keep the four 131st and 132nd Infantry companies out of the withdrawal of all American troops from the operation, and keep them in the battle. As far as Wolf was concerned, Sanborn and his 132nd Regiment counterpart Davis had disobeyed the 3 July withdrawal order of their commander-in-chief, General Pershing.

'You damned old fool, Joe,' said Wolf to Sanborn after an exchange of salutes. 'I don't know whether to court-martial you or decorate you!'[220]

Sanborn was trying to explain to Wolf that the order had been an impossible one to obey, when Major-General Bell walked into the room. After Sanborn and Wolf both saluted their divisional commander, a smiling Bell congratulated Sanborn on a job well done, telling him that congratulations had been flooding in from the Australians and the British. He also told him that he'd heard the Australians were recommending a number of American officers and men from the 131st and 132nd Infantry for British gallantry medals.

Sanborn responded that he was similarly recommending a number of his men for American decorations, starting with Corporal Thomas Pope, whom he was proposing for the Medal of Honor, the highest decoration for gallantry that the US Government could bestow. Erroneously known as the Congressional Medal of Honor because it is presented by the President of the United States on behalf of US Congress, this is the only American decoration for gallantry to be awarded in that manner.

The equivalent of the British Victoria Cross, the US Medal of Honor originated in 1862 and was first awarded the following year during the Civil War. Since late 1917, several US Navy sailors had been awarded the Medal of Honor, but no American soldier had yet received the decoration in this war. Pope would be the first.

As a matter of fact, Sanborn told General Bell, the Australians had presented the 131st with 'a souvenir' – the German machinegun 'which was captured under exceptional circumstances of bravery' by Tom Pope.[221] Proposing Pope for the highest award possible was not only warranted by the circumstances. It also meant that the commander of a Medal of Honor winner could not very well be sanctioned for the action in which the medal had been earned.

Thomas Pope would indeed be awarded the Medal of Honor. Based on the same citation from Colonel Sanborn, Pope would also be awarded Britain's Distinguished Conduct Medal, France's Medal Militaire and the French Croix de Guerre. General Pershing, who was so peeved that his troops fought and died under British command at Hamel, would quite deliberately, and petulantly, fail to mention Pope's Medal of Honor, the inaugural US Army Medal of Honor of the war, when he wrote about this episode in his memoirs several years later. Robbing Pope and eighteen other officers and men of the 131st and 132nd who received British medals for their valorous parts in the Battle of Hamel of recognition, Pershing would merely say in his brief reference to the battle, 'It seems needless to add that the behaviour of our troops in this operation was splendid.'[222]

That would be the extent of Pershing's coverage of Hamel, a battle that proved to be the launching pad for the operations that would end the war within four months. And just as Pershing made no mention of the sacrifice, gallantry or success of American troops in the Hamel operation, never once did he mention General Monash in his plodding memoirs, or the value Pershing's own officers placed in fighting alongside the Australians at Hamel and in later battles during this war.

As Colonel Sanborn met with Generals Bell and Wolf at the Molliens-au-Bois HQ, outside the chateau the weary men of the 131st's C and E Companies were drawn up for the inspection of the divisional commander, minus their casualties in the operation. For the two companies, these casualties had been one officer and thirteen enlisted men killed, seven officers wounded or gassed, and ninety-four enlisted men wounded or gassed. Although this represented in the region of 25 per cent casualties, Generals Monash, Rawlinson and Bell all considered the figures low. Bell addressed the survivors, lavishing praise on them and reading aloud the telegrams from Field-Marshal Haig and Generals Monash and Rawlinson.

Monash, very much aware of the historic nature of the shared battle experience in the Hamel salient, had said to Bell in his 5 July cable:

My earnest thanks for the assistance and services of the four companies of infantry who participated in yesterday's brilliant operations. The dash, gallantry and efficiency of these American troops left nothing to be desired, and my Australian soldiers speak in the very highest terms in praise of them. That soldiers of the United States and of Australia should have associated for the first time in such close cooperation on the battlefield is an historic event of such significance that it will live forever in the annals of our respective nations.[223]

Bell ordered Monash's telegram published to all 15,000 men of the 33rd Division, and on 6 July cabled Monash in reply:

The bravery, efficiency and skill of Australian soldiers are fully appreciated by this division and they are known to the whole world. That your soldiers should have spoken in high terms of our men is the highest praise they could wish for. To have fought on the battlefield with Australia, in the brilliant operation of July the Fourth, will forever remain an historic event in the annals of our country.[224]

From General Rawlinson, Bell had received an even more exuberant telegram:

Am anxious to express to you, General Bell, and to all ranks of the 33rd (Illinois) Division, my warm thanks for the gallant part taken by portions of your division in the attack on Hamel and Vaire Wood on Independence Day. I hear nothing but praise of the manner in which your units fought the enemy, and my only regret is that I was not permitted to employ a larger portion of your fine division. Perhaps later on there may be another opportunity.[225]

At the Molliens-au-Bois parade, Colonel Sanborn turned to an aide, who was holding a German rifle. Taking the weapon, Sanborn presented it to Bell, as a gift. 'The first German rifle taken by your troops on the Fourth of July,' Sanborn proudly advised.

Whilst the men of the 131st and 132nd Infantry were the focus of praise, the 108th Engineer Regiment didn't escape commendation, either. Lieutenant-Colonel Roy McGregor, Assistant Director of Medical Services with the Australian Corps, sent a letter to Major-General Maclagan, operational commander for the Battle of Hamel, which Maclagan in turn passed along to General Bell, drawing his attention to the assistance provided on the Hamel battlefield to Australian medical staff by men of the 108th Engineers.

'This assistance,' said McGregor, 'was proferred without being asked for and was of the greatest use on the 4th and on the night of the 4/5th when all our men were very busy or tired from previous heavy exertions.'[226]

Pointedly, there was no telegram or letter of commendation from the Americans' own commander-in-chief, General Pershing, for American troops or units that had taken part in the Hamel operation. Pershing offered no praise, no thoughts or prayers, for the Americans who had bravely fought, bled and died in the service of their country on the Fourth of July. As far as he was concerned, this 'local engagement' had as good as never happened. Neither did Pershing officially congratulate Haig, Rawlinson or Monash on the operation's success.

Pershing also strove to ensure that no report of the role of American troops in the battle would appear in the US press. He wouldn't be entirely successful. Philip Gibbs, after writing an excited 4 July article about the 'British' victory at Hamel, would file another report for the British press the following day, enthusing about the American part in the battle, which would be picked up by American papers. In Australia, reports from Australian war correspondents also celebrated the unique Australian-American victory.

Accounts referring to Illinois' part in the Hamel battle would begin appearing in the Chicago press later in the year. One quoted a letter from Private Frank A. Johnson, a member of the 131st Infantry's Company B. Writing home on 8 August about the 131st's exploits that particular day, Johnson also made reference to the regiment's first battle, alongside the Australians, on Independence Day. The *Chicago Tribune* of 20 December would headline an article based on Johnson's letter, 'Sanborn's Men Won Admiration of Australians.'

A subheading, relating back to General Bell's 2 July exhortation to his men to make good with the Aussies, read, '"Made Good" With Haig's Hardest Fighters in First Battle'. The article went on, quoting Johnson, 'The 131st on that day won the admiration of the Australians. We had been treated kindly before by them, but we still had to make good. After the battle they took us to their hearts as comrades.'

The 131st's commander Colonel Joe Sanborn was himself immensely proud of his men, and of the bond that had been forged between the Americans and Australians in the Hamel operation. 'The Australians freely expressed themselves afterwards to the effect that the only complaint they could make was that our men were too savage and swift,' he later remarked. 'They displayed remarkable dash and endeavoured to be first and foremost in the fight, the Australians said.'

Sanborn happily repeated the comments of Lieutenant-Colonel John Farrell, commander of the Australian 43rd Battalion, to which the 131st's Company E had been attached, who had told him his Illinois boys had done 'excellent work'. Farrell had added, 'Considering it was their first time in action, they fought splendidly.' Sanborn would go on, 'Even more valued than this official praise was the verdict of the Australian soldiers beside whom the Americans fought.'[227]

When Sanborn bumped into an old friend, Dwight S. Harding, in France several months after the battle, Harding would pump him for information about the Hamel operation, and the following 30 March the *Chicago Tribune* would publish an article quoting Harding about his meeting with Sanborn. 'He told me his version of a fight about which I heard a good deal from other sources,' Harding was to say. 'He complied with an impossible order from British head-quarters and went in and ate the Boche alive.'

Sanborn would have told Harding not to mention the Battle of Hamel specifically, for officially neither Sanborn nor any other subordinate of General Pershing was able to comment about the battle, nor even mention Hamel by name. Infuriated by his commander-in-chief's determination to wipe American participation in the Battle of Hamel from the record, Colonel William K. Naylor, the 33rd Division's Chief of Staff, lodged a memorandum with Pershing's HQ. 'This action is deserving of note by all Americans,' he wrote after detailing the division's role in the operation. 'The people of Illinois have just reason to feel proud of their sons for what they did in this engagement. The engagement at Hamel and Vaire Woods can justly be called "Illinois Victory No. 1".'

Naylor was equally determined to point out that praise from Australian fighting men was praise worth shouting about from the rooftops. 'We hear nothing but praise from all sides on the conduct of our men under fire. There are no finer troops on earth, nor have there ever been, than the Australian Corps, and when they are willing to admit the efficiency of the Americans, it is well worth attention.'[228]

Nonetheless, Pershing would persist in denying the 33rd Division due praise for its Independence Day success.

*

'The psychological effect of the Battle of Hamel was electric and startling,' General Monash would write to his wife. 'This battle was the first definite offensive on a substantial scale which had been undertaken by any of the armies of the Allies on any front since the close of the autumn campaign of 1917.'[229]

Overnight, the Hamel operation changed attitudes. 'Its success converted the whole thoughts of the Allies from an attitude of pure defensive to an attitude of offensive, and it began to dawn upon High Command that it was after all possible to do something else but sit down and take the cuffs and kicks of the enemy,' said Monash. Now, everybody wanted to talk to him, and learn from him. 'People came from far and near to hear all about it and find out "how it was done", and GHQ published a special pamphlet describing the battle plan and the new tactical methods which I employed.'[230]

In preparation for the impending visit to his headquarters of French Prime Minister Clemenceau, Monash collected all the figures he could about his Hamel victory. Apart from taking all their objectives in record time, Monash's Australians and Bell's Americans had between them taken 1600 German prisoners. Monash estimated that the Germans suffered a similar number of killed or wounded, making overall enemy casualties around 3200. Australian casualties totalled 800, the majority of these being walking wounded who would return to duty. This amounted to a casualty rate of around 12.5 per cent of the Australian infantrymen who took part in the assault, which Monash and his superiors considered low. Monash would also record that the operation yielded 171 German machineguns, twenty-six mortars and two field guns.[231]

Prime Minister Clemenceau paid his visit to General Monash and the Australian Corps on 7 July, just two days after the last shots had been fired in the Battle of Hamel. A short, stout seventy-eight-year-old with a walrus moustache, Clemenceau strode out enthusiastically when Monash took him to meet troops of the 4th, 6th and 11th Brigades that had taken part in the Hamel battle, just behind the front. 'He made to them a very fine and fiery oration, in very good English,' Monash wrote home to Vic.[232]

Clemenceau told the assembled Australians what the French people had thought of Australian soldiers when they first arrived in France. 'They expected a great deal of you, because they have heard what you have accomplished in the development of your own country,' he said. 'We knew you would fight a real fight, but we did not know from the very beginning you would astonish the whole Continent with your valour.'[233]

Many other Frenchmen were equally keen to praise the Australians and celebrate the small but landmark Hamel victory. On 14 July, Bastille Day, the French national day, the Prefect of the Department of the Somme defiantly and patriotically held a lunch in the ruins of Amiens' town hall, inviting twenty guests including General Monash and representatives of the evacuated metropolis of Amiens and the Australian, British and French armies. There, in the deserted city, the participants toasted the Hamel victory, and the victories to come.

As for American involvement with the Australians, that was to continue. In the short term, the band of the 132nd Infantry joined the band of the Australian 4th Brigade to play at the 4th Brigade's sports day behind the lines at Querrieu on 20 July. At that same event General Monash presented medals to men of the 4th Brigade who had earned them for deeds during the Battle of Hamel. This medal ceremony, held in a field with men of the brigade sitting and standing casually as they watched and applauded proceedings, and with the medals laid out on a table draped with the Australian flag, didn't include the 4th Brigade's two VC winners. Their awards would only be announced in August, with the medals subsequently presented by King George V.

In August, too, men of the US 33rd Division would again fight alongside the Aussies, once more in an offensive devised by General John Monash. The Australian general had begun planning his very next battle almost the moment the Battle of Hamel ended so successfully.

18.

The Lessons of Hamel Applied on 8 August

'August 8th was the black day of the German Army
in the history of the war.'
General Erich von Ludendorff, German commander

ON THE DAY following Bastille Day, 15 July, the German Army launched an unheralded offensive in the Marne sector in the south, against the French Army holding the line there. After the Germans surprised the French defenders and advanced for two days, reaching Chateau-Thierry just sixty kilometres from Paris, the offensive ran out of steam. The French, with American support, promptly made a crushing counterattack which delivered 15,000 German prisoners and 200 field guns on 18 July alone, and which had the Germans making a strategic withdrawal from the salient they had briefly created.

At his Bertangles HQ, General Monash correctly surmised that this was the Germans' last hurrah, that they had expended their last mobile reserves and would not be in a position to mount another similar major offensive on the Western Front in this war. Monash, confident that Fritz had been rocked back on his heels, was determined that it was time to deliver a swift, massive and decisive blow to the belly of the German Army in the Somme sector, and that the Australians should lead it. This was what he had been repeatedly proposing to his army commander General Rawlinson since the afternoon of 4 July.

The response from Rawlinson, at first cautious, turned increasingly positive as it became clear that Monash was being perceived as the new hope for the Allies by political leaders elated by the Hamel victory. But when Rawlinson suggested that a French corps be responsible for the southern part of the offensive, Monash asked for the Canadian Corps to be instead relocated from its current positions – two of its four divisions were then in the front line in the neighbourhood of Arras, well north of the Somme, while the remainder were resting in back areas – to join the Australians in the attack and take responsibility for the southern flank. This would create the most formidable fighting double act of the war. In Monash's view, 'The Canadians and the Australians have never failed to achieve all their objectives strictly according to plan.'[234]

Canada, which had a larger population than Australia, had some 100,000 more men in uniform, but its forces still formed a small part of the overall British Army. The Canucks had, like the Aussies, developed a reputation as fearsome soldiers who were considered the elite among the British forces. The prospect of the Australians and the Canadians going into battle side-by-side was mouth-watering to Monash, who felt he could rely totally on the Canadian commander, General Currie, who'd told Monash his men would always 'deliver the goods'. And they did. Monash also asked Rawlinson for more tanks, aircraft and artillery.

As it happened, since May, Field-Marshal Haig and France's Marshal Foch, the Commander-in-Chief of all the Allied armies, had been discussing a major offensive launched from the British part of the line and spearheaded by the British Army's best troops, the Australians and the Canadians. The repulse of the Germans' Marne offensive told the field-marshals that the time was now ripe for just such a counterstroke.

On the bright summer afternoon of Sunday 21 July, British Fourth Army commander General Rawlinson hosted a top secret conference at his HQ in the village of Flexicourt on the River Somme. The meeting was attended by General Monash and three other corps commanders – Lieutenant-Generals Sir Arthur Currie of the Canadian Corps, Richard Butler of British III Corps, and Sir Charles Kavanagh of the British Cavalry Corps. Senior Tank Corps and air force officers were also in attendance.

At this meeting, in a grand white mansion in the village's main street, Rawlinson told the gathering that a major offensive on the Hamel model proposed by Monash and launched by the British Fourth Army from the Somme sector had been approved. 'Rawlinson unfolded the outline of the whole [Fourth] Army plan,' Monash was to write, 'and details were discussed at great length in the light of the views of each corps commander.'[235]

At the outset of the conference, Rawlinson informed

Monash that earlier requests he'd made to allow the implementation of such an offensive – the transfer of the Australian 1st Division from Flanders to join the rest of the Australian Corps immediately south of the River Somme, and the reduction in the size of the Australian defensive front in the Somme sector – were being granted.

By the time the meeting broke up that evening, the basic elements of the offensive had been agreed: a joint assault by the Australians and the Canadians south of the Somme, with the Canadians on the right of the Australian Corps, British III Corps shoring up the offensive's left flank north of the river, and a corps from France's First Army securing the right flank, south of the Canadians. The Cavalry Corps would follow as a mobile reserve that could be thrown into the exploitation of any weak spot in German defences.

The meeting agreed that a minimum of ten days should be allowed from the moment approval to proceed was received from Field-Marshal Haig before the offensive was launched, allowing time for the four Canadian divisions and the additional Australian division to be transported by train to the Somme and rested for a few days, and for all the ammunition and supplies to be brought in.

Monash and his fellow corps commanders hurried back to their respective headquarters to engage their staff in preparing detailed but highly secret recommendations for submission to Field-Marshal Haig.

Monash had gone into the Flexicourt conference with two concerns – a lack of confidence in the French, and a lack of belief in the cavalry. The day of the gallant cavalry charge was over. Monash had been impressed by the use of the mounted arm in past wars to quickly manoeuvre behind enemy lines and cut off communications and supply lines. But in the era of trench warfare, wire entanglements and tanks, Monash felt the horse soldier had become an anachronism and that cavalry would only be a burden, not a benefit, to the upcoming offensive. In the event, General Rawlinson would allocate a British cavalry battalion to the Australian Corps for the operation, and it would indeed prove a burden to Monash.

Then there was his worry about the French Army's role in his operation. 'My hesitation to accept the French as colleagues in such a battle was based not altogether on theoretical or sentimental grounds,' Monash was to say. Since the Hamel battle, the Australian 2nd Division, which currently occupied the southernmost portion of the Australian front line, had been daily extending its grip on German-held territory east of Villers-Bretonneux, sometimes by hundreds of metres, via the aggressive 'peaceful penetration' that Monash had ordered on 4 July. But, said, Monash, 'No persuasion on my part, or on that of my flank division [the 2nd], could induce the adjacent French division to extend any cooperation in these advances or to adopt any measures to flatten out the re-entrant which, growing deeper every day, threatened to expose my right flank.'[236]

Monash and his men had a lot of time for the French soldier, and, up to this point, the 2nd Division and French 31st Corps troops who were their immediate neighbours to the south had, in Monash's words, enjoyed 'hearty fraternisation' and 'the evolution of a strange common vernacular'. But, said Monash, while the French could be irresistible in attack and dogged in defence, 'whether they will attack or defend depends greatly on their temperament of the moment'.[237]

The temperament of soldiers, and the psychological factors that affect that temperament, had long interested Monash. He knew that men responded to encouragement from the top. A realist, but an optimist, he was a 'glass half full', not a 'glass half empty' man. From the moment he had been given a battlefield command, he had always quite deliberately displayed a positive attitude, no matter what the circumstances facing him. When things went wrong, Monash would encourage men, not admonish them. One of his former aides, Englishman Lieutenant-Colonel F. M. Farmar, said of Monash, and his ability to bring out the best in his men: 'The poorest instrument will respond unexpectedly well with a master-touch.'[238]

Not all divisions, corps and armies were blessed with leaders with Monash's qualities. Indeed, there were no Napoleon Bonapartes in the modern French Army, no leaders for whom the common soldier would give his all. And Monash knew that, faced with weak leadership, entire armies can lose the will to win. This had been the lesson of recorded history, as far back as 49 BC, when an army in North Africa led by one of Julius Caesar's inept deputies during the civil war that eventually brought Caesar to power unexpectedly found itself cut off. The outnumbered Caesarian troops made their wills and prepared for defeat, which of course proved to be their fate.

Without strong leadership, and without the Australian capacity to quickly adapt to changed circumstances, Monash questioned whether the independent-minded French could be relied on to adhere to the sort of strict timetable for each element of the assault that his planned operation, like the Hamel battle, would call for. 'I felt quite unprepared to count upon it,' Monash would confess. However, with the stout Canadians, many of whom were French speaking, advancing on the Australians' right, and a French corps south of them providing a defensive flank, Monash's concern about the French exposing the Australian underbelly during the offensive was allayed. The Canadians, he knew, would not let him down.[239]

Monash's staff worked quickly preparing detailed plans for the August offensive, basing them on the Hamel model. Once again, the plan called for a carefully integrated assault involving an infantry advance, a creeping artillery barrage, tank support, and aircraft for reconnaissance, bombing/strafing and ammunition drops, but on a much larger scale than at Hamel.

The only major change Monash made to the Hamel model was to take on board a recommendation of Australian officers involved in that battle – this time, the blue line establishing the final objective would be drawn at the enemy gun line, ensuring that large numbers of enemy artillery pieces would be captured, limiting the ability of the Germans to shell the newly taken territory whilst it was being consolidated. The offensive's first 'green line' objective was also a considerably longer distance from the jumping-off tape than had been the case in the Hamel operation – nine kilometres away.

Within two days, Monash had completed his planning. 'Towards the end of the third week in July,' he would write, 'I propounded certain proposals to Sir Douglas Haig in the nature of a counter-offensive on a very large scale.'[240] Haig liked Monash's ideas, but asked for time to discuss it with the French, who would have to agree to participate in the south of the offensive by withdrawing some of their troops to make way for the Canadians and by protecting the Canadians' southern flank during the advance with a corps of its own.

While Monash waited for Haig to get back to him, he decided to take a little overdue leave, which General Rawlinson approved after Monash guaranteed that he would cut short his holiday and rush back to his HQ should the field-marshal give permission for the offensive to proceed in the meantime. So, on 23 July, Monash set off for London, accompanied by a single aide, his nephew Captain Paul Simonson. Travelling via Boulogne and Folkestone, the pair arrived in London late that night.

Over the next five days, Monash would have spent time with his London mistress, Lizette 'Liz' Bentwich, who had been a family friend prior to the war, before a telephone call from the British War Office late on a Sunday evening terminated his break – Haig and Foch were in agreement that the Somme offensive was to proceed as per Monash's proposal, launching on 8 August. Monash was not a fan of flying, so an initial proposal from General Rawlinson that he be flown back to France had not met with the Australian general's approval. Instead, a British destroyer had been laid on at Dover to whisk him across the Channel. Back at Bertangles, Monash threw himself into final planning for the offensive. 'I am now in the middle of preparations for a very large battle,' he wrote home to Vic on 2 August. 'It will be a very big show indeed.'[241]

*

The Battle of Amiens, as it became known, began at 4.20 am on Thursday 8 August. In the middle of the assault line, along a seven kilometre front, two Australian divisions swept forward behind a creeping barrage, with a third division coming immediately behind ready to leapfrog the leading pair once they'd gained their primary objectives, to drive on to the final blue-line objective. Each Australian company in the attack was supported by a British tank, whilst, overhead, Australian and British aircraft provided air cover. On the Australians' right, three Canadian divisions also went forward, and on the Aussies' left, two divisions of the British Fourth Army's III Corps. In all, 100,000 men went into the attack between Albert and Moreuil that morning, over a total front eighteen kilometres long from north to south.

The assault was designed to catch the German Second Army completely by surprise, and, to ensure this, tight security had surrounded preparations and troops movements, even down to refraining from referring to any aspect of the operation in telephone conversations. This was in case the Boche had succeeded in tapping into the kilometres of Allied military telephone lines. In addition, Australian troops were only informed at the last moment that the Canadians were going into battle beside them. Up till then, they were told that the Canadians were merely coming to relieve them.

To mask from the Germans the fact that the Canadians were going into the front line in the Amiens sector, once the French troops occupying that part of the line had been quietly withdrawn to make way for them, Australian troops occupied this part of the front line until the Canadians arrived. But then a spanner had been thrown in the works, by the

Germans. As chance would have it, the enemy had mounted a rare patrol across No Man's Land on the night of 4 August. Capturing an Australian sergeant and five men from the 4th Brigade at an isolated forward post, the German patrol had taken them back to their lines for interrogation.

Once General Monash became aware of this, those around him naturally became concerned that the Australians, under questioning, might be forced to reveal that preparations for a major offensive from this sector were nearing their culmination. Nonetheless, Monash was confident that the Aussie prisoners would reveal no more than their names and unit to the Germans, and he opted not to alter any aspect of the assault plan, including its launch date. Within days, German records of the six Australians' interrogation would be captured, and would reveal that the Aussies had indeed done just as their general had expected, stoutly resisting their questioners' best efforts, giving nothing away.

Another small hiccup had come on the afternoon of 7 August when a random German shell set one of eighteen loaded carrier tanks alight as they all sat just north of Villers-Bretonneux waiting to participate in the operation the next day. The billowing black smoke from the fire had attracted German attention, and within minutes their gunners zeroed in on the site. Loads of ammunition and fuel on the other tanks ignited, and before long fifteen carrier tanks, and their loads, had been consumed by a massive bonfire. The Germans no doubt congratulated themselves on some good shooting, but never suspected they had hit anything more than a stationary arms dump. The impending assault of 8 August remained a secret.

For this operation, Monash had set another ambitious target: the attacking divisions were to advance a minimum of nine kilometres into German-held territory, with a maximum advance of eighteen kilometres the aim. All planning for consolidation of the gains was based around these targets. The Australians' primary objectives, marked by a green line on the operation's maps, were gained before 7.00 am. At 8.20 am the next phase of the advance began, with red line and then blue-line objectives progressively reached thirty minutes ahead of schedule. General Hobbs' 5th Division captured its final objective as soon as 12.15 pm.

By 8.00 pm, Monash knew that the Australians had overrun the German Second Army's positions to a depth of eighteen kilometres, taking 8000 prisoners, 173 field guns, thousands of machineguns, hundreds of vehicles, even a complete German railway train mounting a 12-inch gun that had been shelling Amiens. Five German colonels commanding regiments were captured, and near Framerville the entire HQ staff of the German 51st Corps was seized in the late afternoon. This was the equivalent of General Monash's HQ at Bertangles being captured by the Germans.

Among the German corps HQ paraphernalia including papers, equipment and motor vehicles captured intact was a box containing one hundred freshly minted German iron crosses, ready for issue to German troops as bravery awards. As a result, a number of grinning Australian soldiers came back from the battle with iron crosses pinned all over their uniforms.

Australian casualties for the Battle of Amiens were 1200. On the Australians' right, the Canadians had achieved similar successes and similar 'slight' losses, reaching their blue-line objectives almost as quickly as the Australians. General Rawlinson wrote, 'The Canadians have done splendidly and the Aussies even better – I am full of admiration for these corps.'[242]

The Australian and Canadian gains of 8 August involved the deepest penetration of German territory by 'British Army' troops to date in the war. 'The tactical value of the victory was enormous,' Monash would later observe, but on 8 August he did not know what an absolutely crushing blow it had been to the enemy, from the German rank and file up to the most senior levels.[243]

German commander General Erich von Ludendorff would write in his memoirs after the war, 'August 8th was the black day of the German Army in the history of the war. This was the worst experience I had to go through.' At first confounded by the speed, depth and scope of Monash's attack, Ludendorff soon became convinced that 8 August signalled the end for Germany, a view that his emperor Kaiser Wilhelm later confided to him he shared.[244]

Despite the overwhelming success of the Australians and Canadians that day, Monash found he had a problem. On his left flank, the British Army had let him down. Again. The British Fourth Army divisions assigned to the left flank of the advance north of the Somme, the 47th and 58th, had failed to reach their final blue-line objectives. Importantly, the British divisions' failure had left the Chipilly Ridge, on a spur north of the river around which the Somme bent through marshland, in enemy hands. As a result, German artillery stationed on this elevated ground was able to pound the exposed flank of the Australian 4th Brigade, and on 8 August knocked out six of the nine tanks operating with the 4th. Monash didn't blame the British infantryman for this failure, but was scathing in his criticism of what he perceived to be 'faulty' British staff officer coordination and 'faulty local leadership' of British officers on the ground, which he was convinced had caused the failure at Chipilly Ridge.[245]

The solution to Monash's Chipilly problem was about to be provided by a new friend of the Australians – Colonel Joe Sanborn's 131st Infantry Regiment.

19.

The 131st Saves the Day at Chipilly Ridge

'Who was that old devil who personally led his regiment to the attack?'

Major-General George Bell, Commander, US 33rd Division

GENERAL RAWLINSON HAD not released the American 131st Infantry after its participation in the Battle of Hamel. Despite General Pershing's repeated requests that his 33rd Division and other American divisions assigned to train with the British Army be returned to his control, Field-Marshal Haig had hung onto them, and the 131st Infantry and three other American regiments of the 33rd Division had remained under the control of British III Corps, part of Rawlinson's British Fourth Army, attached now to the British 47th Division.

On the night of August 8–9, another of the Fourth Army's divisions from III Corps, the British 58th, attempted to take Chipilly Ridge after British troops had failed to occupy the spur during the day as part of General Monash's 8 August offensive. They were aiming to reach the blue line to link up with the Australians south of them who had succeeded in taking their objectives. General Rawlinson had impressed on the 58th Division that it was imperative the Germans be driven off the ridge so that the left flank of General Monash's northernmost Australian brigade was secured. But, yet again, the British troops failed, and, come daylight on 9 August, Chipilly Ridge was still in German hands.

Monash was determined to seize the ridge, and to use Australian troops to do it. But he was hampered by the fact that the area north of the Somme lay in the territory of another corps, British III Corps. Just as in Roman times a Roman provincial governor was not permitted to lead his troops into a neighbouring province, Monash was not permitted to encroach upon III Corps territory with his troops. He quickly found a way around this.

As it happened, III Corps commander Lieutenant-General Sir Alexander Godley, a onetime superior of Monash's, was to leave his post on 9 August to take command of the British Third Army. Getting on the phone, Monash was able to convince General Rawlinson to temporarily extend his own command to III Corps, to enable Monash to deal with Chipilly Ridge. Now that he also commanded north of the Somme, Monash ordered the Australian 13th Brigade to swing north, march into III Corps territory by crossing the River Somme at Cerisy, and then storm Chipilly Ridge.

That afternoon of 9 August, as the 13th Brigade was on the march, Colonel Joe Sanborn stepped into the picture. Since 6 July, the 131st Infantry and three other American regiments from the 33rd Division had been spending their days conducting training manoeuvres with III Corps. When III Corps' two British divisions had advanced in the 8 August battle, the 131st had been left in the reserve trenches. Now, after bloodied, disillusioned British troops of the 58th Division fell back through the 131st's position after failing to take Chipilly Ridge overnight, on the afternoon of 9 August Sanborn made a decision – the 131st would take the ridge. As it happened, back on 4–6 July, Sanborn's men had been able to see Chipilly Ridge in the distance as they occupied the trenches they had seized on Hamel Ridge with the Australians, never imagining they would be storming the heights of Chipilly four weeks later.

Although all its companies and battalions were now back together, the 131st had been separated from its usual machinegun battalion, and was also without its full complement of Lewis Guns. Despite this, and despite a total lack of artillery bombardment or tank or aircraft support, or the cover of darkness, Colonel Sanborn ordered his men to fix bayonets and follow him. That afternoon, the 131st marched several kilometres, charged through a rain of enemy shells and attacked the Germans, first taking a wood before launching themselves at the enemy troops dug in on Chipilly Ridge who had thrown back two British attacks over the previous twenty-four hours. From trench to trench and emplacement to emplacement, and with Sanborn personally leading the assault, the Americans fought their way up and along the ridge in desperate fighting.

Corporal Jake Allex was an infantryman with the 131st's Company H. At a critical point in the assault, all Allex's officers had been either killed or wounded. So, Allex took charge of his platoon and led it forward until a German machinegun halted them in their tracks and the Americans were forced to ground. Allex went on alone, running towards the machinegun nest as its gunner unsuccessfully tried to cut him down. Jumping into the nest, Corporal Allex killed five Germans with his bayonet. When the bayonet broke off in his fifth victim, he swung his rifle like a baseball bat, clubbing Germans with the butt end. By the time Allex had finished and his men had joined their platoon leader, another fifteen battered Germans in the trench had surrendered to him.

The 131st had taken almost all of the ridge, with heavy loss to their own ranks, when the Australians of one of the 13th Brigade's battalions arrived on the scene. 'Joining the Americans,' General Monash would later write, these Australians 'helped to clear up the whole situation'.[246] Through Joe Sanborn's determination and elan, Chipilly Ridge was taken, Monash's left flank was secure, and Americans and Australians once more occupied front-line trenches together. General Pershing, writing about this event several years later, said that the 131st captured the ridge 'in splendid fashion', but made no mention of the fact that they were joined by the Australians for the last part of the assault. He portrayed it as an exclusively American success.[247]

That night, Colonel Sanborn went back down to the British, reported the ridge taken, then secured food for his men, leading the detail that brought the grub back to his regiment on the ridge. Sanborn personally carried rations in a pack on his back, through a German bombardment. 'Who wouldn't fight like the devil for a commander like that?' said the 131st's Sergeant William Keane several months later.[248]

A grateful General Monash now removed the 131st from British III Corps and attached it to the Australian 4th Division, creating a temporary 'Liaison Force' made up of Sanborn's 131st and the Australian 13th Brigade under Australian Corps command. This Liaison Force was supposedly meant to liaise with British forces on the northern rim of the Australian Somme sector, but, with no confidence in the British Army's ability to secure his northern flank, Monash actually tasked Liaison Force with shoring up the Australian left flank until the next big Australian push east. At the same time, Monash had the command of his subordinate General Maclagan officially extended to also take in the front some kilometres north of the River Somme, inclusive of Liaison Force.

Back in the days of the Roman legions, the Roman equivalents of colonels – tribunes as they were known – routinely led their men into battle, but in modern armies colonels don't usually lead infantry attacks from the front. That task is left to younger, more junior officers. So, when word reached General Bell's 33rd Division HQ at Molliens-au-Bois that an old, white-haired American officer had been seen leading the assault on Chipilly Ridge, Bell asked, no doubt with a sparkle of delight in his eye, 'Who was that old devil who personally led his regiment to the attack?'[249]

For this act, and on General Monash's recommendation, Colonel Sanborn would be swiftly awarded Britain's Distinguished Service Order – the first American recipient of the DSO during this war. The American Distinguished Service Cross would follow, as would, by war's end, France's Legion d'Honneur and Croix de Guerre with Palm, and the Belgian Order of Leopold. 'It was a great finish for his career,' Dwight Harding would later comment in the *Chicago Tribune*.[250]

Sanborn would in turn recommend twenty-two members of the 131st for bravery medals for the fight that took Chipilly Ridge, medals that would be duly awarded. Sanborn would propose America's highest decoration, the Medal of Honor, for Corporal Allex, for his role. As in the case of Tom Pope, approval of the Medal of Honor award would have to come from Washington DC.

Further opportunities for medals for Colonel Sanborn himself would be limited, with his superiors requiring him to remain at headquarters during future operations. When General Monash wrote about the battles of 1918, he would describe how, at Chipilly Ridge, the 131st 'very gallantly advanced in broad daylight and took possession practically of the whole spur'.[251] As for General Pershing, he would make no mention of Colonel Sanborn's personal role in the 131st's bold, brave storming of Chipilly Ridge, which, again, had occurred whilst the American regiment was in overall 'British' command. Pershing would merely comment: 'The 131st Infantry was relieved on August 20th, having advanced over three miles and suffered heavy casualties.'[252]

20.

The King Presents Americans with Medals for the Hamel Battle

'The [Australian soldiers] were not greatly impressed by pomp and circumstance.'
Tim Fischer, former Deputy Prime Minister of Australia

ON THE AFTERNOON of 8 August, General Monash informed General Rawlinson that he was keen to exploit the successes of that momentous day by immediately pushing on east and advancing all the way to what the Allies called the Hindenburg Line, after its creator, General Paul von Hindenburg – the Germans actually called it the Siegfried-Stellung, or Siegfried Line. This formidable structure, rated impregnable by the German press, was the last German line of defence before occupied Belgium, Luxembourg and Germany itself lay open to Allied armies.

General Rawlinson responded that while the whole situation was being considered by higher powers, he was temporarily knocking Monash's idea of continued eastward advance on the head, ordering Monash to instead focus on cooperating in the continued advance of the Canadian Corps on the Australians' right, which was pushing southeast towards Roye. This order resulted in the Australian 1st Division making solid gains over 9–11 August, taking towns and territory from the German Army on the northern flank of the Canadian advance, against increasingly stiff resistance during which many British tanks were knocked out. Meanwhile, to the north, the 10th and 13th Australian Brigades encircled and eradicated German positions in the twisting valley of the Somme, extending and consolidating the Australian gains there.

Sunday 11 August brought a hectic series of meetings for General Monash, who began the day at Chateau Bertangles working on plans for his recommended eastward push. Quite early in the day, Winston Churchill paid him an unheralded visit, to congratulate Monash on the 8 August victory. First Sea Lord during the disastrous Gallipoli campaign, of which he had been an architect, Churchill was now Britain's Minister of Munitions.

At 11.00 am, Field-Marshal Haig arrived at Chateau Bertangles for a short planned visit. Haig came to formally thank Monash for his work to date, bringing General Lawrence with him. This was the first time since 3 July that Monash and Haig had seen each other, and they, and Lawrence, no doubt discussed the performance of the Americans who had fought in league with the Australians, and also discussed American commander General Pershing – Haig was due to meet with him the following day.

While the trio was still in discussion, General Sir Julian Byng, commander of the British Third Army, arrived to join the gathering. Haig, on learning that Monash planned to confer at 2.30 that afternoon with all five of his Australian divisional commanders at Villers-Bretonneux – the Australian 1st Division had its HQ in the town, and the 2nd Division its HQ on its western outskirts – said that he would return for that conference, as he had yet to meet all of these Australian generals.

Just before noon, after Haig, Lawrence and Byng had departed, Monash received a call from General Rawlinson, who told him that the Allied commander-in-chief, France's Marshal Foch, would be arriving for an urgent meeting with Monash that afternoon to give fresh orders regarding the tactical policy of the next few days. With Haig now on the road and out of contact, Rawlinson had set the meeting to take place at Monash's Bertangles HQ at 3.00. On learning from Monash that both he and 'the Chief' would be at Villers-Bretonneux at 2.30 that afternoon, Rawlinson promptly rescheduled the meeting with Foch for the same place.

Duly at 2.30, the Villers-Bretonneux meeting got underway beneath the shade of a stand of trees beside the road, with Field-Marshal Haig, General Lawrence and the Chief of the Imperial General Staff, Sir Henry Wilson, in attendance with Monash, Glasgow, Maclagan, Jellibrand, Rosenthal, Hobbs and their chiefs of staff. Across the road from the conference place stood a bird cage, a POW pen, containing 3000 German prisoners. Along the road poured an endless line of Australian troops, vehicles and prisoners under guard, while, beside the road, the first train to traverse the now-repaired line from Villers-Bretonneux to Amiens steamed past. In the background, Australian field batteries boomed, sending shells towards German targets to the east.

After Haig made a short speech beneath the trees in praise of Monash's 'perfectly worked out' battle plan for the advance to the Hindenburg Line, the open-air meeting began, led by Monash, only for General Rawlinson and his deputy General Montgomery to also drive up and join in. Not long after, Canada's General Currie arrived, followed by Generals Kavanah and Godley, then the Tank Corps' General Elles and the RAF's Major-General Leo Charlton. Hardly had these generals joined the meeting than another three cars drove up, delivering France's Prime Minister Clemenceau, Finance Minister Louis-Lucien Klotz, and Marshal Foch. 'We all squatted down on the grass,' Monash would say, 'while great maps were spread out and Rawlinson commenced to expound the situation and ask for our opinions.'[253]

This meeting was the largest gathering of senior Allied war leaders that ever took place on the Western Front. It doesn't bear thinking about what might have happened had a German shell randomly landed on that meeting under the trees at Villers-Bretonneux. Only days before, on 6 August, Lieutenant-Colonel McSharry, CO of the 15th Battalion and one of the best and brightest of the Australian field commanders, had been killed in just such a manner, out in the open. While helping a wounded man into cover at Vaire-sous-Corbie during a German bombardment, McSharry had fallen victim to that bombardment. For his courage, he would be posthumously awarded a second DSO.

The tragic killing and maiming of many top Allied commanders at the one place and time may not have changed the course of the war, but it would certainly have lengthened it. Luckily, no German shell landed on this conference, at which options for the drive for the Hindenburg Line were talked through before everyone took their leave. General Rawlinson had already told Monash that his desired eastward push could be resumed by the Australians and Canadians on 15 August, and at this meeting informed him that he was going to lend him a British division, the 32nd, to hold the line north of the Somme and so allow the Australian divisions to narrow their front for the push east. But before Monash could focus on the big push, he had to turn his attention to another interruption – this time in the form of a royal visit.

As early as 2 August, Monash had been advised that George V, King of England, would be coming to France to review Australian troops who had won the Battle of Hamel and to personally present British gallantry medals to American officers and men for their deeds during that Fourth of July operation. For security reasons, it was only on 11 August that it was confirmed that the king would pay his visit the following day, when he would also formally knight General Monash.

*

King George's top-secret visit to the front began at 11.30 am on Monday 12 August at the Molliens Chateau HQ of the American 33rd Division. General Bell had ordered Colonels Sanborn and Davis to be in attendance with those of their men of the 131st and 132nd Infantry who were available for presentation with British military decorations for their roles in the Battle of Hamel, plus an honour guard made up of 100 men and their officers from the 33rd Division.

Despite the fact these regiments had taken part in the Battle of Hamel against the wishes and orders of American commander-in-chief General Pershing, who would later play down the battle, Pershing was also in attendance when men from his units were presented with the British medals. For King George was also to present Pershing and his chief of staff General Tasker H. Bliss with decorations – this was all made possible because the American government had only recently ruled that American service personnel could accept foreign awards and decorations. Pershing had motored to Molliens from his General HQ at Chaumont on the Sunday, joining Bliss, who had preceded him. The pair stayed the night at Chateau Molliens with General Bell. This was the first time Pershing and Bell had met in the flesh since the Battle of Hamel, and Pershing was clearly still seething about the way the men of the 131st and 132nd had been used by the British on the Fourth of July.

Knowing this, over dinner Bell went into colourful detail about their Independence Day exploits. 'Their services had been urgently requested, general,' Bell stressed, 'and they acquitted themselves well.'[254]

When the king arrived at Bell's HQ on the Monday morning, medal recipients well enough to attend had been brought in – from the trenches on Chipilly Ridge, in the case of the 131st Infantry. They joined the American troops of the honour guard, who were drawn up in a hollow square at the rear of the chateau. Eleven officers and men from Sanborn's 131st and eight from Davis's 132nd received British medals. The British Distinguished Conduct Medal had been conferred upon the 131st's Corporal Thomas Pope. But, as Pope was still confined to a hospital bed in England as he recovered from his gassing on 5 July, he was not present for the presentation by the British sovereign.

Three rooms in the chateau had been set aside for King George's use, and, shortly after his arrival, Generals Pershing and Bliss were invited to join him in one of them. Dressed in the uniform of a British field-marshal, including, like John Monash and his Australian generals, riding boots and breeches, the slight, neatly bearded king presented Pershing with the Grand Cross of the Order of the Bath, and Bliss with the order of St Michael and St George. Had Pershing and Bliss been British, the king would have draped the orders around their necks, but as they were Americans, who had been traditionally averse to royal ceremony ever since ditching the king's predecessor George III a century and a half before, George V simply handed the decorations to the generals in their presentation cases.

'I am anxious to have as many American troops as possible serve with the British Army, general,' King George told Pershing. 'Their presence has an excellent effect in stimulating the morale of our men. Although Britain's troops have never lost spirit, they have been sorely tried. I am not a politician, and I do not see things from their point of view, but I think it would be advantageous to have some Americans serving with my armies. I hold friendly sentiments for America, and it would mean a great deal after the war to be able to say that the two English-speaking peoples had fought side-by-side in this great struggle.'

'I entirely agree, Your Majesty,' Pershing replied, 'that friendly relations ought to be stronger after the war, but we are forming an American army of our own and will require practically all our troops as soon as they can be brought together.'

'I appreciate that fact,' King George persisted, 'but I hope that some of your divisions might remain with the British Army.'

'I can make no promises in that regard,' Pershing, equally persistent in his view, came back.[255]

The king and the American generals then adjourned outdoors for the medal presentation ceremony. Members of Colonel Sanborn's regiment who had medals pinned on their chests by the king on the steps of the chateau this sunny summer's day included Sergeants James Krum, Raymond Powell and Albert Erhardt, Corporals Andrew Schabinger and Harold Zyburt, Private William Linskey, and stretcher-bearer Christopher Keane.

Among members of the 132nd recognised by the British for their Hamel exploits were medical officer Lieutenant Frank Schram, 2nd Lieutenant Harry Yagle, Sergeant Frank Kojane, Corporals Albert Painsipp and John De Smidt, and Private Harry Shelly. General Pershing would record that the American medal recipients were immensely proud at the honour bestowed on them by the British sovereign. It was an occasion the men of the 131st and 132nd would remember for the rest of their lives.

As King George moved on, Pershing departed for a scheduled meeting with Field-Marshal Haig, where he intended demanding the return of his troops, irrespective of what the king had said. As for George V, he arrived at British III Corps HQ at Querrieu at 12.15, where he inspected representatives from the British 12th, 18th, 47th and 58th Divisions drawn up in drill order and steel helmets. By a little after 1.00, His Majesty was lunching in the open on a rise near Querrieu overlooking Villers-Bretonneux. Running a little late following lunch, shortly after 2.00 pm the king was driven up the shady avenue to Chateau Bertangles, which was lined with hundreds of captured German weapons and vehicles, the horse-drawn vehicles complete with their teams.

General Monash was surprised that the king arrived with a small entourage of just a knight of the realm and a military aide from the Fourth Army. As he stepped down from the open car, King George was greeted by Monash, then took the Royal Salute from the honour guard and formally inspected the guard with the general. All the while, official Australian photographer Captain Wilkins was snapping away; Monash had made a point of having him on hand to record the occasion.

In addition to ensuring the event was recorded on film, Monash had taken his usual preparatory care in stage managing the king's reception at Chateau Bertangles, arranging for 500 Australian Corps men who had participated in the Battle of Hamel and another 100 from the Royal Garrison Artillery to be present. Now, in the quadrangle outside the chateau, these 600 troops bussed in for the event stood waiting at attention, rifles on their shoulders. Among those men were the newly promoted Company Sergeant-Major Ned Searle and other Australians decorated for their heroic deeds during the Battle of Hamel, who had received their medals from General Monash in July.

Two Australian Corps men would receive the Victoria Cross as a consequence of the 4 July operation. The first, the 1000th VC ever awarded, went to the 15th Battalion's Two-Gun Harry Dalziel, who had survived his grave head wound but was still in a serious condition in an English hospital. Said Dalziel's citation when his VC was gazetted in London on 16 August, four days after King George's visit to the Australian Corps, 'His magnificent bravery and devotion to duty was an inspiring example to all his comrades, and his dash and unselfish courage at a most critical time undoubtedly saved many lives, and turned what could have been a severe check into a splendid success.' The second Hamel VC went to Jack Axford of the 16th Battalion, who, in September, would be presented with his medal by the king at Buckingham Palace.

Meanwhile, Harry Dalziel's 15th Battalion colleague Ned Searle had to be satisfied with the Military Medal, and promotion. Ned's medal citation noted, 'His coolness and courage throughout were most inspiring, and had a steadying effect on his men.' Knowing my great-uncle Ned, he may well have joked that he hadn't realised that VCs were rationed to one per battalion per day. But the fact that he had souvenired the uniform of the German officer he captured almost certainly counted against him. Likewise, Frank Shaw, whose efforts also seemed worthy of the Victoria Cross, was presented with the Military Medal. By venturing as far as the quarry on 4 July, contrary to orders, he is likely to have cost himself a higher award. Searle's company commander, Captain Ernest Bradley, was awarded the Military Cross, then the officer's equivalent of the Military Medal.

The king, after moving along the lines of decorated Australian soldiers, stopping every now and then to chat with one soldier or another, Searle and Shaw among them, climbed the steps to open French windows and entered one of the reception rooms, where he was introduced by Monash to their host, the white-bearded marquis. Back out on the steps, Monash presented his divisional commanders and senior staff to His Majesty, while, crowded at the chateau's upper windows, junior members of the corps staff watched proceedings.

A square of carpet had been laid at the top of the steps, with a small table and footstool placed on them, in preparation for Monash's official investiture as a Knight Commander of the Bath (KCB). Monash, in his memoirs, remembered this carpet as being located in the middle of the quadrangle outside the chateau, but as photographer Wilkins recorded on film, it was at the top of the steps, in front of the open French window used by the king.

The royal investiture of knights traditionally involves the use by the monarch of a sword, but King George had not come equipped with one, and a sword did not form part of the battlefront equipment of Australian officers. So, a frantic search for a sword, of any description, was instigated in the chateau. An epee, a fencing rapier, apparently the property of monsieur the marquis, was produced, and with Monash dropping his right knee onto the footstool and bowing his head, King George tapped him lightly on each shoulder with the rapier, dubbing him Sir John, in front of Monash's smiling officers and staff. After Monash rose, the king took the insignia of the knighthood from the small table and presented it to the general, then shook him warmly by the hand. After giving a short speech in praise of Monash, the king then asked the victorious general to conduct him on a tour of the collected war trophies.

George took particular interest in the captured German transport horses. 'I hope that they will soon learn the Australian language,' he remarked to Monash with a smile.[256]

And then the royal Rolls pulled up in front of the chateau steps, and the king and his two companions clambered in.

'Three cheers for His Majesty!' called the commander of the honour guard to all the assembled troops, as the car slowly drove off. 'Hip-hip!'

The response from the Australian infantrymen was so unenthusiastic it was barely audible.

'Three cheers for His Majesty!' the commander of the guard repeated with irritation. 'Hip-hip!'

This time, the cheers were a little louder, but more ironic than patriotic. It was a reminder, says Monash biographer and former Australian deputy prime minister Tim Fischer, that Australian soldiers 'were not greatly impressed by pomp and circumstance'.[257]

The royal visit had lasted just half an hour. Now, General Monash and his men could get back to winning the war.

*

Early in the afternoon of that same Monday 12 August, General Pershing met with Field-Marshal Haig aboard Haig's advance headquarters train near Wiry-au-Mont, and Pershing and his aide Colonel Carl Boyd lunched with Haig and his senior staff officers in a railway dining car. 'We chatted about everything except the object of my visit,' Pershing would later complain. Several days earlier, Pershing had written Haig a letter in which he had said he wanted the return of at least three of the five American divisions then undergoing training with the British Army, for an attack he was planning for his new American First Army against a German salient at St Mihiel. Following lunch, Haig took Pershing to the railway car he used as his office, and at last addressed the subject of the American general's letter.

'I understood, Pershing,' the field-marshal said, 'that the American divisions had been sent to be trained, and to serve on the British front. Now, just as they have become useful, it is proposed that they be taken away. I had hoped that these divisions would remain, and would be disappointed to have them removed.'

Pershing countered by reminding Haig of the original understanding they had, that these American troops were at all times to be under Pershing's orders, and that they were to remain behind the British front while in training and only be used in battle to meet an emergency. The Australian attack at Hamel had been an offensive action, one that in no way could be characterised as an emergency, and yet troops of the 131st and 132nd Infantry had been thrown into that attack.

'We are all fighting a common enemy, Marshal Haig,' Pershing went on. 'In my opinion, the best way to help toward victory is for the Americans to fight under their own flag and their own officers. I assure you that your desire to have American troops is fully appreciated, and I regret the necessity which impels me to make this decision just at this moment, but in accordance with our agreement I must insist on having them.'

'I acknowledge the understanding we had,' Haig unhappily responded. 'And, although I need your troops, I realise your position, and your reasons for their withdrawal. Pershing, of course you shall have them. There can never be any difference between us.'[258]

When Pershing left the train, it was with the agreement that Haig would give him back three of his divisions as soon as British replacements could be brought in to fill their places behind the lines. Sure enough, on 23 August the 33rd Division would be withdrawn from the Somme and from General Read's American II Corps, despatched north to Toul, just west of Nancy in the Lorraine region. Two other American divisions were also withdrawn and sent north to join Pershing's First Army.

This would leave Read, who had started with five divisions, with just two, the 27th and 30th, which were then still officially on attachment to the British Army and undergoing training behind the lines in the Ypres sector in Flanders. Having given Pershing the minimum that he'd asked for – the return of three of his five divisions – and no more, Haig fully intended employing the remaining two American divisions to best effect while he had them.

To complicate matters, General Rawlinson had just advised the Chief that General Currie was now privately refusing to take his Canadian Corps against the Hindenburg Line with the Australians on 15 August as Monash planned. Currie was asking for the Canadians to be sent back to their past stomping ground, in the Arras sector, from where he wanted to launch his own drive to the Hindenburg Line.

General Monash, when he wrote about this episode several years later, would be most gracious about Currie's demand to go back to Arras. He said he understood completely that Currie wanted his men to advance through territory they were familiar with. But Monash, and many others in the know, must have suspected that Currie didn't want his Canadians to again share the limelight with the Aussies, nor be the subject of direct comparison between the successes of the Australian and Canadian Corps. The nearest Monash came to criticising Currie would be when he wrote, 'Corps commanders were inclined to be jealous of any encroachment upon their frontiers, or upon the tactical problems in front of them.'[259]

Diplomatically, Monash never expressed his disappointment in Currie, to him or anybody else, but he was clearly frustrated by the setback to his own offensive plans when Rawlinson acceded to Currie's demand. The Canadians progressively pulled out and headed north, leaving two Canadian divisions temporarily under Monash's command until the transfer was completed in late August – for several weeks Monash controlled eight divisions and 200,000 men, by far the largest Allied corps command of the war.

Once all the Canadians had returned to Arras, another two divisions would be needed to take their place beside the Australians when Monash launched his strike east. Putting off the 15 August start date for Monash's planned next offensive to allow for the changeover, Rawlinson would make a suggestion to Haig – in place of the Canadians, why not give

Monash the two American divisions that remained under British control, for the Australian general's Hindenburg Line campaign? But that was still several weeks, and several battles, away.

21.

The Loophole in General Rawlinson's Orders

'The only alternative was to do nothing and attempt nothing. That would have been the worst of bad generalship.'
Lieutenant-General Sir John Monash

ON 20 AUGUST, the French opened a large attack against the German Army in the south. The following day, the British Third Army, commanded by General Byng and now with elements of the American 33rd Division attached, launched a similarly major assault, opposite Albert north of the Somme and immediately above the British Fourth Army's part of the line. In conjunction with Byng's Third Army assault, General Monash had agreed that his 3rd Division's 9th Brigade would advance the Fourth Army front line on the Third Army's right flank to match the British gains and level out the front line.

This all went according to plan, but in the late afternoon of 21 August the Germans fiercely counterattacked the south of the now advanced British front line. The Germans drove back the Third Army's British 47th Division, with which a young Bernard Law Montgomery, the future field-marshal, was a lieutenant-colonel and senior staff officer. This British retreat exposed the left flank of the Australian 33rd Battalion to the south of the 47th Division. The 33rd held its ground but was at risk of being surrounded until the 34th Battalion joined it, after which the two Australian units jointly repelled the German attack and restored the situation.

With German commanders and resources occupied by these two Allied offensives, and with an eye on the change of season, General Monash was keen to resume his major drive east from his Somme sector, so that, combined, the Germans would be confronted by multiple Allied offensives that could potentially advance all the way to the Hindenburg Line. The stated strategic objective for Monash's own planned offensive was, 'To make the line of the Somme useless to the enemy as a defensive line, and thereby render probable [the enemy's] immediate enforced retreat to the Hindenburg Line.'[260] But he had to strike now, while the weather held.

It had been no coincidence that the Roman legions had traditionally campaigned in Europe between March and October each year. After that, the autumn weather closed in, with rain, snow and ice making roads, rivers and mountain crossings impassable. Nothing much had changed in 1900 years. By 21 August 1918, said Monash, 'The autumn was upon us; not more than another eight or nine weeks of campaigning weather could be relied upon.'[261]

Monash was aware that many senior British commanders were satisfied that German offensive operations had been rebuffed. They were counselling waiting out the winter and going on the offensive in the spring of 1919, augmented by the many more American divisions scheduled to arrive in France by that time. The Australian general was not content to wait. To Monash, momentum was everything. Pausing was perilous – once you have your enemy off balance, pursue him, prevent him stopping to regain his balance, to catch his breath, to reinforce, and to make a stand.

Restrained by General Rawlinson from embarking on another major eastward thrust to deliver the German Army another powerful blow in the mould of 8 August, over 13–20 August Monash had his divisions force the Germans on the Somme back from one strongpoint, wood or ruined village after another and to keep snapping at their heels, all with the excuse of straightening the Australian front line. At the same time, he rotated his Australian units to give their men a break out of the line.

Frustrated by intransigence on the part of General Rawlinson at Fourth Army HQ, and using the feigned premise that a new major operation would deny the Somme to the German Army as a winter line of defence, Monash embarked on a plan to put his troops on the east bank of the twisting River Somme in an assault by two divisions, General Glasgow's Australian 1st Division and the British 32nd, with strong tank support. On 21 August, Monash communicated this plan to his corps at a conference of his senior commanders including tank and flying corps officers, with the operation to be undertaken in two days' time.

At dawn on 23 August, Monash launched this latest assault. In what became known as the Battle of Chuignes, Australian and British troops took all their objectives, seizing the Chuignes Valley against stubborn resistance and taking 3100 prisoners and two complete railway trains, one mounting a 15-inch gun that fired shells weighing almost a tonne over a range of thirty-two kilometres – the largest such weapon captured by any army during the war.

'I was at this stage sorely perplexed by the uncertain attitude of the Fourth Army,' Monash was to write. By 'Fourth Army' read 'Rawlinson'. Said Monash, 'I was all for pushing on enthusiastically, and received General Rawlinson's approval to do so on August 24th.' Elated, Monash told his staff to make the necessary plans. 'But on the very next day he [Rawlinson] announced a diametrically opposite policy, which greatly embarrassed me.' In a written communication received by Monash on the 25th, Rawlinson declared that the Fourth Army, inclusive of the Australian Corps, had done its fair share of the fighting and would now mark time and let other armies take a share of the burden.[262]

Monash was furious, and determined to circumvent Rawlinson's decision. Monash's legal training came to the fore as he cunningly used Rawlinson's own words to justify his subsequent actions. 'There was one saving clause in the [Fourth] Army attitude,' Monash would write, 'and this fortunately gave all the loophole necessary for the continued activity which I desired to pursue. It was this: "Touch must be kept with the enemy".' As far as Monash was concerned, 'It was sufficient to justify an aggressive policy on my part.' Monash would resume the advance east, and while the German Army continued to retreat in the face of Australian aggression, the Australians would continue to 'keep touch' with them, chasing them all the way to the Hindenburg Line.[263]

From the early hours of 27 August, vigorous Australian patrolling found that a number of enemy posts east of the new Australian front line had been abandoned by the Germans. This was just the excuse Monash was looking for; the Boche had played right into his hands. 'I ordered an immediate general advance along my whole front. There followed a merry and exciting three days of pursuit, for the enemy was really on the run.'[264] Despite heavy rain on days two and three, and stiff resistance from German machinegun teams, the progress was rapid, until 29 August, when the Australian Corps came to a bend in the Somme where the Germans had blown most of the bridges, effectively halting the Australians' eastward advance.

Monash had been expecting this. To his mind, any German commander who failed to eliminate the bridges in the Australians' path would have been incompetent. Ever since the taking of Chipilly Ridge, Monash had been thinking about a back-door solution to this potential problem – an attack from the north to take the opposite bank of the river at Péronne.

*

To find out what the hell Monash was up to, on the afternoon of Friday 30 August General Rawlinson paid a visit to Monash at his advance HQ, which was then located in a collection of houses in the Somme village of Glisy. Monash explained the Australian Corps' gains of 27–29 August to Rawlinson, then calmly laid out how, the following day, he was going to launch an operation to take the Somme riverside town of Péronne north of the river, and a fortified hill on Péronne's northern outskirts called Mont St Quentin. This hill was key to the operation. The rocky mount overlooked the area north, south and east of Péronne, and artillery located at the ancient fortress atop it commanded the Somme for kilometres around.

Monash's plan was as clever as it was bold. While the British 32nd Division made it appear that it was striving to cross the river opposite Péronne, the Australian 3rd Division would take Bouchavesnes Ridge northeast of Clery, and the 2nd Division would swing up through the 3rd Division's new positions then turn south to attack Mont St Quentin and Péronne from the north, with the 5th Division in support. As Monash was to admit, it was like a battle plan out of the playbook of Confederate general Stonewall Jackson.

Because the Australian Corps' advance had outstripped much of its artillery and the 5th Tank Brigade had almost run out of serviceable tanks, Monash's troops would be going against Mont St Quentin over open territory with limited artillery support and no tanks. And the final assault would be undertaken by just three understrength Australian battalions out of the thirty-five taking part in the operation. Worse, it was known that elite troops from one of the best and last German reserve divisions, the Second Prussian Guards, the equivalent of Britain's Grenadier Guards, bolstered by German volunteers from a host of other units, occupied the trenches below Mont St Quentin. The proud Kaiser Alexander Regiment held the summit. The defenders had orders from General von der Marwitz to hold Mont St Quentin at all costs.

When Rawlinson heard Monash's intention, he burst out

laughing and openly mocked him. 'And so you think you're going to take Mont St Quentin with three battalions! What presumption! However, I don't think I ought to stop you. So, go ahead, and try! And I wish you luck!'[265]

Rawlinson clearly thought Monash had bitten off more than he could chew this time, and probably expected him to come out of the exercise chastened and a little more acquiescent. Perhaps defeat at Mont St Quentin would leave Monash prepared to bow to his army commander's wisdom in future and rein in his ambitions for the Australian Corps. Give a man enough rope, and he will hang himself, so the old saying goes.

Monash's Australians took that rope, and, after bitter fighting that lasted until 3 September, took Bouchavesnes Ridge, Mont St Quentin, Péronne, and all the high ground overlooking that town. Quite early in the battle, stiff German resistance halted the advance of the 2nd Division's 5th Brigade and caused Monash to throw in his lone reserve brigade, the 6th. 'The only alternative was to do nothing and attempt nothing,' Monash would later say. 'That would have been the worst of bad generalship, and it was an occasion when risks must be taken.'[266]

The 6th Brigade finished what the 5th had begun, taking Mont St Quentin in bloody hand-to-hand fighting that left it strewn with German dead. Equally bitter fighting was experienced in Péronne. Three Victoria Crosses were awarded to Australians in the taking of Mont St Quentin, and four in the taking of Péronne. German commander General von der Marwitz, a vastly experienced Prussian cavalry officer and formerly adjutant to the Kaiser, was shocked and devastated by this defeat, especially when told that his defenders on the mount had outnumbered their Australian attackers three to one. The German commander had put the best men he had on Mont St Quentin, and considered both it and Péronne unassailable. He knew that he faced the Australians there, but despite a healthy respect for the Aussies and their commander Monash, like General Rawlinson the Boche general underestimated them both.

Monash had set out 'to open a wide gate through which the remainder of the Fourth and Third Armies could pour', after which they could turn north and south behind the German front line and roll it up. It had been tough going for a while, but the Australians had executed their general's brilliant and scorned plan to perfection. Now, to prevent tens of thousands of its troops being overrun from the rear, the German Second Army east of the Somme was forced to evacuate trenches and towns, and began a disorganised retreat, fleeing 'helter-skelter', in Monash's words, thirty kilometres over clogged roads to the protection of its Siegfried Line.[267]

General Rawlinson meanwhile lavished praise on the Australian 2nd Division, which took Mont St Quentin, telling Monash: 'I am filled with admiration at the gallantry and surpassing daring of the 2nd Division in winning this important fortress, and I congratulate them with all my heart.'[268] What his congratulatory message didn't say was that, using the loophole in General Rawlinson's orders, Monash, and his Australian Corps, had yet again shown how to bring the end of the war closer. On 31 August, the day after the storming of Mont St Quentin and Péronne, Paris newspaper *Le Figaro* ran the story of the assault under the headline 'Australians in Péronne'. The French press was always quick to praise Australian troops for their successes, unlike the British press at that time.

On 11 September, Monash would write to his wife, 'In connection with the present counter-offensive the London press started very badly, and, in fact, in several striking instances attributed successes achieved by the Australians to other [British] troops who had previously failed in the same tasks. I made very serious remonstrations about this to Perry Robinson of *The Times*, to Rawlinson, to Lawrence, and to the Chief of the Imperial General Staff, Sir Henry Wilson, telling them plainly that my own appeal to my troops was the prestige of the Australian arms, and that, unless the performances of the Australians were justly placarded, I would not hold myself responsible for the maintenance of their fighting spirit. I put it plainly that they are by nature and instinct sportsmen, and that they would refuse to go on playing any game in which their scores were not put up on the scoring board.'[269]

Monash's complaints would result in the British press giving the Australians their due by the time he wrote to his wife, allowing him to focus on the next stage of his drive east. 'Before the end of the first week of September,' Monash was to say, 'the Somme had ceased to hold our further interest. It had become a thing that was behind us, both in thought and in actuality. The enemy was once more on the move, and it became our business to press relentlessly at his heels.' On all fronts now, the enemy was making a general retreat to the Hindenburg Line.[270]

22.

The Aussies and Yanks Go Against the Hindenburg Line Together

'Feed your troops on victory.'
Lieutenant-General Sir John Monash

As the German Army retreated and the Australian Corps continued its pursuit, General Monash had departed the luxury of Chateau Bertangles in mid-August and moved his headquarters further and further east to keep up with his advancing troops. Firstly to Glisy, then to a wrecked chateau at Mericourt, and then on 8 September to an uncomfortable camp of small wooden huts on a rise near Assevillers. There, he received a constant flow of curious celebrity visitors wanting to learn more about the Australian victories, from Winston Churchill to Sherlock Holmes' creator Sir Arthur Conan Doyle to leading Australian artist Arthur Streeton. Field-Marshal Haig also dropped in regularly, and former Australian Corps commander General Birdwood, now commanding the British Fifth Army, came to congratulate Monash.

There at the Australian Corps' Assevillers HQ on 13 September, General Rawlinson conferred with his three corps commanders, Generals Monash, Butler (British III Corps) and Braithwaite (British IX Corps), and a plan was discussed for a joint assault, while the weather still allowed, on the Hindenburg Outpost Line, which was the first of four lines of defences that made up the kilometres-deep Siegfried Line.

By this stage, the British 32nd Division had been transferred to the Fifth Army after doing good work with the Australian Corps. This left Monash with just his five Australian divisions. For the assault on the Hindenburg Outpost Line, he would employ his 1st and 4th Divisions. Company Sergeant-Major Ned Searle of the 4th Division's 15th Battalion had survived all the battles of July, August and September, and was looking forward to 'having a go at the Inderbugs Line'.[271] As was General Monash.

Concerned that, as a result of attrition, only eight serviceable tanks remained for the Australian Corps' assault, Monash assigned his 3rd and 5th Division machinegun battalions to the 1st and 4th Divisions, doubling his machinegun resources. He also ordered the manufacture of as many dummy tanks as possible by his engineers and pioneers, which created great competition in the fake tanks' design and construction. At dawn on 18 September, as the Australians advanced behind a massive creeping barrage and in drenching rain, the Germans saw the best of these dummy tanks, made of wood and hessian, sitting in the gloom. Unable to differentiate between real and fake tanks at a distance, German observers would massively overestimate the number of armoured vehicles coming for them, and German morale in the trenches plummeted.

The 1st Division overran the trenches and emplacements of its assigned portion of the Hindenburg Outpost Line before nightfall on 18 September, by which time the 4th Division was within 500 metres of the Outpost Line but had halted in the face of murderous enemy fire. Pausing to catch its breath, the 4th Division resumed its attack in darkness at 11.00 pm, and that night it, too, took all its assigned objectives and reached the blue line.

On their flanks, the Australians were again let down by poor performance from the British troops involved in the assault, who were meant to advance at the same rate and to the same blue line as the Australian Corps. On the Australians' left, British III Corps failed to take any part of the Outpost Line, and was bogged down, leaving the Australians' northern flank dangerously exposed. On the Australians' right, British IX Corps had only reached the day's first red-line objective, with the blue-line final objective still well ahead of it.

The Australians took close to 5000 prisoners that day, a number of whom surrendered without a fight. One of the captives was a German battalion commander, and General Monash, who spoke fluent German and always interrogated senior prisoners personally, asked the German colonel why his men had given up without any show of resistance.

'Well, you see,' said the *oberst*, 'they are dreadfully afraid of the Australians. So they are of the tanks. But when they saw both of them coming at them *together*, they thought it was high time to throw up their hands.'[272]

Having achieved their objectives, the Australian 1st and 4th Divisions were relieved and withdrawn, being taken by bus and train to a riverside location to the southwest,

between Amiens and Abbeville, for recreation and recuperation. General Monash's plan was to let these two divisions
rest over the winter, so that they could come back fresh,
reinvigorated and reinforced for a final campaign in 1919.
No one knew at the time that the war had less than two
months left to run, so it would eventuate that the combat
services of these two veteran Aussie divisions would no longer
be required. Nonetheless, one last great effort lay ahead for
General Monash's Australian divisions still in the line.

*

On 18 September, even while the battle for the Hindenburg
Outpost Line was still being fought on the Australian-British
front, Monash spoke with General Rawlinson and explained
that, of necessity, he would be resting the 1st and 4th
Divisions once they had achieved their objectives that day,
replacing them in the line with two of his remaining three
Aussie divisions.

'I will thus be left with insufficient resources to maintain
an immediate pressure upon the enemy,' he told Rawlinson.

In response, Rawlinson had a suggestion. 'There is a
possibility,' he said, 'of obtaining, very shortly, the services
of the II American Corps' two divisions.' This was the same
II Corps that had until recently included the 33rd Division,
whose men had proven such good comrades-in-arms to the
Australians. Rawlinson, who clearly had previously discussed
with Field-Marshal Haig the idea of giving Monash the
American 27th and 30th Divisions, now asked, 'Monash,
would you be prepared to accept the responsibility of taking

this force under your command for the continuance of the operations?'

Monash seized on the suggestion. He would later say: 'I had no reason to hesitate. My experience of the quality of the American troops, both at the Battle of Hamel and on the Chipilly spur, had been eminently satisfactory. It was true that this new American corps had no previous battle service, but measures were possible to supply them with any technical guidance which they might lack.'[273] In other words, he felt he could whip the Americans into shape for the operation.

The number of troops involved was also attractive to Monash. American divisions at that time contained close to twice as many men as Australian and English divisions at full strength. Bringing these two American divisions under Monash's command would add tens of thousands of fresh combat and support troops to the Australian Corps for the Hindenburg Line campaign. The Australian divisions had been heavily reduced by the campaigns of 1918; following their latest battle, the victorious but battered 1st and 4th were well under strength. So, unsurprisingly, Monash promptly accepted Rawlinson's offer.

'Submit a proposal,' Rawlinson then instructed him, 'for a joint operation to take place towards the end of the month by these two American and the remaining three Australian divisions, with the object of completing the task of breaking through the Hindenburg defences.'[274]

Monash wrote and submitted his proposal that same day.

*

The main Hindenburg Line defences in front of the Australian Corps were built around a north-south Napoleonic canal system, called the Canal de St Quentin, which merged with the Canal de l'Escaut to the north. This canal created a formidable physical barrier which the Germans had built into their Hindenburg Line defences. Monash felt that a direct assault on the canal itself would prove costly in terms of casualties. He had a better idea. Known to study maps and aerial reconnaissance photographs for hours, Monash had already looked for, and spotted, a weak link in the Hindenburg Line, which happened to be opposite the failed line of advance of the British III Corps assault of 18 September.

At the point in question, the St Quentin Canal disappeared into a hill, flowing beneath the slopes in a tunnel, known as the Bellicourt Tunnel because the hill village of Bellicourt sat astride it, before reemerging into the open 6500 metres to the north. In that tunnel, the Germans had moored barges which provided accommodation for German regiments defending the line, deep beneath the hill and impervious to Allied shelling or bombing. If an attacking force could successfully assault and take that hill, this would create a passage over the top of the canal far more useful than any bridge.

In the Monash plan, the two American divisions would lead the assault, with British Fourth Army support on their flanks, advancing to the hill over the tunnel against German trenches and emplacements to a green-line primary objective. The Australian divisions coming behind would then leapfrog the Americans and drive over the tunnel to the blue-line objective, which would be beyond the fourth line of the Siegfried defences, several kilometres east of the canal.

Directly on the heels of the assault, engineers from all the Australian and American divisions would build a minimum of four roads over the tunnel hill. This would create a wide and deep breach in the Hindenburg Line, a breach through which the British Third and Fifth Armies could pour to wrap up the rest of the Hindenburg Line from the rear.

Monash's proposal was quickly approved by Haig and Foch. The day after the Australian submitted his plan, 19 September, Rawlinson came to Monash's Assevillers HQ. Monash's assault involving the five Australian and American divisions could go ahead as proposed, with the exception that the taking of the last line of German defences, known as the Beaurevoir Line, would not be an objective on the first day of the assault. Rawlinson felt that aiming to overrun all three remaining German lines of defence in the one day was asking a bit much, even of the apparently superhuman Aussies.

Rawlinson had been made aware by Field-Marshal Haig that the French in the south and British and Belgian armies to the north would also attack the Hindenburg Line in their sectors about the same time that the Australian-American assault was launched, so he had decided that his British IX Corps should make a direct assault on the canal as part of the Fourth Army contribution to what would be an almost simultaneous multi-pronged assault the length of the Hindenburg Line. British XIII Corps had recently been transferred to Rawlinson's command, and, instead of the poorly performing III Corps, which would be replaced in the line by the Americans, XIII Corps would be the unit tasked with passing through the opening in the Hindenburg Line created by the Australian and American 'shock troops'.

With the date of the great multi-pronged assault set for 29 September, Monash and his staff immediately commenced work on the planning for the second operation of the war, after the Battle of Hamel, in which American forces would go into battle under overall Australian command, although this would involve much larger numbers and be on a much grander scale than at Hamel, which now lay well behind the Allied front line. In this latest operation, Monash would wield 200,000 troops, 200 tanks and 1000 artillery pieces.

To facilitate close cooperation between the Americans and Australians, General Read relocated his American II Corps headquarters to nearby General Monash's HQ. Read, who was 'reserved, agreeable and courteous' in Monash's view, was prepared to stand back and let the experienced Australian general take the lead, making no attempt to impose his will or ideas on Monash as he prepared for the operation. 'He very generously took upon himself the role of spectator,' Monash was to say, 'so that I might not be hampered in issuing orders or instructions to his troops. At the same time, I am sure that in his quiet, forceful way he did much to ensure on the part of his divisional commanders and brigadiers a sympathetic attitude towards me and the demands I had to make of them.'[275]

On 11 September, General Pershing's new American First Army had finally seen action, in the attack on the Germans at St Mihiel. That same First Army would subsequently join the French in a 26 September attack between Verdun and Rheims. These events made the Americans now under Monash's command all the more anxious to get into the fray. But, as much as Monash valued the enthusiasm and fighting spirit of the Americans, he did have concerns about the efficient internal management and discipline of their units, and the lack of American familiarity with the way Australian units worked and fought. Joe Sanborn's 131st and Abel Davis's 132nd Infantry had been schooled in both at Hamel, but with those regiments now in a different sector, the Australians would have to bed in a new and much larger group of keen but green Yankee student soldiers.

To overcome these concerns in the little over a week that he had available to him before the joint assault, Monash proposed a liaison body, the Australian Mission, made up of Major-General Maclagan of his now relieved 4th Division, with 216 experienced officers and NCOs from the 1st and 4th Divisions, who were to be spread across the American corps, division, brigade and battalion headquarters. Their job would be to advise their American counterparts on Australian methods and tactics, so that the forces of the two countries could integrate easily during the battle ahead.

General Read readily agreed to this idea, which was implemented at once. But Read quite deliberately failed to inform his superior General Pershing that he was doing this. Pershing had developed such a jingoistic distaste for foreign advisers that he had recently vetoed a plan to send British and French officers with experience in trench warfare to the US to help train recruits there, and he would surely have scuppered the idea of the Australian Mission to his 27th and 30th Divisions had he known about it. It seems that Pershing may never have learned of the Australian Mission and its work.

General Monash, at a 23 September conference at his HQ,

explained his plan for the upcoming battle to General Read, Read's divisional commanders Major-General John F. O'Ryan of the 27th Division and the 30th Division's Major-General Edward M. Lewis, and their senior officers. Monash delivered this briefing as he would to his Australian commanders, only to be deluged with questions from the Americans when he had finished. From experience, Monash's Australian commanders knew exactly what he was talking about when he briefed them, but his operational language was as clear as mud to the Americans. Monash was forced to run through the plan again for them, this time in fine detail, using a blackboard, to explain terms and tactics and to graphically illustrate what he expected of the American troops.

There was one element that Monash stressed above all else to the listening American generals and colonels – this was the vital importance of the 'moppers up', the troops who came behind the first wave in Australian assaults. To maximise the speed and maintain the momentum of an assault, Australian troops of the first wave passed over enemy first line trenches once they had dealt with defenders, leaving any enemy who remained skulking in dugouts or emplacements to be handled by tanks and the 'mopper up' troops of the second wave. This included posting men at dugout and tunnel entrances to flush out occupants. If mopping up was not thoroughly and efficiently carried out, enemy troops would be left in the rear of the first wave – men who could emerge and attack them from behind.

Monash knew that, at the Battle of Hamel, Americans of the 33rd Division had been more interested in dashing forward to the attack than staying back to mop up, a proclivity they would again display in their next campaign to the north. American commander-in-chief General Pershing had been told of the propensity of his troops to rush forward, beyond set objectives or into their own side's artillery barrages, that they displayed during the Battle of Hamel. Yet he took no steps to discourage it. He would write of the 33rd Division in 1931, downplaying this ill-disciplined tendency, and characterising it as a positive: 'This division afterwards displayed the same eagerness to get at the enemy at several hard-fought engagements during the trying days of the Meuse-Argonne offensive.'[276]

General Monash felt that this habit, unless checked by their officers, had the potential to create unnecessarily high numbers of American casualties, and could put the overall success of an operation in jeopardy. This issue would be particularly important on 29 September because, from German documents captured by the British Third Army to the north, Monash had learned the detailed layout of that part of the Hindenburg Line that faced him. 'The whole defensive system [is] provided, on quite an exceptional scale,' Monash told the American commanders at the 23 September conference, 'with underground shelters, galleries, passages and dugouts.'[277] As a consequence he instructed the American commanders to allocate fully half their men to mopping up duty. The Americans left this conference assuring Monash that they 'got it'.

Extensive troop movements were involved in preparations for the 29 September attack, as the Americans came down from the north and the Australians moved out of the line to be replaced by divisions from the French First Army

261

and relocated north to that part of the line that faced the Bellicourt Tunnel and had previously been occupied by British III Corps. Uniquely, for a period of five days while these movements were underway, there were no Australian troops in the front line on the Western Front, for the first time in the war since they had initially gone into the line in April 1916 following their withdrawal from Gallipoli.

*

Monash was holding a joint conference of all his Australian and American commanders on 26 September when Field-Marshal Haig turned up unexpectedly. He came to watch, and to impress on participants the fact that, if successful, this operation would hasten the end of the war. Clearly, of the trio of attacks scheduled for three days' time, it was this Australian-American operation for which Haig held the highest hopes.

But before the main operation could be launched, there was an obstacle to overcome that went back to 18 September. This was when British III Corps had failed to reach its blue-line objective, the northern part of the Hindenburg Outpost Line attacked by the Fourth Army that day. Their failure had left the front line at that point 1000 metres behind the new front line created by the Australian Corps to their south.

To rectify this and finish the job, in the process level-ling out the front line for the start of the main operation on 29 September, General Rawlinson instructed Monash to send the American 27th Division on 27 September to attack that part of the Hindenburg Outpost Line in his path that still remained in German hands. Rawlinson also told Monash to base all planning around the assumption that the Americans would take this objective and the front line would be even for the jumping off of all forces on 29 September.

Monash never normally made assumptions, but now he was forced by Rawlinson's order to base his battle plan on the assumption of success by inexperienced American troops. 'For the first time,' Monash was to say, 'I had to gamble on a chance. It was contrary to the policy that governed all my previous battle plans, in which *nothing* had been left to chance.'[278]

One of the key elements of Monash's detailed planning for 29 September covered the 1000 artillery pieces that would provide the creeping barrage for his Australian-American assault. The artillery, infantry and tanks had to be provided with detailed maps showing the coordinates for the start point and the successive lift points of the massive barrage on the day of the main battle. Hundreds of maps were prepared, printed and distributed to all artillery, infantry and tank commanders down to battery and platoon level, marked according to the assumption that the American 27th Division would reach the 18 September blue line in its 27 September attack.

This preliminary American assault duly commenced at 5.30 am on 27 September, supported by a creeping barrage and British tanks, with the objective of reaching and taking the German trench system in front of what had once been Quennemont Farm and Gillemont Farm. To rapidly identify the extent of enemy ground taken in advances, General Monash had recently schooled his own troops in a system where they fired orange flares into the sky when Australian reconnaissance aircraft flew by, and the Americans were introduced to this system. As the morning of 27 September unfolded, Monash received conflicting reports about the American division's progress. General Read's HQ was telling him that American troops had reached their objectives, but Australian aircraft were seeing no orange flares rising from all the strategic points where the Yanks ought to be, such as Gillemont Farm.

It transpired that elements of two battalions of American 27th Division troops had in fact reached their furthest objective, the village of Le Catelet, well to the east. But in their enthusiasm to reach their main objective they had ignored Gillemont Farm, leaving it, and its defenders, behind them. Breaking Monash's golden rule by failing to mop up en route, these men of the 27th had allowed Germans to emerge from underground hideaways in their rear. Of course, these Fritzes were soon attacking the Americans from behind.

The American troops in Le Catelet found themselves surrounded in the village, and although they refused to surrender, their advance had been for nothing, and their position was perilous. As a consequence, much of the Hindenburg Outpost Line in General Monash's path remained in German hands. The American assault proved a waste of time and lives, and failed to meet the assumption of ground secured by day's end that had been forced on Monash by Rawlinson.

With this knowledge, Monash hurried to General Rawlinson's HQ and sought a postponement of the 29 September main assault to give the 27th Division time to send in more troops to make a second attempt at completing the taking of the Outpost Line, and free the trapped American battalions, before the main attack began. Rawlinson responded that a postponement was not possible, as planned attacks by all British, French, American and Belgian armies were tied to a coordinated schedule. Although Monash managed to obtain more tanks from Rawlinson for the 27th Division's use, fresh troops from that division would have to rapidly advance 1000 metres against the enemy on 29 September to liberate their surrounded colleagues, reach the old blue line and catch up with the Australians and the creeping barrage, all before continuing with the main assault.

*

All through this period, General Monash had striven to keep two secrets from his men, after finding himself, as he said, 'in a sea of troubles'.[279] Earlier in the year, the British War Office had decreed that, because of decreasing troop numbers, all brigades in divisions made up of men from around the British Empire were to be reduced from four battalions to three, with men from the abolished battalion distributed among the others. Monash's predecessor General Birdwood had, in May, been about to implement this order when Monash took over the Australian Corps.

Monash, considering this a typically stupid Whitehall pen-pushers' solution to the problem of falling battalion strengths, had ignored the abolition order for months. He knew that, while some Australian battalions had a history going back only two or three years, their surviving men were fiercely proud of their units, their sacrifices and their victories, and would resist disbandment. 'The private soldier,' said

Monash of his Australians, 'valued his battalion colour patch almost more than any other decoration.'[280]

This proved the case. After the abolition was forced on Monash in October via an order from above, received on 19 September in the middle of the Hindenburg Line campaign, the men of eight Australian battalions slated for abolition would go on strike. One of the units set down for disbandment was the 42nd Battalion, which had participated in the Battle of Hamel victory. Its survivors were destined for the 43rd Battalion. Only the 59th and 60th Battalions would merge without demur. For now, Monash received permission from General Rawlinson to put off the matter of battalion abolition for several weeks until the Hindenburg Line campaign had been wrapped up, keeping news of it from his rank and file to prevent his troops from being distracted from the task at hand.

Then there was Monash's second secret. On 16 September, two days before his Hindenburg Line campaign began, the general had received a communique from the War Office telling him that 6000 of his Australians who had served continuously since 1914 were to be sent back to Australia for six months' special furlough. This would become known as 1914 Leave. It would transpire that this had been initiated by Prime Minister Hughes. The War Office was securing ships to take these men home, and Monash was told that the withdrawal order affecting these men could come through with just forty-eight hours' notice.

For the moment, Monash also failed to tell his men about this. Whilst good news for the 6000, this special leave would be a wrench both for men who would be going and those staying. It would also deprive Monash of 6000 of his best men. Determined that there would be no distractions from the task at hand, for his troops or himself, Monash kept the subject of 1914 Leave under wraps as he focused on 29 September.

*

When the time came, 29 September proved one of the most trying days of General Monash's military career. After Zero Hour at 5.50 that misty morning, all began well; very well in fact. At the canal, the British IX Corps attack, meant as a diversion to draw German attention away from the main Bellicourt Tunnel assault, achieved surprising success. Using all manner of contrivances, British troops of the 46th Division had crossed the canal in several places and were fighting on its east bank. On the right of the Australian-American assault, the American 30th Division seemed by 10.00 am to be on track to fighting its way to its green-line objective by 11.00, when the following Australian 5th Division was scheduled to leapfrog it and push on to the blue-line objectives east of the tunnel.

Then, at 11.10 am, Monash received a disturbing message: his 5th Division's advance on the right had been held up because the Americans of the 30th Division ahead of it were locked in desperate fighting in the town of Bellicourt, above the tunnel, against German troops the Americans had failed to mop up in their wake and reinforcements brought in along the canal in boats by the Germans.

Two minutes later, the Australian 3rd Division reported

from the left that it was still dug in west of the tunnel because troops of the American 27th Division were bogged down ahead of them, west of Gillemont Farm. It later eventuated that only two of the six American battalions involved in the advance had succeeded in catching up with the creeping barrage as planned. These battalions had rushed on over the tunnel to gain their green-line objectives, but yet again over-eager Doughboys had failed to mop up in their rear. As large numbers of German troops emerged from their hiding places behind them, these American battalions soon found themselves in trouble. Meanwhile, most of the British tanks assigned to the 27th Division's assault had been knocked out by a combination of German artillery and landmines.

In the south, the 5th Division's advance guard came up on the rear of the German forces that had trapped Americans of the 30th Division in Bellicourt. In fierce hand-to-hand fighting, the Australians overwhelmed the Germans in their path, fought their way through the village, mopping up all the way, and liberated large numbers of American troops. As the Australians pushed on, bent on achieving their blue-line objectives east of the canal, the Americans in Bellicourt, instead of sticking to General Monash's plan and staying where they were and consolidating their position at the green line, excitedly joined the Australians in their advance east of the main Hindenburg Line.

Thus, by hook and by crook, the southern part of the Bellicourt Tunnel fell into Monash's hands. But to the north it was a different story. The 3rd Division found itself having to achieve the 27th Division's objectives before it could proceed to achieve its own. By 2.00 pm, General Monash knew that the 3rd was partly astride the tunnel, its front line now running obliquely from northeast to southwest, with the tunnel's northern entrance still in German hands.

With a number of isolated parties of American troops of the 27th Division known to be cut off in German territory, Monash decided he couldn't use artillery in his efforts to take the northern tunnel defences, as that risked shelling these Americans. Forced by events to throw out his original carefully structured battle plan, late in the day Monash brought his reserve division, the Australian 2nd, up by bus from near Péronne to within striking distance of the tunnel. He also ordered the withdrawal of all American troops of the 27th and 30th Divisions who could be reached, officially for rest and reorganisation but in reality to get them out of his hair. It was only with some difficulty that those Americans who had unofficially attached themselves to rampaging Australian units were convinced to pull out of the fight and return to the rear.

Monash's worst fears about the Americans and their potential to fail to mop up in their rear had come to pass, with expensive consequences for the American divisions involved, and headaches for Monash. Yet, he was not overly critical of them. 'They demonstrated their inexperience in war, and their ignorance of some elementary methods of fighting,' he was to say. 'For these shortcomings they paid a high price.' Still, he felt they were 'entitled to high credit for a fine effort'.[281]

With the Americans pulling back, Monash ordered his 3rd Division to that night swing left, despite torrential rain, and combine with the northernmost elements of the 5th

Division to attack German northern tunnel defences from due south the following day, without the benefit of artillery support or tanks. On 30 September, the soaked 3rd Division fought halfway to its objectives through a tangle of muddy trenches in desperate hand-to-hand combat with bayonet and grenade, whilst the 5th Division gained ground to the east. By nightfall on 1 October, in Monash's view driven by his subordinate General Gellibrand's personal tenacity, the day's objectives including the northern entrance to the canal tunnel had been secured by the 3rd Division, with more than 3000 German prisoners taken by the Australians before another two days had passed.

The Allies' first breach in the main Hindenburg Line had been made, and while the fourth and last line of Hindenburg trenches, the so-called Beaurevoir Line, remained in German hands for the moment, the 50th Division of the British XIII Corps was able to pass through the gap created over the top of the tunnel by the Australians and Americans, swing left, and envelop and wrap up the main Hindenburg Line defences to the north.

Many remaining lost parties of American soldiers including wounded were recovered by the 3rd Division from the previously German-held territory, but when Australian patrols reached Le Catelet, where men from two battalions of the American 27th Division had been reported cut off days earlier, no trace of the Yanks was found. The Germans had just pulled out of Le Catelet, in such a hurry that they had left their own wounded behind. A senior Boche officer taken prisoner on the last day of the assault informed General Monash when he questioned him that the German Army had taken 1200 American officers and men of the 27th Division prisoner in and around Le Catelet, after which they had been quickly shipped east, before the Australians could free them. Those 1200 Americans had paid the price for their impetuosity and were now on their way to POW camp in Germany.

The men of the Australian 3rd and 5th Divisions had done magnificent work, but they were exhausted. Monash knew it, and withdrew them to join his 1st and 4th Divisions resting southwest of Amiens. They were replaced in the line by a single division, the 2nd, Monash's last remaining Australian division. It linked up with the British 32nd Division, which was now a part of IX Corps. The 2nd wasn't just a place-filler; there was still work for the Australian infantrymen to do before the Hindenburg Line was fully breached.

Over 3 and 4 October, the 2nd Division assaulted and took a 6000-metre length of the Beaurevoir Line, the fourth, most easterly and final of the 'impregnable' Hindenburg Line defences, in the process taking another 1800 German prisoners. They did this despite tough resistance, despite most of the remaining 5th Tank Brigade machines being knocked out by German artillery in the attack, and despite most of the small, two-man Whippet light tanks that were also assigned to the assault finding the German trenches too wide to cross and proving of little assistance to the Australians. All four strands in the Hindenburg Line had now been cut by the Aussies. The way to Germany now lay open to the Allies, and the German Army was soon in wholesale retreat.

General Pershing, in his memoirs, would characterise the 29 September battle for the Bellicourt Tunnel as essentially an American victory. Here is how he depicted the assault:

'Good reports came in regarding the operations on the 29th of our II Corps (Read), which was with General Rawlinson's British Fourth Army. With both the 30th (Lewis) and 27th (O'Ryan) Divisions in line, this corps formed the main wedge in the attack against that portion of the German line that included the Bellicourt tunnel of the Cambrai-St Quentin Canal.'

Pershing continued his misleading narrative by saying: 'The [American] II Corps, attacking on September 29th against stiff resistance, gallantly captured the ridge of the tunnel, which was part of the Hindenburg Line. The 30th Division did especially well. It broke through the Hindenburg Line on its entire front and took Bellicourt and part of Nauroy by noon of the 29th. The Australian 5th Division coming up at this time, continued the attack with elements of the 30th Division and the line advanced a considerable distance. The 27th Division, due to no fault of its own, had been unable to take full advantage of the accompanying barrage, which was laid down over 1000 yards ahead of the line from which the troops started the attack. Despite the handicap, it took the enemy trenches of the Hindenburg Line south of Bony, captured the Knoll, and established its line south from that position to a point just west of Gillemont Farm.'[282]

Whilst Pershing did mention the role of the Australian 5th Division in the assault, he failed to mention that of the Australian 3rd Division that day, or the subsequent role of the Australian 2nd Division. He neglected to admit that both his 27th and 30th Divisions failed to meet their objectives, or that many of their men had to be rescued by the Australians. He likewise did not reveal that 1200 of his men from the

27th had been taken prisoner by the Germans in the battle. Neither could he bring himself to say that the American divisions were under overall Australian command leading up to and during the battle, or that the assault was masterminded by General Monash.

*

On 5 October, Monash withdrew his 2nd Division and sent it by bus and train southwest, to join its four brother Australian divisions for a long overdue rest. The 2nd was replaced in the line by the American 27th and 30th Divisions, with General Monash yielding command of the American troops back to their own General Read.

That same day, the German Government commenced secret negotiations with the Allies for an Armistice that would bring an end to the war. That Armistice would eventually come into effect at 11.00 am on 11 November. Right up to that time, the fighting, and the dying, would continue. American troops would be engaged to the bitter end, but the Australian Corps had fought its last battle and won its last victory.

*

In expectation of further fighting, on 5 November the well-rested Australian 1st and 4th Divisions commenced to march east, and General Monash proceeded towards the chateau at Le Cateau that had been the HQ of his adversary General von der Marwitz, commander of the German Second

Army. Von der Marwitz had been relieved of command of the Second Army on 22 September and sent to take over Germany's Fifth Army, which was facing American troops on the Meuse. Monash was still en route to Le Cateau on 11 November when word reached him that the Armistice had finally been signed at 5.00 that morning, in a French railway carriage, and would come into effect at 11.00 am. The war was over.

Monash was to say that in their great battles and victories from 8 August to 5 October, the AIF lost 5000 men killed. This toll from the two-month period of nonstop victory compares to a total of 61,000 Australians killed throughout the war, from the first deaths in New Guinea in 1914 through Gallipoli in 1915 to the last casualties on the Western Front in 1918. Monash considered this a small price to pay for final victory.

From the day the United States entered the war in April 1917 to the Armistice in November 1918, the US lost close to twice as many service personnel as Australia did in the entire war. Certainly, America committed many more men to the conflict, but General Monash was of the firm view that many American casualties during this war were due to the over-exuberance of American rank and file and the inability of their officers to impose the discipline necessary to keep men out of friendly barrages and to hold back to mop up in the wake of their advances. Years of battle experience had taught Australians to uniformly keep a respectful distance from friendly bombardments and to follow orders to thoroughly mop up rather than go charging ahead in search of glory.

Monash confessed in his memoir of the battles of 1918 that he drove his men hard towards the end, as he saw total victory within his grasp. He had become uncharacteristically quiet and introspective by the time 11 November came, and his hands were seen to have developed a faint shake. Had the war lasted into 1919, as many expected it would, Monash may have by that time been invalided out of his Australian Corps command. Perhaps he had foreseen this and drove himself even harder than his men to achieve swift success.

When he'd taken command back in May, it had been with a simple mantra: 'Feed your troops on victory.' And this was what he did. 'They came to believe,' he was to say of his Australian soldiers, 'because of success heaped upon success, that they were invincible.'[283] That belief began with the halting of the Germans in their tracks outside Amiens in March. It had been fed by the crushing ninety-three-minute victory in the Battle of Hamel that had put the Australian Corps and the Allied armies generally on the offensive in the summer of 1918. From Hamel forward, with an ironclad belief in themselves and their general, the Australians fought their way east and truly did feast on victory.

23.

The Heroes Return: Ned Searle

'The wrong one came home.'
Elizabeth Annie Searle, mother of Ned Searle

COMPANY SERGEANT-MAJOR NED Searle was one of the 6000 Australian soldiers granted 1914 Leave. He was notified that he was going home on 5 October, the same day that the Australian 2nd Division came out of the line and secret Armistice negotiations began between German and Allied representatives. Ned had helped lead D Company as the 15th Battalion took the village of Cerisy during the Battle of Amiens on 8 August. In September he had steadied his men during a German gas attack when the 15th was advancing near Jeancourt. He had participated in the 18 September assault on the Hindenburg Line.

By 12 October, Ned and other Australians embarking on 1914 Leave were aboard the Canadian troopship *Prince George* when it sailed from the French port of Le Havre for Southampton on the south coast of England, where they went into temporary camp. On the last day of the month,

Ned and his mates boarded the 6500-tonne troopship *Port Lyttleton* at Southampton, and on 1 November the ship sailed for Australia via the Mediterranean.

It is intriguing to speculate what would have happened had the war lasted into 1919. Had that been the case, the following southern summer the men on 1914 Leave back in Australia would have been required to re-embark for France to join the northern spring campaign against a German Army that had used the winter to regroup. Australians like Ned Searle had given their all in the summer and autumn of 1918, and maybe, just maybe, a good number of them would have had their fill of the killing, and would have refused to return.

As it turned out, the war only had days left to run as the *Port Lyttleton* entered the Mediterranean. When the remainder of the 4th Division was marching east with General Monash on 10 November, Ned and his comrades aboard the troopship steaming towards the Suez Canal were informed that the Armistice was expected to take effect the following day.

Ned and a number of his mates asked their officers to turn the ship around and head for France so that the 4th Division men could celebrate the end of the war with their comrades. When this request was turned down, larrikin Ned decided to hijack the ship and force the captain to sail it back to France. Ned and several friends dressed in captured German military attire, with Ned looking especially authentic in his German officer's uniform and jackboots. Armed with his German artillery Luger and a thick German accent, and with his Military Medal pinned to his chest, Ned led the attempt to take over the *Port Lyttleton* and turn her around.

The hijackers' disguises proved too good. Word spread like wildfire that German stowaways were trying to take over the ship. Hundreds of Australian soldiers came at the run. Ned and his mates were quickly overpowered and disarmed, and as the venture's leader he was about to be thrown overboard when his protestations that he was in reality Company Sergeant-Major Ned Searle MM of the 15th Battalion only just saved him from a watery grave. Someone produced a camera, and, all smiles, the 'hijackers' and their 'captors' gathered for group snapshots. No disciplinary action was taken against Ned or his companions.

Even though the war was now officially over, it wasn't for Ned and the other 5999 men on 1914 Leave. No one knew for sure whether the Germans would keep to the Armistice agreement and withdraw all their troops back into Germany within two weeks, then disband their army, surrender their navy and make Kaiser Wilhelm II abdicate. After landing back in Australia in December, Ned remained in camp in Melbourne until the following February, when he and his comrades received their discharges. Back home to Westbury in northern Tasmania went Ned, with his Military Medal, but without his two brothers Viv and Ray, who lay buried on distant foreign shores.

Ned was well received back home, with everyone wanting to buy him a drink. As one of just two men in the town who could drive a motor vehicle in 1919, he was soon offered the job of driver of the town's new motor ambulance. He had learned to drive while doing a stint as a member of a Traffic Control unit, then a form of AIF military police working behind the lines, after he was discharged from hospital and before he returned to the 15th Battalion. Ned, the expert killer, would fulfil this role as Westbury's ambulance driver, aiding the sick and injured, for years to come.

When the State Governor paid Westbury a visit in 1920, Ned led a parade of local World War One veterans. The Governor came to unveil a monument on the village green that listed local members of the AIF who had lost their lives in the conflict, including Ned's brothers Viv and Ray. Ned wore his sergeant-major's uniform, but, because his khaki trousers had worn out, he borrowed a pair of riding breeches from a Westburyite who had served in the Light Horse.

Although he kept a photograph of former girlfriend Win Watson until the day he died, in September 1921 Ned married Westbury girl Agnes Drake, a descendant of noted colonial artist John Glover and daughter of a Westbury baker. Ned and Agnes had two children. To please his mother, in remembrance of one lost brother Ned named his firstborn, a girl, Vivian, a Latin name which, ironically, means 'alive'. In remembrance of his youngest brother, Ned named his second child, a boy, Ian Ray.

Ned's mother, Elizabeth Annie, never got over the battle-field deaths of Viv and Ray, and refused to have any dealings with the Australian Government, whom she accused of taking her boys from her. Ned himself cleaned up his act once he married, settled down and had a family. No more drunken antics or larrikin pranks for him. Yet, no matter what Ned did to gain his mother's approval, Elizabeth Annie never warmed to her eldest son, and never ceased to mourn her lost boys. Years after the war, Elizabeth Annie told her granddaughter Gwen Lovatt, 'The wrong one came home.'[284]

In his sixties and seventies, Ned did seasonal farm work in the Westbury district, riding to and from farms on the back of a truck with other locals, who would remember him as a hard worker, and good company with a fine singing voice. Ned rarely spoke about his war experiences, but once in a while, when his grandson Craig Searle prodded him with questions, he would open up.

On one occasion, Ned told the story of the German lighting a cigarette for him in the tunnel beneath Hill 60. On another, he made the confession that he had smashed his own hand to delay his return to the front. He also told Craig about the arrival of the Yanks to fight beside him on the Somme, and recalled a game German soldier who would clamber from his trench on the Western Front some mornings, sit on a chair in the open and shave, before returning to his trench. Ned and his Australian mates so admired the Fritz's pluck they didn't have the heart to fire a shot at him.

Ned Searle, one of the heroes of Hamel, passed away in September 1967, at the age of seventy-nine. His funeral was well attended and he was buried in a Westbury churchyard. Ned may well have been heartbroken by his mother's lack of acceptance once he came home, and if he'd had the opportunity he might have readily changed places with his dead brothers. Instead, Ned lived silently for half a century with the same sort of guilt that haunted many heroes of the Great War who survived to come home when so many friends and loved ones did not.

24.

The Heroes Return: Thomas Pope

'The last surviving World War One Medal of Honor winner.'
New York Times

ON 22 APRIL 1919, Corporal Thomas Pope was sufficiently recovered after being gassed in July 1918 to be back with the 131st Infantry when it paraded at Larochette in Luxembourg in front of the AEF commander-in-chief, General Pershing. At this parade, Pershing finally acknowledged the Hamel battle by awarding the Medal of Honor to Tom Pope. At the same medal ceremony, Pope was presented with his British Distinguished Conduct Medal and his French Medal Militaire and Croix de Guerre.

On this occasion, too, General Pershing presented the 131st's other Medal of Honor winner Jake Allex with his medal, for his valour in the taking of Chipilly Ridge. Because the 131st had again been under British command at that time, in his memoirs Pershing would also skip over the Chipilly Ridge fight and Jake Allex's courageous act, just as he all but ignored the Battle of Hamel.

The 131st was about to go home, and five days after Pope and Allex received their Medals of Honor the regiment commenced a transfer by rail to the French port city of Brest. From another French port, Le Havre, which was the centre of British Army evacuation from Europe, Major-General George Read of II Corps worked as General Pershing's appointee in administering the withdrawal and repatriation home to the US of all American troops. Read's major command of the war, II Corps, would have several notable commanders during the 1940s, Generals Omar Bradley, Mark Clark and George S. Patton.

Tom Pope, his CO Colonel Sanborn and the rest of the men of the 131st sailed from Brest that April aboard the USS *Kaiserin Auguste Victoria*, a confiscated German ocean liner. Back in Chicago, Tom moved in with his brother J. J. on Overhill Avenue, in Norwood Park West, immediately south of Edison Park, and resumed work for the Cook County Highway Department, now as district foreman.

In 1923, Tom became president of the Combat Medal Men, an organisation made up of Medal of Honor winners across the United States. At no time did Tom court publicity or interviews. It was enough to share his experiences with his fellow soldiers in the exclusive Medal of Honor club. After the Veterans Administration was founded by the US Government in 1930, Tom joined the VA as a contract officer and adviser, a post he held for the rest of his career as he focused on helping fellow vets. Later in life, following retirement, Tom settled in the Los Angeles, California suburb of Woodland Hills, to be closer to family members – his daughters had given him a clutch of grandchildren to dote on.

Tom moved back to Chicago later in life, and ended his days in the Edward Hines Jr. Veterans Administration Hospital in the suburb of Maywood, where he passed away from congestive heart failure on 17 June 1989. He was ninety-four years of age – which would surely have surprised the doctors who treated him in 1918 and 1919 for serious gas inhalation, which usually resulted in life-shortening lung problems. Pope in fact long outlived most of the other heroes of Hamel. As a Medal of Honor winner, he was buried at Arlington National Cemetery, Virginia, the burial place of presidents and heroes, with full military honours.

When he died, Tom Pope was the oldest surviving US Army World War One Medal of Honor recipient, being literally the first and the last member of this elite club. His passing earned him obituaries in the Chicago press and both the *New York Times* and *Los Angeles Times*. The latter said, in part, 'Although he saw action for only two days in World War I, Pope received commendations from four nations as well as the highest honor his country could bestow . . . He became one of ninety-five US soldiers to receive the Medal of Honor in the war and was the last surviving one.'[285]

Tom, one of the heroes of Hamel, was survived by three daughters, eight grandchildren, and eleven great-grandchildren. He is remembered in his Chicago birthplace Edison Park via a plaque on a marble pillar in Monument Park, which lists Pope and other locals who served their country.

As for Tom's colourless, churlish and unimaginative commander-in-chief General Pershing, he served as America's most senior soldier until his retirement in 1925, ending his career with the extremely high rank of General of the

Armies – technically, a six-star general. He died in 1948. Today, Pershing sits high in the US military pantheon, remaining officially the second-highest-ranking general in American history after George Washington, and ahead of illustrious later American generals such as Patton, Dwight D. Eisenhower and Douglas MacArthur. In his 1931 memoirs, Pershing mentioned the Australians once. This was the reference to the Australian 5th Division in his misleading account of the Bellicourt Tunnel assault. Never once did Pershing refer to General Monash, nor to any other Australian commander or soldier.

It is possible that Pershing played an influential role in the organisation of the 1929 burial at Arlington National Cemetery of Private Henry Johnson, the black US soldier who was awarded the Croix de Guerre for bravely fighting off a German patrol and saving a comrade whilst on guard duty when attached to the French Army in the Argonne on 14 May 1918. As Johnson at the time of his death had not a single US gallantry medal to his name, nor even a Purple Heart in recognition of the wounds he received, it is astonishing that in 1929, with segregation rife in the US, Johnson, a black man, was buried at Arlington, and with full military honours. This leads to the conclusion that either Pershing or Johnson's former regimental commander, the liberally-minded Colonel William Hayward, who became US Attorney for the District of Southern New York after the war, or both men, could have been instrumental in Johnson's Arlington interment.

As fate would have it, in 2015, after a decades-long campaign led by Democrat senator for New York Chuck Schumer and others, President Barack Obama awarded

Henry Johnson a posthumous Medal of Honor for his May 1918 actions. Ninety-seven years after the event, this posthumous award put Johnson ahead of Battle of Hamel hero Thomas Pope as the first US Army awardee of the Medal of Honor in the First World War.

25.

The Heroes Return: Harry Dalziel

'He used to get headaches and really couldn't do
anything physical.'
Frank Dalziel, youngest son of Harry Dalziel VC

AGAINST THE ODDS, Harry Dalziel had survived his serious
head wound. But even if he had been entitled to 1914 Leave
in October 1918, he would have been too unwell to take
advantage of it. As it happened, having enlisted in January
1915, Dalziel fell short of the six-month furlough entitlement
by a matter of weeks. Receiving extensive medical treatment
in England he remained in hospital until January 1919, when
he was finally discharged after nine months, and sent home.
The hole in his skull remained, but by this stage skin had
grown over it.

Back in Australia, Dalziel was based for several months in
Brisbane, where he was discharged from the AIF in July 1919.
While undergoing medical treatment in Brisbane, Harry
fell for local military nurse Ida Ramsay of the staff of the
17th Australian General Hospital. When Dalziel returned

home to Atherton on the Atherton Tablelands by train in the winter of 1919, his fame as a VC winner preceded him, and cheering crowds were waiting to greet him at every station he passed through from Townsville to Atherton.

Unable to resume his physically demanding former job as a fireman on steam locomotives, Harry now worked on 'Carmelbank', a small farm outside Atherton, all the time wooing Ida Ramsay in Brisbane. The following year, on 8 April, the couple married at the Congregational manse in South Brisbane. Harry was eligible for a soldier settlement grant, and the newlyweds took up a plot of land beside the railway line to Tolga, calling it 'Zenith', and running it as a mixed farm with both crops and a few head of stock. They proceeded to have three children, two sons and a girl.

The problem with soldier settlement plots was that they were always small and often on marginal land, meaning that working them was always hard work and frequently an uneconomic proposition. In Harry's case there was another problem, his health. 'He was sick all the time,' his youngest son, Frank, would later recall. 'He used to get headaches and he really couldn't do anything physical.'[286]

Because the site of his head wound was still sensitive, even though his hair had grown back over it, Harry wasn't able to properly wash the area, and Ida, the experienced nurse, would carefully clean it. Harry's sensitive state meant that the children were rarely allowed to have anything to do with him. Nonetheless, Frank would remember being fascinated by the sight of his father's war wounds as a child – one a scar on the back, the other the injury to the right hand.

Meanwhile, most of the physical work at Zenith fell to Harry's wife, putting an enormous strain on the marriage. Unable to cope with married life and his inability to contribute to working the farm, within a few years Harry left his wife and children and drifted south into New South Wales. For a time, Harry and his younger brother Vic, who had briefly served as a private in the 9th Battalion towards the end of the war, again teamed up, this time digging for gold at Bathurst.

Failing to strike it rich, Harry ended up working in a Sydney factory. In the early 1930s, as the Great Depression struck, Ida fell ill, and Harry returned to Queensland to help his wife and their children, settling in Brisbane. Out of work for some years, in 1933 Harry joined the Citizens Forces, the army reserve. With the rank of sergeant, he served in the Brisbane-based 9th/15th Battalion, which was a composite of his old battalion the 15th and his brother's 9th Battalion. Harry always looked forward to the annual Anzac Day commemorations each April, attending the Dawn Service and the subsequent march through the streets of Brisbane, when he was as relaxed and cheerful as his children ever saw him. 'He loved meeting up with everybody,' said Frank.[287]

Harry also served as a member of the King's Colour escort at the opening of Queensland State Parliament, and in 1938 was a guest in the Anzac Day march through the streets of Sydney. By that stage, Harry had developed a reputation as a songwriter, having written poems and songs during long stints in hospital over the years. Some of his songs, including 'A Song of the Tableland' and 'Love Time, Merry Love Time', were published in England. He also developed a talent for painting and pottery.

When the Second World War broke out, Harry enlisted in the 2nd AIF, and, with the rank of sergeant, was assigned to the 29th Infantry Training Battalion. As a Victoria Cross winner, he was used primarily by the army to tour around speaking at recruitment and war-bond rallies, and addressing recruits in training camps. On 6 November 1942, with the twenty-fourth anniversary of the end of the First World War looming, Harry sat down and wrote a brief account of the day he became Two-Gun Harry at Hamel in 1918 and won the VC, revealing for the first time the story of how the German soldier thanked him for saving his son's life that day.

Harry never spoke about the war with his children. They learned from someone else, possibly their mother, that their father had been among a pile of bodies which American troops were burying when he was found to be still alive.

Following the Second World War, in 1956, the year of the Melbourne Olympics, the sixty-three-year-old Harry Dalziel travelled to England aboard the liner *Orcades* with other Australasian Victoria Cross holders to be among the 301 VC winners from around the British Commonwealth attending Victoria Cross centenary celebrations in London. Following the London event Harry took a side trip to France, on 4 July visiting Hamel and the site of the battle thirty-eight years before. The town of Hamel had long since been totally rebuilt and expanded, and the countryside around it was now lush farmland, with no hint of the death and destruction that had been visited upon this pretty, peaceful corner of France decades before.

After laying a wreath at Hamel's war memorial, Harry went looking for Pear Trench and other reminders of his desperate and almost fatalistic exploits that 4 July day in 1918 with two revolvers, a dagger and Tilly Lewis. But Harry was disappointed. The trenches had gone. While Hamel Ridge was still there east of the town, there weren't enough recognisable landmarks from the war days for Harry to be able to pinpoint where he had walked, fought, crawled and almost died.

Returning to Queensland, Harry received a military pension once he retired to the town of Oxley, where he resumed his painting, poetry and pottery. On 24 July 1965, seventy-two-year-old Two-Gun Harry Dalziel, one of the heroes of Hamel, was receiving treatment at the Repatriation General Hospital at Greenslopes, Brisbane, when he suffered a massive stroke and died. He was given a funeral with full military honours, and cremated at Brisbane's Mount Thompson Crematorium.

Forty-five years later, in 2010, Harry's by then elderly children put his VC and other service medals, plus the military memorabilia he had collected over the years including the original of his 1942 account of the Battle of Hamel, up for auction. The Victoria Cross being classified Category A by the Australian Government, by law it could be purchased by an overseas buyer but could under no circumstances leave Australia.

In the event, Harry's VC and collection were bought by West Australian media mogul and philanthropist Kerry Stokes, for $525,000. Stokes donated Harry's medals to the Australian War Memorial in Canberra, where they are today on display. Harry would no doubt have thought that a perfect result.

26.

The Heroes Return: Jack Axford

'I wasn't full of rum at the time, for I've never had a drink
in my life, though I did work in a brewery for eight years.'
Jack Axford VC

LIKE NED SEARLE, Jack Axford sailed back to Australia
on 1914 Leave in November 1918, arriving on Australian
soil that December. Returning by train to Kalgoolie on
23 December, Jack was met by his family, the mayor and a
large crowd, but he could not be induced to make a speech.

Discharged from the AIF on 6 February 1919, and keen
to forget the war, Jack went back to his old labouring job
at the Boulder Brewery. But he was ambitious for qualifi-
cations, and hearing that he was eligible to train as a fitter
and turner under the Vocational Training Act, he quit the
brewery job and was hired as an apprentice at the Kalgoorlie
Foundry. Only after he had started work there did Jack
discover that he was too old to be an apprentice, by one
week. Despite public protests on his behalf, the government would not make an exception for him and Jack was

discharged, becoming unemployed through no fault of his own.

'I had a crook spin on the eastern goldfields immediately after the war,' he later remarked about this episode. Unable to find work there, Axford moved to Perth. All he wanted was 'a home of his own, to live a peaceful life, and rear a family', he later told a reporter, and he did everything he could to avoid the limelight as one of only sixty-four Australians awarded the Victoria Cross during World War One.[288]

Western Australia was then run by the conservative Nationalist Party. Jack, meanwhile, leaned left in politics, and in 1921 was put on trial for participating in a Perth labour movement march and singing 'The Red Flag', a march charged down by mounted police. Jack was arrested while trying to help a woman who'd been knocked over by a police horse. Convicted, he was let off by the magistrate with a caution after a public outcry in his favour. Subsequently staying away from politics, Jack found a job as a clerk with Massey Harris Pty Limited.

The socialist Labor Party returned to power in WA in 1924, and when a state government position as a commissionaire, or doorman, came up with the Mines Department in Perth in 1926, Jack applied, government jobs then being considered jobs for life. Jack won the post, subsequently working his way up to a clerical position in the department's records office. For recreation, Jack, ever the gambler, would go to the horse races at weekends, in his own words, 'trying to pick winners'. Generally, he kept his own company, shying away from ex-service organisations, but he did accept the occasional invitation to dine and march in Anzac Day and St Patrick's Day parades with other Australian VCs.[289]

Having fallen in love with Perth shop assistant Lily Foster, Jack's secure new government job gave him the courage to pop the question, and the couple was married at St Mary's Cathedral on 27 November 1926. They would have two sons and three daughters. Jack's Victoria Cross no doubt helped him gain the post of appointments clerk to Minister for Mines John 'Happy Jack' Scaddan in 1932. Scaddan, by then a Nationalist Party member, had been a young Labor Party premier of the state during the war. Now, everyone wanting an appointment with the minister had to apply to Jack Axford VC. With Labor regaining power in 1933, Axford went on to hold this post for close to a decade.

In the years leading up to World War Two, Jack joined the army reserve, and in June 1941, with two younger brothers serving overseas, forty-seven-year-old Jack went to the enlistment office and signed up. '"Jack" Axford, VC of 1918, Is Back Again in Khaki,' the local press proudly announced.[290] Made a sergeant, Jack was posted to the army records office in Perth. In September 1945, he turned up in court in uniform and smiling at the magistrate, in support of his fifteen-year-old son Norman, who was fined for riding his bicycle 'no hands'.

After being discharged from the army in 1947, Jack returned to the Mines Department's records office. In 1950, Perth reporter Arthur Bennett interviewed him, but had little luck when attempting to pump Jack for details of the Battle of Hamel exploit that had earned him his VC. 'It was just an incident in a fight,' said Jack dismissively. But then he smiled, as he added, 'And I wasn't full of rum at the time, for I've never had a drink in my life, though I did work in a brewery for eight years.'[291]

Four years later, Jack grabbed national headlines and broad public sympathy by turning down an invitation to meet Queen Elizabeth II when she visited Perth, after the powers-that-be refused to extend the invitation to his wife. Jack did accept an invitation when the British Government threw its lavish 1956 celebrations to mark the Victoria Cross centenary. He joined Harry Dalziel and other Australian VC holders, and their wives, when they sailed to England for the event.

In 1981, three months after wife Ivy died, Jack again journeyed to England, this time for a reunion of the Victoria Cross and George Cross Association. On 11 October that year, eighty-seven-year-old Jack Axford suffered a heart attack between Dubai and Hong Kong whilst aboard an aircraft returning from the London gathering, and died. His body was cremated in WA with full military honours. Four years later, Jack's family donated his VC and other war medals to the Australian War Memorial in Canberra.

27.

The Heroes Return: Joseph Sanborn

'The men of the 131st will forever hold as their
slogan the comment of their [Australian] comrades in
arms . . . "You'll do us, Yanks, but you're a bit rough!"'
Colonel Joseph Sanborn, Commander, 131st US Infantry

COLONEL JOSEPH SANBORN returned to the US with his
men in 1919, and went home to Chicago to reunite with his
wife, Julie, and two daughters. He immediately started work
on a book about the 131st Infantry's war exploits, enlisting
the aid of the regiment's operations officer, Captain George
N. Malstrom. The resultant work, *The 131st US Infantry
(First Illinois National Guard) in the World War: Narrative,
Operations, Statistics*, was published by Sanborn in Chicago
later that year. In putting this work together, he clearly set out
to gain the 131st recognition for its pioneering role in the US
war effort on the Western Front, recognition which General
Pershing had denied it and would continue to deny it.

In his book, Sanborn gave lucid accounts of all the
regiment's engagements, writing with particularly fond

remembrance of the unit's baptism of fire in the defining fight alongside the Australians at Hamel. He declared: 'The men of the 131st will forever hold as their slogan the comment of their [Australian] comrades in arms in that Fourth of July battle: "You'll do us, Yanks, but you're a bit rough!"'[292]

Feted as a war hero in his home town, Sanborn was promptly offered the post of State Tax Commissioner for Illinois, which he accepted. The 131st Infantry Regiment now returned to National Guard status, with Sanborn still its CO. In March 1921, Sanborn was forced to step down as commander of his beloved 131st because the previous December he had exceeded the state government's legislated retirement age of sixty-five. He would continue on the rolls of the National Guard and continue to receive promotions. Sanborn also resigned as Tax Commissioner that same year, one that had been trebly traumatic for him – Julie died in 1921, too.

To keep busy, Joe returned to his family company, J. C. Sanborn Co., which he presided over until 1925, when he finally gave up business. He continued with the National Guard until April 1931, when he retired, at the age of seventy-six, with the rank of lieutenant-general. Three years later, seventy-nine-year-old Joe Sanborn passed away in Chicago, survived by his second wife and two daughters.

Sanborn never revealed whether he knew that his regiment's participation in the Battle of Hamel had come about because General Pershing had been blindsided by both the British and by his own corps commander, George Read. Sanborn was probably unaware of it at the time, but it's likely Read or General Bell filled him in after the war.

28.

The Heroes Return: John Monash

'Monash was the greatest strategist in the Army.'
David Lloyd George, Prime Minister of Great Britain

AS THE HUMBLED German Army retreated out of France, Belgium and Luxembourg in the wake of the commencement of the 11 November Armistice, the Allied armies followed on their tail, marching east almost 300 kilometres all the way into Germany itself to become an army of occupation along the Rhine. To assist the transport and supply of these hundreds of thousands of Allied troops, Germany had been forced by the terms of the Armistice to hand over 5000 locomotives and 100,000 pieces of rolling stock.

The armies of France and the United States duly occupied two of the three sectors established along the Rhine, and representative units from the British Army the third. General Currie's Canadians were stationed on the northern extremity of the British sector, beside the frontier with the Netherlands, which had remained neutral throughout the war. With British corps filling the gap in between, General Monash's Australian

Corps was chosen to occupy the southern part of the British line, just outside Mainz, a German city that had originated as a Roman legion base. Coincidentally, in Roman times, the best troops were always placed on the right extremity of the battle line, and the next best on the left extremity; and so it was with the Australians and Canadians in the British occupation line along the Rhine.

General Monash was not to join his troops. Summoned to London by his prime minister, Billy Hughes, Monash overcame his previously declared reluctance to work in a government post and accepted an offer from Hughes to take charge of the demobilisation and return home of all troops in the Australian Imperial Force. Surrendering command of the Australian Corps to General Hobbs, Monash took up his new post in a London office on 1 December and assembled a new staff to administer the 'demobbing' and repatriation of his nation's army. Expecting this job to last some time, Monash sent for wife Vic and daughter Bertha, and they joined him in England in early 1919.

In the meantime, on 28 December Monash attended a dinner for sixty-eight guests hosted at Buckingham Palace by King George V for visiting US President Woodrow Wilson. At the dinner, held in the palace's Banquet Hall, Monash sat with author Rudyard Kipling on one side of him and Lord Burnham, proprietor of London's *Daily Telegraph*, on the other. Immediately opposite sat South African Prime Minister Louis Botha, artist John Singer Sergeant and Winston Churchill. Monash met President Wilson at the dinner, but had no opportunity to talk at length about the way Australians and Americans had fought alongside each other as brothers at Hamel, Chipilly Ridge and assaulting the Hindenburg Line. 'My five minutes with the president,' Monash told his wife, 'were quite formal.'[293]

During 1919, Monash led Australian troops on horseback at the 25 April Anzac Day commemoration in London, and again in July's great Victory Parade through the streets of the British capital. He also dashed off his revealing memoir *The Australian Victories in France in 1918*, taking just four weeks. By late 1919, it had become apparent that his wife was very ill, and he took her home, landing back in Melbourne that December. The diagnosis was dire – Vic had terminal cancer. She died the following February.

Prime Minister Hughes turned his back on Monash following the war, and no Australian Government post or award was offered him. In August 1920, Monash accepted the job of general manager of Victoria's State Electricity Commission, resigning all directorships that might conflict with the post, later becoming SEC chairman. He was appointed honorary vice-chancellor of the University of Melbourne in 1923, and elected president of the Australian Association for the Advancement of Science the following year, a post that benefited from his innovative mind.

Monash's daughter, Bertha, married a dentist in 1921, and gave Monash four grandchildren. Meanwhile, Monash brought mistress Liz Bentwich out to Australia. But when he attended the races at Flemington with Liz on his arm, tongues wagged furiously. So, rather than move Liz into his Toorak home and ignite a scandal, he installed her in a suite at the swish Windsor Hotel in the city, where she would live for the rest of Monash's life. Whilst it was an open secret that Monash and Liz were lovers, she was never included in official invitations sent to the general. In his later years, Monash travelled openly outside Australia with Liz at his side.

First suffering a heart attack at his Toorak home on 29 September 1931, after a series of subsequent strokes Sir John Monash died on 8 October that year. He was sixty-six years of age. His body lay in state at Queen's Hall in Melbourne's Parliament House before an 11 October funeral procession wound through the streets to Brighton Cemetery. In that procession, with a quarter of a million silent people lining the route, thousands of his former soldiers preceded his coffin, which was borne on a gun carriage and was followed by his horse, with the general's boots reversed in the stirrups. Field guns boomed out a salute, as military aircraft conducted a fly-past overhead.

Monash died just as Nazism was beginning its rise in Germany. Within two years, Hitler would be Chancellor of Germany. Within eight years, the tactics pioneered by Monash at the Battle of Hamel, of rapid surprise assaults utilising closely coordinated tanks, infantry, artillery and air power, would be employed by the German Army. They would call it *Blitzkrieg*, or lightning war.

Ironically, Monash had a close attachment to the swastika, which became the symbol of Nazi Germany after his death. During World War One, each British Army corps commander was required to choose a symbol to represent him and his corps, just as Roman generals had done: Julius Caesar's symbol was the elephant, Pompey the Great's a lion with a sword in its paw. British generals tended to choose animals or birds. Monash selected the swastika, then an ancient and mystical eastern symbol. It was the one and only thing that John Monash, the Jewish-Australian general, had in common with Adolf Hitler the antisemitic dictator and genocidal maniac.

Today, John Monash is remembered in Australia via Monash University, Monash Children's Hospital and the Monash Freeway, all in Melbourne, and scholarships in his name. An equestrian statue of Monash stands outside Melbourne's Shrine of Remembrance. His chief of staff during World War One, Thomas Blamey, was Australia's most senior soldier in World War Two. Becoming Australia's first and only field-marshal, Blamey worked closely with America's General Douglas MacArthur in the conduct of the war in the Pacific against former World War One ally Japan. Critics of the way Blamey treated his officers and men during the New Guinea campaign described him as 'reckless', 'shabby', 'cowardly' and 'childish'.[294] The best that can be said of Blamey is that he was promoted above his abilities after Monash's death, and that he made a better number two than he did a number one.

Despite the many reminders of Monash around Melbourne, in Australia few would know who Monash was or what he did. Unlike many countries, Australia does not have a highly visible military culture. Apart from the annual Anzac Day commemorations, which have taken on a quasi-religious importance to Australians, we don't go in for military parades. We don't give military veterans a highly venerated status; even the handful of living Australian Victoria Cross holders, whilst respected, come second to sporting stars in Australian affections. General Monash got that right – Aussies are sportsmen and sportswomen at heart. Which might explain why, when push comes to shove, they make such fearsomely competitive soldiers.

For several years, former Australian deputy prime minister Tim Fischer has led a worthy campaign to have General Monash posthumously promoted to field-marshal. It's a campaign that has not gathered much interest or traction. Mr Fischer might have better luck if he was trying to have an Australian sporting star elevated to sainthood.

Meanwhile, in France, Monash's memory is venerated by those who know the history of the Great War. In contrast, in Britain today the name of Monash, the Australian general who showed the British how to fight, does not even appear at the Imperial War Museum, or in official published histories of World War I. British generals get all the British Great War coverage, and credit, not a Jewish-Australian former militia officer. Yet, in 1968, Britain's Field-Marshal Viscount Montgomery wrote of Monash, 'He possessed real creative originality and the war might well have been over sooner, and certainly with fewer casualties, had Haig been been relieved of his command and Monash appointed to command the British Armies in his place.'[295]

British Prime Minister David Lloyd George had recognised this fact some time earlier, but not soon enough to implement the change suggested by Montgomery and appoint Monash in Haig's place. Lloyd George wrote in his 1933 *War Memoirs*, 'No doubt, Monash would, if the opportunity had been given him, risen to the height of it, but the greatness of his abilities was not brought to the attention of the [British] Cabinet.' Only after the war was Lloyd George made aware of what he called Monash's 'genius for war', and learned that the Australian was, in his words, 'the greatest strategist in the Army'. Lloyd George put the fact that he was not told about Monash's abilities at the time down to the professional jealousy of generals at the top of the British Army who could not bring themselves to take orders from a man who 'was a civilian when the war began'. Let alone an Australian, and a Jew.

In the United States, Monash's Hamel and August the 8th battle tactics are taught in some academic institutions, but, just as General Pershing wrote Monash out of his memoirs, Monash's skills, and his influential role in the conclusion of World War One, and the fact that American forces of up to division strength fought under the Australian general's brilliant command three times in 1918, are little known. Just the same, some modern American academics do recognise Monash's military genius. 'The greatest general Australia has produced,' says Eliot A. Cohen, Professor of Strategic Studies at Johns Hopkins University in Baltimore, 'and an equal of any during the world wars.'[296]

As for the Battle of Hamel, yes, in contrast to the larger numbers of combatants involved in the better-known battles of WWI, it was a small affair. However, the overall numbers on both sides, taking in infantrymen, tankers, artillerymen, pioneers, engineers, airmen, HQ staff, etc, were similar to the number of men who took part in the 1644 Battle of Naseby between Oliver Cromwell and King Charles I in the English Civil War.

And just as Naseby was a turning point in that conflict,

Hamel was a turning point in the Great War, a stunning early Allied victory in 1918 and the model for the larger battles of August, September and October that brought Germany to her knees. The Battle of Hamel was also an engagement that cemented an alliance that has seen Australian troops serve beside American troops in every war that America has participated in since 1918, something no other country, not even Britain, can claim.

Perhaps this book will go a little way towards shining new light on General Monash and the other Australian and American heroes of Hamel, without whose genius, dash, endurance and extraordinary courage one of the most brilliantly conceived and perfectly executed battles of World War One, and perhaps of all time, could not have taken place.

Author's Note

The Term 'Digger'

THE TERM 'DIGGER', referring to the Australian soldier, came out of World War One. No one knows who coined it, although one theory is that it was applied by New Zealand soldiers at the front because of the Australians' industrious trench digging. 'Digger' came to be used by war correspondents, and was particularly popularised by Charles Bean in his wartime despatches and later books about the war, and by bestselling Australian authors of the era such as poet C. J. Dennis, whose 1918 book about a World War One veteran's struggle to reassimilate after coming home from the war was entitled *Digger Smith*.

However, in all the many contemporaneous diaries, letters and accounts written by World War One Australian soldiers that I have consulted in the research for this book, and in the World War One war diaries of the Australian battalions, brigades and divisions of the AIF, I never found the men on the ground describing themselves or their comrades as Diggers. Accordingly, in this work I have refrained from using the term.

Appendix

Australian, American and British Units Involved in the Battle of Hamel

AUSTRALIAN

4th Infantry Brigade (4th Division) – 13th, 14th, 15th and 16th Battalions

6th Infantry Brigade (2nd Division) – 21st, 22nd, 23rd and 24th Battalions

11th Infantry Brigade (3rd Division) – 41st, 42nd, 43rd and 44th Battalions

4th Machinegun Battalion

4th, 5th, 7th, 8th, 10th, 11th, 13th and 14th Artillery Brigades

Pioneer units

No. 3 Squadron, Australian Flying Corps

AMERICAN

Company C, 131st Regiment, 66th Brigade, 33rd 'Prairie' Division, attached to Australian 42nd Battalion

Company E, and one platoon of Company K, 131st Regiment, 66th Brigade, 33rd 'Prairie' Division, attached to Australian 43rd Battalion

Company A, 132nd Regiment, 66th Brigade, 33rd 'Prairie' Division, attached to Australian 13th Battalion

Company G, 132nd Regiment, 66th Brigade, 33rd 'Prairie' Division, attached to Australian 15th Battalion

108th Engineers Regiment, 33rd 'Prairie' Division, attached to Australian Corps

BRITISH
5th Brigade, Tank Corps
Special Company, Royal Engineers
Elements of Nine Artillery Brigades
No. 9 Squadron, Royal Air Force

Notes

Chapter 1: The English War Correspondent's Mission

1–3. Gibbs, 'Battle-Cry "Lusitania"', in Pease, *Illinois in the World War.*

Chapter 2: The Australian General's Plan

4. The percentages are Monash's, from *The Australian Victories in France in 1918.* General Pershing, in *My Experiences in the World War,* noted that two of the fifty-three 'British' divisions (including Dominion and colonial troops) were so understrength as to appear on paper only.
5. Monash, *War Letters.*
6. A. K. Macdougall in an Introduction to the 2015 edition of Monash's *War Letters.*
7. From a Foreword to the 1935 edition of Monash's *War Letters.*
8. Montgomery, *A History of Warfare.*
9. Monash, *War Letters.*
10–13. Monash, *The Australian Victories.*
14–16. Monash, *War Letters.*
17–18. Monash, *The Australian Victories.*
19–20. Monash, *War Letters.*
21. Fischer, *Maestro John Monash.*
22. Monash, *The Australian Victories.*
23–24. Fuller, *Tanks in the Great War.*
25. Reinforcement figures from Bean, *Official History of Australia in the War of 1914–1918.*
26. Monash, *The Australian Victories.*
27. Cutlack, Foreword to 1935 edition of *War Letters.*
28–29. Monash, *War Letters.*
30. Introduction to 2015 edition of *The Australian Victories.*
31. Pease, *Illinois in the World War.*
32–36. Monash, *The Australian Victories.*
37. For many years, neither of the two African-American soldiers involved in the 14 May fight was awarded a single American decoration. Then,

in 1998, after a concerted public campaign, both were posthumously awarded Purple Hearts. See Chapter 24 for details of a subsequent award of the Medal of Honor to one of these men.

Chapter 3: The American Colonel's Orders

38. Sanborn.
39. Cooper, *Haig*.
40. Pease.
41. Rule, *Jacka's Mob*.
42–43. Pease.
44. Cooper.
45. 6 July 1918 letter to General Monash, in Pease, *Illinois in the World War.*
46. Sanborn.
47–48. Monash, *War Letters.*
48. Sanborn.
49. Monash, *War Letters.*
50. Bean, *Official History.*
51–52. Sanborn.
53. Bean, *Official History.*
54. Bean, *Official History.* He didn't name the war correspondent involved. It would have been either Keith Murdoch or Gordon Gilmour.
55–57. Sanborn.
58. Bean, *Official History.*

Chapter 4: The Australian Sergeant's Reluctance

59. Vegetius, 'Selection and Training of Levies', *De Re Militaria.*
60–62. Dando-Collins, *Crack Hardy.*
63. Tanks gained their title after the British government described them as 'water tanks' whilst they were being developed, to fool enemy spies.
64. One of those forced to capitulate was the 14th Battalion's Private Roy Holloway, from Victoria. Wounded in the foot, an embittered Roy raised his hands as Germans swarmed into his trench after his comrades had departed. His bitterness was directed not so much at the Germans but at his own side – at the tanks that had let him down, and the generals who sent him on this doomed one-way mission in the first place. Even before this battle Roy had lost confidence in the higher-ups. 'They just fool us about just like we are a lot of school children,' he'd written home with contempt. With hundreds of other captured survivors of the First Battle of Bullecourt, Roy spent the rest of the war at a POW camp at Soltau in northern Germany, where the severe German commandant kept them on a starvation diet and banned them from lighting fires in winter. Like Ned Searle, Les Holloway's girlfriend ditched him while he was serving overseas, in Les's case while he was a POW! Holloway's

words and experiences are in a 31 January 2012 letter to the author by his son Les Holloway.

65. Dando-Collins, *Crack Hardy*.
66. Fuller.
67. Monash, *The Australian Victories*.
68. Fuller.
69. Courage recommended using forty-eight tanks, plus three in reserve. This was upped by General Rawlinson to fifty-eight for the operation.
70–71. Monash, *The Australian Victories*.

Chapter 5: The Objections of General Courage

72. Monash, *War Letters*.
73. Introduction to 2015 edition of Monash's *War Letters*.
74. Monash, *The Australian Victories*.

Chapter 6: The American Corporal's Destiny

75. Sanborn.
76. Pease.
77. Sanborn.

Chapter 7: The Blindsiding of General Pershing

78. Pease.
79. Dando-Collins, *Crack Hardy*.
80–81. Craig Searle to author, 7 June 2017.
82. Monash, *War Letters*.
83–85. Pershing, *My Experiences of the World War*.
86. Pease.
87–89. Monash, *The Australian Victories*.
90–92. Pease.
93. Bean, *The Official History*.
94–95. Pease.
96. Dando-Collins, *Pasteur's Gambit*.
97. Monash, *War Letters*.
98. Pershing.
99. Cooper.
100. Pershing, and Cooper.
101. Pershing.
102–106. Monash, *The Australian Victories*.
107. Ibid., and Bean, *Official History*.
108. Pershing.
109. Monash, *The Australian Victories*.
110. Bean, *Official History*. He didn't identify the war correspondent concerned.
111. Cooper. Haig noted all this in his diary.

112. Monash, *The Australian Victories*.
113. Monash, *War Letters*.
114. Bean, *Official History*.
115. Monash, *The Australian Victories*.
116. Bean, *Official History*.

Chapter 8: The Gamble of Two-Gun Harry
117–118. Pease.

Chapter 9: The Countdown to Z Hour on the Fourth of July
119–120. Monash, *The Australian Victories*.
121. Pease.
122. Dando-Collins, *Crack Hardy*.
123. *Sunday Times*, 29 June 1941.
124. Monash, *War Letters*.
125. Monash, *The Australian Victories*.
126. General Monash only asked for American infantrymen, not machine-gunners.
127. 15th Battalion War Diary.
128. Pease.
129–131. Monash, *The Australian Victories*.

Chapter 10: The Hell of the Opening Barrage
132. Monash, *The Australian Victories*.
133–134. Gibbs.
135. Monash: *The Australian Victories*.
136. 15th Battalion War Diary.
137. Sanborn.
138. Gibbs.
139. Sanborn.
140–141. Pease.
142. Dalziel's personal account.
143. Pease.

Chapter 11: The Assault on the Left Flank
144. Gibbs.
145. Sanborn.
146. Monash, *The Australian Victories*.
147. Pease.
148. Pease.
149. Sanborn.
150–152. Pease.
153. Sanborn.

154. Gibbs.

155. Lt.-Col. R. S. McGregor's letter, 7 July 1918, contained in Pease.

156. Sanborn.

157–159. Pease.

Chapter 12: The Assault in the Centre

160. Pease.

161. Henry Dalziel gave the number of twenty-three German machineguns at Pear Trench, in his account of the battle.

162. Pease.

163. Dalziel's personal account.

164–166. Pease.

167. Shearer wrote in his diary about tending to Dalziel.

168. Dalziel.

169–170. Gibbs.

171–172. Pease.

173. 15th Battalion War Diary.

174. Pease.

175. Fuller.

Chapter 13: The Consolidation, Morning of the Fourth of July

176–177. Monash, *War Letters*.

178. Monash, *The Australian Victories*.

179. Pease.

180. Gibbs.

181–182. Pease.

183. 15th Battalion War Diary.

184–185. Dalziel.

186. Pease.

187. Monash, *The Australian Victories*.

188. Pease.

189. Gibbs.

Chapter 14: The Reaction of General Pershing

190–191. Pershing.

Chapter 15: The Afternoon of the Fourth of July

192. 15th Battalion War Diary.

193. The 4th Brigade's war diary mentions the 15th Battalion raid at 2.00 pm, but says it was carried out by an officer and eight other ranks. The 15th Battalion's war diary, which is likely to be the most accurate, states the raid was carried out by a non-commissioned officer and eight other ranks.

194. Pease.

195. Gibbs.
196. Diary of Sydney Young.
197–200. Gibbs.
201–202. Pease.
203–204. Monash, *The Australian Victories*.

Chapter 16: The German Counterattacks That Night
205. 15th Battalion War Diary.
206–207. Dalziel.
208. Sanborn.
209. *Stars & Stripes*, 28 March 1919. It was initially believed that Pope's brave act took place during the initial assault on 4 July, but American military historians now agree it was during the German counterattack, as described here.
210. Pease.
211. Monash, *War Letters*.
212–213. Sanborn.
214. Fuller.

Chapter 17: The Immediate Repercussions
215. 15th Battalion War Diary.
216. Pease.
217. Sanborn.
218–219. Pease.
220. Dwight S. Harding, *Chicago Tribune*, 30 March 1919.
221. Pease.
222. Pershing.
223–226. Pease.
227. Sanborn.
228. Pease.
229. Monash, *War Letters*.
230–231. Monash, *The Australian Victories*.
232–233. Monash, *War Letters*.

Chapter 18: The Lessons of Hamel Applied on 8 August
234. Monash, *War Letters*.
235–237. Monash, *The Australian Victories*.
238. Monash, *War Letters*.
239–240. Monash, *The Australian Victories*.
241–242. Monash, *War Letters*.
243–245. Monash, *The Australian Victories*.

Chapter 19: The 131st Saves the Day at Chipilly Ridge
246. Monash, *The Australian Victories.*
247. Pershing.
248. *Chicago Tribune*, 27 January 1919.
249–250. *Chicago Tribune*, 30 March 1919.
251. Monash, *The Australian Victories.*
252. Pershing.

Chapter 20: The King Presents Americans with Medals for the Battle of Hamel
253. Monash, *The Australian Victories.*
254–255. Pershing.
256. Monash, *The Australian Victories.*
257. Fisher.
258. Pershing.
259. Monash, *The Australian Victories.*

Chapter 21: The Loophole in General Rawlinson's Orders
260–268. Monash, *The Australian Victories.*
269–270. Monash, *War Letters.*

Chapter 22: The Aussies and Yanks Go Against the Hindenburg Line Together
271. Dando-Collins, *Crack Hardy.*
272–275. Monash, *The Australian Victories.*
276. Pershing.
277–281. Monash, *The Australian Victories.*
282. Pershing.
283. Monash, *War Letters.*

Chapter 23: The Heroes Return: Ned Searle.
284. Dando-Collins, *Crack Hardy.*

Chapter 24: The Heroes Return: Thomas Pope
285. 21 June 1989.

Chapter 25: The Heroes Return: Harry Dalziel
286–287. *Sydney Morning Herald*, 6 July 2016.

Chapter 26: The Heroes Return: Jack Axford
288–289. *Sunday Times*, 13 August 1950.
290. *Sunday Times*, 29 June 1941.
291. *Sunday Times*, 13 August 1950.

Chapter 27: The Heroes Return: Joseph Sanborn
292. Sanborn.

Chapter 28: The Heroes Return: John Monash
293. Monash, *War Letters.*
294. Paull, *Retreat from Kokoda.*
295. Montgomery.
296. 2015 edition of Monash's *The Australian Victories.*

Bibliography

BOOKS

Bartholomew, E., *First World War Tanks*. Oxford, Shire, 1986.

Bean, C. E. W., *Anzac to Amiens*. Canberra, AWM, 1946.

Bean, C. E .W. (editor), *Official History of Australia in the War of 1914–18*. Canberra, AWM, 1919–42.

Chataway, T. P., *The History of the 15th Battalion AIF During the Great War of 1914–1918*.

Brisbane, Brooks, 1948.

Cooper, D., *Haig*. London, Faber & Faber, 1935.

Czechura, G., and J. Hopkins-Weise. *A7V Mephisto: The Last German First World War Tank*. Brisbane, Queensland Museum, 2008.

Dando-Collins, S., *Crack Hardy: From Gallipoli to Flanders to the Somme, the True Story of Three Australian Brothers at War*. Sydney, Vintage, 2011.

Dando-Collins, S., *Legions of Rome: The Definitive History of Every Imperial Roman Legion*. London, Quercus, 2010.

Dando-Collins, S., *Pasteur's Gambit: Louis Pasteur, Australasia's Rabbit Plague, & a Ten Million Dollar Prize*. Sydney, Vintage, 2008.

Dennis, C. J., *Digger Smith*. Sydney, Angus & Robertson, 1918.

Fischer, T., *Maestro John Monash: Australia's Greatest Citizen General*. Melbourne, Monash University Publishing, 2014.

Fuller, J. F. C., *Tanks in the Great War, 1914–1918*. New York, Dutton, 1920.

Keiza, G., *Monash: The Soldier Who Shaped Australia*. Sydney, ABC, 2016.

Laffin, J., *Guide to Australian Battlefields of the Western Front, 1916–1918*. Kenthurst, Kangaroo, 1992.

Lloyd George, D., *War Memoirs of David Lloyd George*. London, Ivor, Nicholson & Watson, 1933.

Lynch, E. P. F., *Somme Mud: The War Experiences of an Infantryman in France, 1916–1919*. Sydney, Random House, 2006.

Mays, H., 'Dalziel, Henry, 1893–1965', *Australian Dictionary of Biography*. Canberra, National Centre of Biography, ANU, 1981.

Monash, J., *The Australian Victories in France in 1918*. Melbourne, Black Ink, 2015.

Monash, J., *War Letters of General Monash*. Melbourne, Black Ink, 2015.

Montgomery, V., *A History of Warfare*. Cleveland, World Publishing, 1968.

Paull, R., *Retreat from Kokoda*. Melbourne, Heinemann, 1958.

Pease, T. C. (editor), *Illinois in the World War: An Illustrated History of the Thirty-Third Division*. Chicago, States Publication Society, 1921.

Pedersen, P., *Monash as Military Commander*. Melbourne, MUP, 1985.

Perry, R., *Monash: The Outsider Who Won a War*. Sydney, Random House, 2004.

Pershing, J. J., *My Experiences in the World War*. New York, Stokes, 1931.

Remarque, E. M., *All Quiet on the Western Front*. London, Putnam, 1929.

Rule, E. J., *Jacka's Mob: A Narrative of the Great War*. Melbourne, Military Melbourne, 1999.

Sanborn, J. B., and G. N. Malstrom, *The 131st U. S. Infantry in the World War: Narrative, Operations, Statistics*. Chicago, Illinois National Guard, 1919.

Scott, E. J., *Scott's Official History of the American Negro in the World War*. Chicago, Homewood Press, 1919.

Serle, G., *John Monash: A Biography*. Melbourne, MUP, 1982.

Smith, G. (editor), *Military Small Arms*. London, Salamander, 1994.

Smithers, A. J., *Sir John Monash*. Sydney, Angus & Robertson, 1973.

Tuchman, B., *The Zimmermann Telegram: How the USA Entered the Great War*. London, Constable, 1959.

Vegetius (Flavius Vegetius Renatus), *The Military Institutions of the Romans*. Harrisburg, Military Service Publishing, 1944.

DOCUMENTS

Axford, T. L., War Service Record, Series B2455, National Archives of Australia, Canberra.

15th Battalion War Diary, Australian War Memorial, Canberra.

Roster of the Illinois National Guard on the Mexican Border 1916–1917, Pritzker Military Museum & Library, Chicago.

Searle, E. G., War Service Record, Series B2455, National Archives of Australia, Canberra.

PERSONAL DIARIES, LETTERS & ACCOUNTS

Holloway, R. V. – Private Collection (L. V. Holloway).

Searle, E. G. – Private Collection (C. Searle).

Searle, F. V. – Private Collection (C. Searle).

Searle, R. V. – Private Collection (C. Searle).

Shearer, J. H. – Australian War Memorial, Canberra: AWM3DRL/3362.

Young, S. B. – Mitchell Library, State Library of New South Wales, Sydney: MLMSS 985.

NEWSPAPERS

Barrier Miner, Kalgoorlie, 1918–1921

Chicago Daily Tribune, 1918–1920

London Gazette, 1918

Los Angeles Times, 1989

New York Times, 1989

Stars & Stripes, Paris, 1919

Sunday Times, Perth, 1918–1950

Sydney Morning Herald, 2010–2016

WEBSITES

aph.gov.au: 'Parliament of Australia – Henry Dalziel'

firstworldwar.com: 'Private Henry Dalziel VC'

History.Net. World War I: 'Battle of Hamel'

sherwdipillyrsl.org.au/Pages/Dalziel One.html: Henry Dalziel's personal account of the Battle of Hamel

Index

Index